*Local Knowledges,*
*Local Practices*

PITTSBURGH SERIES IN COMPOSITION,
LITERACY, AND CULTURE

*David Bartholomae and Jean Ferguson Carr,*
*Editors*

# Local Knowledges, Local Practices

*Writing in the Disciplines
at Cornell*

EDITED BY

Jonathan Monroe

University of Pittsburgh Press

*For Gabriel and Holly*

Published by the University of Pittsburgh Press, Pittsburgh, Pa., 15260
Copyright © 2003, University of Pittsburgh Press
Manufactured in the United States of America
Printed on acid-free paper
10 9 8 7 6 5 4 3 2 1

Library of Congress Cataloging-in-Publication Data

Local knowledges, local practices : writing in the disciplines at
Cornell / edited by Jonathan Monroe.

    p.      cm. — (Pittsburgh series in composition, literacy, and
culture)

Includes bibliographical references and index.

   ISBN 0-8229-4196-1 (alk. paper)

   1. English language—Rhetoric—Study and teaching—New York
(State)—Ithaca. 2. Interdisciplinary approach in education—New
York (State)—Ithaca. 3. Academic writing—Study and teaching—
New York (State)—Ithaca. 4. Cornell University. I. Monroe,
Jonathan, 1954- II.

Series.

PE1405.U6L63 2003

808'.042'071174771—dc21        2003007697

# CONTENTS

Contents    *vii*

# PREFACE

I would found an institution where any person can find
instruction in any study.

EZRA CORNELL, 1865

In 1966, a century after the university's founding by Ezra Cornell and its
first president, Andrew Dickson White, and a half-century after the initial publication of *The Elements of Style* (1918), the classic writing guide coauthored by
Cornell professor William Strunk and his student, E. B. White, Cornell revital-
ized the teaching of freshman writing by replacing a program based solely in the
Department of English with freshman humanities courses taught in nine departments. By 1975, the program had grown to fifty different courses in seventeen
departments. The Knight Foundation's endowment of the Writing Program in
1986 ensured its capacity to provide intensive training and skilled supervision to
instructors from many disciplines. Now in its fourth decade, Cornell's writing
program has involved a series of ever-broadening attempts to create and nurture
the teaching of courses in which such writing will occur. In July 2000, thanks to
a December 1999 grant for endowment from the Knight Foundation for the purpose of further internal development and national and international outreach,
the Knight Program was formally renamed the John S. Knight Institute for
Writing in the Disciplines. Housed in the College of Arts and Sciences, the Institute administers freshman and upper-division writing seminars, tutorial writing classes, and seminars in the teaching of writing for students throughout the
university. More than thirty academic departments and programs participate
annually.

## First-Year Writing Seminars

In general, Cornell students are required to take two First-Year Writing
Seminars, each of which has a maximum enrollment of seventeen. Most students fulfill the writing requirement in the first year. One-third of the seminars
are taught by faculty, professorial or lecturer, located in the sponsoring departments. The remaining two-thirds are taught by graduate student teaching assis-

tants, also located in the sponsoring departments. In the thirty-six years since its inception, the First-Year Writing Seminar program has grown to include over one hundred courses serving three thousand undergraduates each semester. Taught by individual faculty and graduate students from departments and programs located in the humanities, social sciences, expressive arts, and sciences, each seminar adheres to a program-wide set of guidelines published in a print and on-line brochure that students use each semester to select their First-Year Writing Seminars: (1) at least thirty pages of writing; (2) at least six, and at most about twelve, writing assignments; (3) at least three opportunities for serious revision, not mere editing, of essays; (4) ample classroom time spent on work directly related to writing; (5) reading assignments small enough to permit regular, concentrated work on writing; and (6) individual conferences.

## The Writing Workshop

The Institute's Writing Workshop provides a small corps of senior lecturers whose positions support many important features of the Institute. Perhaps most importantly, Workshop faculty offer their own particular kind of First-Year Writing Seminar, An Introduction to Writing in the University, a non-discipline specific seminar for students who might struggle in the environment of other seminars. Directed by Joseph Martin, the Workshop enrolls about 130 students in Writing 137 each fall semester. In the spring, most of those students go on to other writing seminars, while a few are encouraged to take Writing 138. Through the Institute's walk-in service, directed by Mary Gilliland, a staff of undergraduate and graduate tutors provides an almost daily support for students throughout the university who wish additional help with writing or language use. Realizing that a growing number of students come from backgrounds in which English is the second language, the Workshop also has on its staff Judith Pierpont, an expert in ESL instruction. While Elliot Shapiro has taken on increasing responsibility for coordinating the Institute's training of new graduate student instructors of First-Year Writing Seminars, several Workshop instructors, among them Barbara LeGendre, have developed their own specialized, upper-level writing seminars that are taught as part of the English department's Expository Writing, English 288-89.

## Upper-Division Writing-Intensive Courses

After the freshman year, Cornell students can receive further intensive writing instruction through programs and courses supported by the Knight Institute as well as in courses offered by the College of Agriculture and Life Sciences, the College of Engineering, and the School of Hotel Administration. The Knight Institute is engaged in several major initiatives that reflect different and complementary ways of making upper-level writing training available to students in various fields. The oldest of these, English 288–89, coordinated by English department senior lecturer Stuart Davis, uses Institute and English department resources to offer cross-disciplinary writing courses to all Cornell students regardless of major or college. More recently, since its establishment in 1988, the Institute's Writing in the Majors program brings writing into departments and disciplines where it might not otherwise be richly used in advanced undergraduate courses. Based on the premise that language and learning are vitally connected in every field, Writing in the Majors extends the Institute's discipline-based approach to advanced courses in all spheres of the curriculum. An essential ingredient of the program's success has been the Institute's support of additional teaching assistants, drawn from the professor's own discipline, to ease the burden of responding to student work. Since 1997, thanks initially to funding from the Knight and Park Foundations, which the university is now committed to continue on a permanent basis, the Institute offers thirty Writing in the Majors courses per year. Finally, in fall 2001, thanks to a 1999 grant for endowment from the Knight Foundation and matching commitment from Cornell, the Institute launched a new sophomore-level program which, when fully implemented, will make available an additional thirty writing-intensive seminars annually. Limited to a maximum of fifteen students per course, and facilitated by the Institute's new coordinator of sophomore seminars, these faculty-taught "gateway" seminars offer sophomores early mentoring experiences in their prospective majors within an interdisciplinary context that encourages expanded cross-departmental collaboration.

## Training and Development for the Teaching of Writing

The Knight Institute seeks in a variety of ways to support and improve the teaching of writing at Cornell. All Teaching Assistants new to the First-Year Writing Seminar Program (about eighty-five each year) are required to take Writing 700: Teaching Writing, a course in the theory and practice of writing instruction. Teaching Writing introduces new instructors of Cornell's First-Year Writing Seminars to the challenges of teaching writing in courses that both introduce students to particular fields of study and develop the sophisticated writing skills students will need throughout their undergraduate careers and beyond. An important complement to Teaching Writing is the Institute's TA Peer Collaboration Program, which encourages graduate student teachers from participating disciplines to work together to define and discuss their own terms for what constitutes successful writing and writing pedagogy in their chosen fields. During the academic year, faculty members from the departments offering First-Year Writing Seminars act as course leaders for graduate students who are teaching seminars. Additionally, the Institute's annual Faculty Seminar in Writing Instruction allows five or six Cornell faculty to meet with each other and Institute staff to devise ways to improve writing instruction at Cornell while teaching First-Year Writing Seminars in Cornell's six-week summer writing program—a mixture of theory and practice that provides an excellent environment for thought about writing. Most recently, to enhance our understanding of what the teaching of writing across the disciplines will look like in the twenty-first century, the Institute welcomed onto its staff in fall 2001 our new coordinator of electronic communication and assessment, Joel Kuszai. The new coordinator's principal responsibilities include (a) research and development of opportunities for computer-assisted writing instruction and distance learning capabilities, and (b) the development of a longitudinal study of the teaching of writing at Cornell in collaboration with a small subset of veteran institutions from the Institute's annual Consortium for Writing in the Disciplines.

## The Cornell Consortium for Writing in the Disciplines

Established in 1997 with a three-year pilot grant from the Knight Foundation, the Institute's Consortium for Writing in the Disciplines received additional funding in Knight's recent grant for endowment to ensure the Consortium's continuation as a national and international resource for discipline-specific approaches to writing instruction. This goal was also addressed in June 1999, three weeks prior to the third annual Consortium, when the Knight Institute hosted the Fourth National Writing across the Curriculum Conference. Now in its seventh year, the Consortium offers a forum for the study and development of writing in the disciplines at all levels of the curriculum, facilitating in-depth, productive dialogues among participants from a wide range of colleges and universities, both public and private. To assure meaningful collaboration over time, each institution normally participates in the Consortium for two years, sending to Cornell each June a team of three representatives—a faculty member from a particular discipline, a writing program administrator, and a college or university-level administrator.

In June 1999, the Consortium served as an occasion for the initial presentation of many of the essays in *Local Knowledges, Local Practices*. As an integral part of the most comprehensive school in the Ivy League and the land-grant university for the State of New York, the Knight Institute occupies an uncommon, even unique position from which to engage the developmental needs of a broad range of institutions. As we work to maintain, develop, and strengthen our own programs internally, we are acutely aware of the extent to which responsive dialogue must respect the particularity of different writing and institutional cultures, and grateful for the expanded conversation the Consortium continues to allow. We hope the essays that follow will serve to further the spirit of open-ended, cross-disciplinary exchange and interaction that has made possible such a rich culture surrounding the teaching of writing at Cornell for the past four decades. The Institute's continuing effectiveness and enduring influence will continue to depend first and foremost on the depth and range of the Cornell faculty's commitment, as evidenced in the essays that make up *Local Knowledges, Local Practices,* to the idea of writing as a complex, heterogeneous activity, one integral to thinking and learning across all disciplines, from cornerstone to capstone.

# ACKNOWLEDGMENTS

If the many hands involved in the making of *Local Knowledges, Local Practices* haven't exactly made light work, they have nonetheless made that work a genuine pleasure. First and foremost, I thank my Cornell colleagues in the Knight Institute and the dozen departments represented herein for their distinctive contributions, their exemplary attention to the integral role writing plays in learning, and their ongoing commitment to the shared enterprise of teaching writing and writing to learn in their respective fields. Many thanks as well to the two readers of the manuscript for the University of Pittsburgh Press for their detailed, helpful suggestions, which have benefited both individual contributions and the shape of the book as a whole.

I am especially grateful to my predecessor, Harry Shaw, who has since gone on to chair the Cornell Department of English, and now serves as senior associate dean of the Arts College, and to former Arts College dean and university provost, Don Randel, now president of the University of Chicago, for inviting me to take on the role of director of the Knight Writing Program in 1992; to my colleagues in the Department of Comparative Literature for release time to continue well beyond the original three-year term for which I initially agreed to serve; and to former Arts College dean Phil Lewis, former Cornell University presidents Frank Rhodes and Hunter Rawlings, and the central administrations of the Arts College and the university for their enduring support of the Knight Institute and their understanding and appreciation of the Institute's vital role in undergraduate education at Cornell and in preparation of the future professoriate.

Katherine Gottschalk's energetic, creative, effective leadership of our First-Year Writing Seminars, which remain the cornerstone of the Knight Institute–sponsored courses, has given me the necessary time and mental space to conceive and develop the present volume and oversee the Institute's dramatic growth and expansion over the past five years, especially. I am much indebted to her collegiality, reliability, and good humor, and grateful to have had such a gem of a colleague to work with in close proximity for the past ten years. While the joint location of the offices for Writing Workshop director Joseph Martin and Writing in the Majors director Keith Hjortshoj in Rockefeller Hall, across the street from the Institute's headquarters on the Cornell Arts quad, has prevented the same frequency of day-to-day interaction, their contributions to the quality and development of the Institute's work have been no less indispensable, and are equally appreciated.

A special thank you to David Bartholomae, chair of the English department at the University of Pittsburgh and coeditor of the University of Pittsburgh Press's Composition, Literacy, and Culture series, for his initial expression of interest in a book that would bring to light the distinctive tradition of the teaching of writing at Cornell. His insights and suggestions for developing the project at various stages, and his continuing engagement with our annual Consortium for Writing in the Disciplines, have been a source of inspiration. The Institute's annual Faculty Seminar in Writing Instruction, from which I learned a great deal myself as a participant in 1986, has been fortunate to be able to rely on the able and inspiring leadership of James Slevin (Georgetown University). We are grateful as well to Jim and to Nancy Sommers (Harvard University) for their continuing contributions to the Consortium, as also to representatives from the participating schools in the Consortium, from whom all of us in the Institute have learned so much over the past five years.

My heartfelt thanks to the Institute's program assistant extraordinaire, Dorothy Clark, for making the Institute such a fun, productive place to work, and to our incomparable administrative manager, marathon man Bruce Roebal, for his steadfast dedication in preparing the manuscript at various stages. Many thanks as well to Deborah Meade, editor at the University of Pittsburgh Press, for her patience and expertise through the book's final phase.

Finally, I wish to express my special gratitude to A. Richardson Love III, former director of Development of Education Programs for the John S. and James L. Knight Foundation, for his abiding interest in and substantive encouragement of our work. All of us in the Knight Institute and at Cornell generally remain profoundly indebted to the Knight Foundation for its continuing, magnanimous support.

# PART ONE

---

## *Cultures of Writing*

From Cornerstone to Capstone

# Local Knowedges, Local Practices

## *An Introduction*

JONATHAN MONROE

Director, John S. Knight Institute
for Writing in the Disciplines

ᑀ Readers familiar with William Strunk and E. B. White's classic, *The Elements of Style,* may still associate Cornell and the teaching of writing—even over three-quarters of a century after its initial publication in 1918—with that book's enduring legacy. Yet in the past thirty years, Cornell has been the site of a remarkably sustained and successful experiment that the book's legendary authors could scarcely have anticipated. Administrative arrangements for the teaching of writing at Cornell have evolved from the Freshman Humanities Program (1966), to the Freshman Seminar Program (1974), to the John S. Knight Writing Program (1986), to the John S. Knight Institute for Writing in the Disciplines (2000). During each phase, Cornell faculty and graduate students have contributed to an increasingly rich appreciation of the diversity of writing practices across the disciplines.

In 1984, the first published evidence of this experiment became available in the form of *Teaching Prose,* a collection by eight teachers and administrators affiliated with Cornell's Freshman Seminar Program. Edited by former director Fredric V. Bogel and then associate director, now director of First-Year Writing Seminars, Katherine K. Gottschalk, *Teaching Prose* served for fifteen years (before going out of print in 1999) as a valuable resource for the program's training course for graduate students, Teaching Writing. Although, by the early 1980s, the Freshman Seminar Program already included courses from a wide range of departments beyond the original nine involved in the Freshman Humanities Program first offered in 1966, *Teaching Prose* included no mention of disciplines or disciplinarity. With two exceptions—Russian professor Patricia Carden and Writing Workshop senior lecturer Keith Hjortshoj, a Cornell Ph.D. in anthropology who has served since 1988 as director of Writing in the Majors—the volume's contributors all had their primary academic training and institutional affiliations in the field of English. As valuable as *Teaching Prose* proved to be, it left untapped and unexplored the particular, discipline-specific cultures of writing in fields other than English, which for over three decades have given the teaching of writing at Cornell its most distinctive character.

In conceiving within this context the purpose and potential value of *Local Knowledges, Local Practices*, my perspective has been shaped by two experiences in particular. First, as an assistant, then associate, professor from 1986 to 1992, I served my home department of Comparative Literature as a faculty course leader for graduate students teaching First-Year Writing Seminars. Second, during my first term as director of what was then the John S. Knight Writing Program, from 1992 to 1995, I served as a section leader and codesigner, with First-Year Writing director Katy Gottschalk, of Teaching Writing, which enrolls some forty graduate students each summer and thirty more each fall. It was especially in negotiating the very challenging demands of teaching graduate students from a range of disciplines how to teach writing that I came to appreciate firsthand the importance and potential benefits of cultivating and foregrounding more effectively the program's distinctive multidisciplinary character. Beyond the perennial challenge of balancing theory and practice—a binary that has lost some of the fierce bite it once had in the eighties and early nineties—the most pressing issue that needed to be addressed between 1992 and 1995 was the perception on the part of many graduate students from fields other than English that the writing practices and perspectives of their particular disciplines were either underrepresented or wholly absent from our training materials. Having supervised roughly a dozen comparative literature TAs each semester for six years, and served for three years thereafter as my home department's director of graduate studies, I was struck especially by the frustrations of two graduate students with whom I worked in the summer of 1993 who expressed vehement resistance to *Teaching Prose* and the dominance of what they felt to be an English department perspective and pedagogical agenda in our assigned reading materials, syllabi, and assignment sequences. Although the heated opposition of these two graduate students was exceptional, they were not alone among their peers, especially those from non-literature departments, in feeling that the writing program's goal was to turn all new instructors, from any department, into English teachers. Given the apprenticeship status of graduate students in relation to their own disciplinary cultures, and the complex processes of acculturation they must negotiate into the discipline-specific writing practices, protocols, and conventions of their chosen fields, it is not surprising that this perceived goal registered with some frequency as an unwelcome detour and distraction.

Bringing the rich potentialities of Cornell's multidisciplinary approach to articulation more fully, and putting this approach into practice more effectively, required some significant revisioning. Above all, we came to understand the importance of cultivating more extensively and incorporating more inclusively the discipline-specific experiences, insights, practices, and authorities of Cornell faculty representing a wide range of disciplines. What attracted me initially to the Knight Writing Program was its rich array of course offerings across so many fields. Yet the full implications of this shared responsibility for the teaching of writing across the disciplines had remained, until the late 1980s and 1990s, more latent than manifest, more curricular fact than programmatic reflection, more departmental and individual commitments than collective, institutional conversation within a national and international context. As director of the Knight Writing Program, now Institute for Writing in the Disciplines, for the past eleven years, I would identify our increasingly explicit attention to questions of disciplinarity and more inclusively multidisciplinary orientation as the single most needed and significant change during that time. Demonstrating the rare mix of disciplinary cultures that make the teaching of writing at Cornell what it is, *Local Knowledges, Local Practices* offers the fruits of this multidisciplinary decentering and discipline-specific explicitation through examples of what Donald Schön has called "reflective practice." This book represents over a dozen different disciplines, each with its own locally determined dialectic between theory and practice, research and teaching.

The distance traveled from *The Elements of Style*, which some teachers of First-Year Writing Seminars at Cornell continue to use as a reference, to *Teaching Prose*, which also remains for us a useful resource, to *Local Knowledges, Local Practices*, speaks volumes about the history and current state of the art of writing instruction not only at Cornell, but throughout the United States and abroad. With its seven undergraduate and four professional schools and colleges, and its uniquely hybrid status as private and public (as part of the State University of New York system), Cornell has been called the most complicated university in the country. Given this complexity, and the widely varied demands of writing across so many disciplines at an institution where "any person may pursue any study," it is perhaps not surprising that Cornell should have evolved a content- and discipline-based approach to the teaching of writing roughly a decade before the terms "writing across the curriculum" (WAC) and "writing in the disciplines" (WID) began to gain currency. Because of Cornell's long-standing tradition involving courses from so many distinctive disciplinary cultures, it seemed clear by the mid-1990s that there could be substantial benefits from a volume that would engage, more self-consciously and deliberately, this rich diversity of perspectives. In tandem with the efforts that have resulted in the present volume, the second most important inflection of the Knight Program during the past decade, which led to its renaming in 2000 as the Knight Institute for Writing in the Disciplines, has been toward an increasing awareness of, and engagement with, the larger context of WAC and WID approaches throughout the nation and abroad. It was, above all, as a result of our annual consortium's contributions to this ongoing conversation, and to the increasing influence of WAC and WID movements generally, that copublishers *Time* and *The Princeton Review* named Cornell, in the 2001 issue of *The Best College for You*, their College of the Year among private research universities.

In the spirit of continuing innovation as well as respect for the received traditions that I had the good fortune to inherit as director from my two immediate predecessors, and indeed from the writing program's entire thirty-seven-year history, *Local Knowledges, Local Practices* shares with its companion volume, *Writing and Revising the Disciplines* (Cornell University Press, 2002), the goal of encouraging faculty from a wide range of fields to represent themselves, to speak and write in their own voices about what it means to practice and teach writing from the varied perspectives of their distinctive disciplinary cultures. Based on the Knight Distinguished Lecture Series, which I organized at Cornell in the fall and spring of 1998–1999, *Writing and Revising the Disciplines* includes chapters by nine of Cornell's most distinguished faculty, three each in the physical sciences, the social sciences, and the humanities. They offer a combination of career autobiographies and state-of-the-discipline addresses focused on the role of writing in each scholar's field at the turn of the millennium. Integrating scholarly reflection on their particular fields with more concerted attention to pedagogical practices, *Local Knowledges, Local Practices* offers practical examples of the wide variety of ways in which Cornell faculty encourage their students not merely to assimilate and reproduce their particular disciplinary writing practices, but to explore and question these in ways at once respectful and open-ended. Exemplifying that broader understanding of scholarship, which Ernest Boyer has characterized as encompassing the discovery, integration, application, and sharing of knowledge, the two volumes together offer a forum for Cornell faculty to represent the scholarly and pedagogical concerns, the specific conjunctions of local knowledges and local practices, that make up their distinctive contributions to writing, the production of knowledge, and the teaching of writing within and across their respective fields.

## *Administering Writing at Cornell*

Appropriately, since the history of graduate student training in the teaching of writing at Cornell could not be written without her, Katherine Gottschalk, Walter C. Teagle Director of First-Year Seminars, offers a brief history of writing instruction at Cornell focused especially on her role in developing Teaching Writing, a course she first pioneered with former Freshman Seminar Program director, professor of English Rick Bogel, and has since overseen through many iterations both with my predecessor, Harry Shaw, and with me. As Gottschalk's chapter makes clear, the training of graduate student teachers at Cornell, coordinated closely with faculty-taught seminars, is one of the university's most important functions. Recognizing graduate student teachers as, in Gottschalk's words, "a wellspring of the Knight Institute's vitality," Teaching Writing plays a critical role in preparing Cornell's graduate students to become leaders in the future professoriate. In taking the Knight Institute's discipline-specific approach with them to other colleges and universities, they have the potential to have a far-reaching impact on the role of writing instruction throughout the nation. Putting into practice on the front lines the tenacious attitude, as Gottschalk puts it, "that studying writing means not just the study of form and grammar but the development of ideas and inquiry through writing," Teaching Writing continues to evolve to meet the needs of the many disciplines that make the Knight Institute such a dynamic part of the university. Through close work with faculty "course leaders" from all participating departments, the vast majority of whom teach First-Year Writing Seminars themselves, and the TA Peer Collaboration Program, the Knight Institute offers an important opportunity for faculty and graduate students to work together in a common enterprise that values the diversity of perspectives and contributions each discipline has to offer.

As Keith Hjortshoj makes clear in "Writing without Friction," his account of the fifteen-year history of Writing in the Majors, of which he is the director, ongoing innovation and an inductive, experimental approach have from the outset shaped and informed that program's reason for being. In contrast to the Institute's much larger-scale First-Year Writing Seminar program, through which students fulfill a two-course requirement, the Writing in the Majors program has to date, as Hjortshoj points out, no "general standards for writing and teaching across the curriculum," preferring instead to trust faculty to "put work with language into solution with learning," so that writing might be experienced "as a privilege, not as a burden." Writing in the Majors has developed on a case-by-case basis through courses self-selected by faculty, graduate students, and undergraduates. It has drawn voluntary participation thus far from over one hundred faculty members and has successfully avoided the tensions sometimes associated with WAC programs. The effectiveness of this approach, which has allowed Writing in the Majors to grow over the past decade from a pilot program of fifteen courses on soft funding to a permanently funded program of thirty courses annually, has led to new challenges. Among these is the challenge of engaging and evaluating more programmatically and systematically—without losing the approach's adventurous, experimental edge—what Hjortshoj refers to as the "great variation in the roles of written language among disciplines and levels of instruction," as well as "striking patterns across the curriculum—patterns obscured by the assumption that academic disciplines or clusters of disciplines represent separate realms of discourse."

In expanding the Institute's investment in Writing in the Majors over the past five years, particularly in the sciences and the social sciences, one of our primary interests has been to encourage an appreciation for the rich diversity of writing practices not only among but within particular disciplines, including that quality of serious play that Hjortshoj has called the "exploratory sense of the term 'experiment': to try something new and see what happens." Like our First-Year Writing Seminar and Writing in the Majors programs, the Institute's new Sophomore Seminar program, now in its second year of implementation, is governed by respect for the autonomy of individual faculty and participating departments. As Stephen Donatelli, Sophomore Seminar Coordinator, and I work to develop the discipline-specific, student-centered approach this new program is designed to make available, we will continue to emphasize an exploratory sensibility through interdisciplinary clusters of seminars focused on particular issues (e.g., ethics, the environment, race and ethnicity) that will excite the imaginations of faculty and students alike. Taught by members of Cornell's tenure-stream faculty working in close collaboration with one another, and with a ceiling of fifteen students per course, each Sophomore Seminar is intended to serve as gateway course into a particular discipline within an expressly interdisciplinary context. With approximately fifteen such courses representing over a dozen departments already approved for 2003–2004, the Institute is well on the way to achieving its goal of thirty Sophomore Seminars annually by 2005–2006.

Too recent a development to be represented by a contribution to the present volume, the newly emergent Sophomore Seminar program shares with both Gottschalk's and Hjortshoj's chapters, and also with Harry Shaw's "Finding Places for Writing in the Research University: A Director's View," an emphasis on the value Cornell attributes to the particularity and diversity of writing practices across the disciplines. Shaw further highlights the Institute's capacity, by means of discipline-specific approaches to the teaching of writing at all levels of the curriculum, to provide a counterweight to institutional and disciplinary pressures toward intellectual isolation and the fragmentation of knowledge. In preferring to focus on "concrete, institutionally situated (which is to say, historical) practices," Shaw understands the writing program administrator's ideal as to "let others do the talking" while making a few "expertly chosen institutional changes." Like Shaw, I have felt exceptionally fortunate in having as my predecessor someone who placed such a premium on the role of listening. All of us in the Knight Institute, as well as many faculty members at Cornell, have benefited a great deal in this regard from another expert listener, Georgetown University's James Slevin. Shaw brought Slevin to the program in 1986 to direct the annual Faculty Seminar in Writing Instruction, from which dozens of Cornell faculty, including myself, have since drawn insight and inspiration. As the "keystone of the course" for the past fourteen years, Slevin's one-on-one work with Cornell faculty each summer has continued to inspire recognition that, in Shaw's words, "attention to writing can enrich learning in all the disciplines pursued at a major research university." By supplementing Slevin's efforts in recent years with visits to the Faculty Seminar by such nationally known figures as David Bartholomae and Nancy Sommers, I have sought to expand the Knight Program's dialogue with other influential voices in the field of writing instruction in ways that will, in Shaw's words, help "capable people deal with real problems." This goal is also addressed through the two yearlong postdoctoral fellowships we have awarded each year since 1997 with Knight Foundation funding.

In conceiving and launching Writing in the Majors, Shaw proceeded on the basis of a principle that continues to inform our approach to this day, namely that the way to "get instructors interested in making writing a focal point of courses they already teach" is "to make it appear plausible that by concentrating on writing, they could . . . teach the subjects of their expertise more successfully." By "turning writing over to people in various academic fields," as Shaw puts it, Writing in the Majors has been able to make inroads into disciplines that once might have seemed unlikely prospects for sustained interest in questions of writing. In recognition of the Institute's expanded influence in this regard, and its growing role throughout the university community as a result of the new Knight funding, the directorship of the Institute has recently been redefined and reconfigured within the College of Arts and Sciences, as of fall 2000, under the title of associate dean. While this newly expanded role reflects the Institute's increasing impact on the lives of Cornell faculty, graduate students, and undergraduates, its primary function continues to be, in Shaw's words, "to create places where others [can] address substantive problems."

## Writing and Teaching Disciplinary Cultures

*Local Knowledges, Local Practices* attests to the Knight Institute's commitment to listen to the disciplines themselves—to encourage faculty from these disciplines to speak of writing and the teaching of writing in their own terms and in their own voices. With this fundamental principle and guiding purpose in mind, I invited this volume's contributors to make presentations at the June 1999 consortium as the basis for the chapters included herein, and deliberately offered very little in the way of specific instructions. Intent on avoiding a cookie-cutter, one-size-fits-all response that might in any way compromise the imaginations of the contributors and the disciplinary effects that might emerge, I preferred to allow faculty of such diverse talents and interests to give shape to their own concerns. Thus, I asked colleagues from participating disciplines to write what I referred to as "thought pieces" or examples of "reflective practice" based on their experiences teaching First-Year Writing Seminars and/or Writing in the Majors courses. These pieces, I hoped, would open onto issues concerning the relationship between scholarship and teaching in varying disciplines and how each scholar perceives his or her field's disciplinary culture and writing practices. Since all of these colleagues were scheduled to teach Knight Program–sponsored courses that fall or spring, I suggested they might draw especially on those most recent experiences, including such materials as the course syllabus, writing assignment sequences, a specific assignment or two, and samples of student writing representing the quality and style of learning they wanted to model and encourage. Given the range of fields participating in the Knight Institute in both first-year and upper-division courses, my objective was to allow the variety of forms and contents of the contributions to exemplify the diversity of concerns and approaches that give writing at Cornell its particular richness and texture.

Organized alphabetically by field, the chapters that follow demonstrate remarkable commonality, as well as diversity. I have said that the Knight Institute views its most important function as the task of listening to faculty from across the disciplines. In *Local Knowledges, Local Practices*, the faculty have spoken. When we listen to faculty from such a range of disciplines talk about teaching writing and what's in it for them, what do they say? What do the chapters in this collection tell us? What do faculty get out of teaching these (admittedly labor-intensive) courses? Why does participation in the Cornell program remain strong?

According to the evidence assembled here, First-Year Writing Seminars and Writing in the Majors courses share at least three primary functions, each of which is emphasized to varying degrees by virtually all of the volume's contributors: a) to improve student writing for both specialists in particular fields and a broader public; b) to introduce students to received disciplinary forms and norms not merely for the sake of imitation and replication, but to call these practices and their underlying assumptions into question; and c) in the process, to open up the discipline itself to other disciplinary perspectives and real-world concerns felt all too often by the faculty to be bracketed or ignored as a result of the university's compartmentalizing, often isolation-enforcing disciplinary structures.

## *Writing in the Sciences*

Speaking to these concerns, Elizabeth Oltenacu values her First-Year Seminar as a place to affirm "the discipline imposed by the constraints of science," but also the importance of how those outside of animal science perceive the field, and of conveying "technical information into layperson's terms." She wants to emphasize, as well, how "issues of importance to the layperson will force animal scientists to think and write differently about their field . . . reflect more on the ethical implications." Finally, she wants her First-Year Writing Seminars to help students "integrate subject areas and skills that will face them in the working world" and work against compartmentalization of learning.

This collection's most striking example of resistance to such compartmentalization is perhaps Michael Spivey's Writing in the Majors course in cognitive science, which places a premium on interdisciplinary conversation involving five distinctive disciplinary cultures—psychology, neurobiology, computer science, philosophy, and linguistics—as well as "interdisciplinary subfields." Spivey asks his students to do journal entries, formal debates, and a major term paper, and sees it as his primary task to teach students about the five disciplines and "what the field of cognitive science knows about the major cognitive skills," while introducing students to "fundamental methodologies and perspectives of the five contributing disciplines." As is compellingly evident in the excerpts he includes from a prize-winning piece of writing by senior Elizabeth Tricomi, Spivey is successful in encouraging his students to include "logical argumentation," "compelling linguistic examples," and "scientific experimental evidence."

Spivey's emphasis on cultivating an interdisciplinary writing culture that will "*question* the facts" is a value that is affirmed in Paul W. Sherman's "Teaching Behavioral Ecology through Writing." In his Writing in the Majors course on behavioral ecology, a branch of evolutionary biology, Sherman wants his writing-intensive section to offer students "multiple, unhurried opportunities to synthesize and demonstrate their knowledge," a challenge he says they are so eager to accept that his writing-intensive courses and sections are "consistently oversubscribed." Noting that writing has become integral to pedagogy in all his courses as "an essential part of scientific communication," he, like Oltenacu, wants his students to learn to address not only colleagues but also "the broader scientific community and the public." Having begun teaching writing-intensive courses out of frustration and dissatisfaction with traditional teaching of science, he now regularly assigns oral participation and frequent writing projects, "pounces" on first drafts, strongly encourages collaboration among classmates, reviews five hundred to six hundred short essays per term, builds in peer reviews and peer editing as part of the scientific process, and has his students work on grant proposals (for example, to the National Geographic Society) incorporating everything from hypotheses and methodologies to appropriate data, bibliography, and budget. Integrating more writing allows him to track the development of his students in real time, engage them in an ongoing dialogue, help them generate their own research questions, and see how they are progressing with "thorough information gathering, careful thought, and clear and concise exposition." Emphasizing the importance of distinguishing "levels of analysis," a concern similar to government professor Matthew Evangelista's emphasis on competing/alternative explanations and interest in conversation across the disciplines, Sherman demonstrates an acute awareness of the different writing demands students face every day in moving across the curriculum. Like Oltenacu and many other contributors to the volume, he is deeply concerned with relevance in what he calls the "'real world' of science," focusing, for example, in the last three weeks of each term on Darwinian medicine and staging "a student-led symposium" in which students "use their 'basic' knowledge to address 'applied' problems."

## Writing in the Humanities

While the Knight Institute has found remarkable and inspiring interest among scientists in developing innovative assignments and uses of writing in the service of learning at all levels of the curriculum, funding constraints have, by and large, limited support of writing-intensive efforts in the humanities, where an interest in writing would be more readily assumed, to First-Year Writing Seminars. Such an interest is in evidence in the chapters by English department colleagues, Daniel R. Schwarz and Paul Sawyer. Focusing on questions of "citizenship, value, and self-understanding," Paul Sawyer's "Freshman Rhetoric and Media Literacy" explores the relationship between "specialization and liberal education" and the role of the university as "a place not of liberal but of professional education." Seeing his course as a "place for exploring the nature of rhetorical engagement in general," dealing with "context, audience, and occasion . . . communities, genres, and interactions," he concludes his chapter with excerpts from a prize-winning student essay on Jonathan Kozol's *Amazing Grace* that links "rhetorical readings to political meanings," moves beyond "the expertise of any single discipline," and questions "the conventional limitations of politics-as-usual as constructed by the mass media." Daniel R. Schwarz, meanwhile, argues for the value of his advanced First-Year Writing Seminar in "The Reading of Fiction" as a place to teach students close reading and the ability to "think independently and challenge accepted truths," skills "transferable not only to other disciplines but to . . . future careers." Echoing the concerns of anthropology professor Billie Jean Isbell and government professor Mary Katzenstein, Schwarz's goal is not to create more professors within his field but to make students "productive citizens," in part through consideration of such writing issues as "formal problems of point of view," and in part through creating "a community of inquiry where each student understands learning as a process, takes responsibility for being prepared each day, takes his assignments seriously."

As is clear in linguist John Whitman's "Translation and Appropriation in Foreign Language and Writing Classrooms," First-Year Writing Seminars work especially well as sites for serious disciplinary and cross-disciplinary play. Asking what useful commonalities there are "between the teaching of foreign languages and teaching writing," Whitman argues that the "broad sense of translation provides models for a type of language appropriation . . . important for teaching academic writing." He discusses the role of writing in foreign language learning through the linguist's distinction between "procedural" and "declarative" knowledge, and in so doing, provides an excellent example of useful thinking about writing generated from within his own particular disciplinary frame of reference, with his own disciplinary terminology, a distinction also strongly manifest in the chapter by sociologist Michael Macy. An especially compelling consequence of Whitman's reflection in this regard is his recognition of the difficulties involved in applying assessment models for what counts as good writing across disciplinary boundaries. Distinguishing the "appropriation" model of language teaching from the "initiation" model of teaching writing, of "appropriatory versus initiatory thinking," Whitman explores the benefits of transferring "the activity of language appropriation to writing entirely within the world of English." To that end, he has his students do rewriting exercises and especially exercises in inter-genre translation, as, for example, in the recasting of the Orwell essay, "Shooting an Elephant" into play form, with students performing roles in skits they have written. These exercises in rewriting, genre appropriation, and "dramatic adaptation" give students a sense of power, Whitman discovers, freeing them to rewrite even canonical materials in ways that help them understand that "any type of language learning involves establishing ownership . . . appropriation."

Like Whitman's focus on Orwell in India, Ross Brann's Writing in the Majors course in Near Eastern studies, described in his "Writing Religion at Cornell (Reflections of a Penitent Professor)," opens onto questions of cross-cultural translation and appropriation. Stressing "the critical function of student revisions" in effectively cutting across the disciplines—and through cultural biases—his course on North African Islamic culture emphasizes writing "not properly considered a skill at all but a significant, transformative vehicle for thinking and learning itself." Tensions concerning the transformative power of language and thinking, "good" writing, and disciplinary appropriation surface as well as concerns in Jennifer E. Whiting's chapter, "Cultivating Dialectical Imagination." Calling into question the disciplinary specificity of the goals of "precision, clarity, and rigor" in philosophy (as compared, for example, to legal writing, or "writing in the natural and social sciences"), Whiting notes that much great philosophy, such as that of Wittgenstein or Nietzsche, takes the form of "cryptic or paradoxical remarks." In that context, she fears that an unquestioned emphasis on these traditional values of "good" writing in general and good philosophical writing in particular might "encourage reductive habits of mind." Since truths, she writes, "may be messy or paradoxical . . . vagueness and indirection may in some cases serve truth-respecting and/or communicative functions." For Whiting, "philosophical writing" involves an "articulation of one's own views in response to imagined views," and the cultivation of "philosophical imagination." Accordingly, in her First-Year Writing Seminar, she explores issues of voice, character, and claims, challenging students, like government colleague Matthew Evangelista, or biologist Paul Sherman, to cultivate "appreciation of views opposed to one's own," to "recognize the complexity of issues and to resist superficial solutions to deep problems," and to value "intellectual integrity" and "rigor." Echoing Whitman's notion of translating between genres—here between dialogue and a "straightforward argumentative piece"—she invites her students to cultivate "dialectical discussion with themselves and with each other" that will draw them "into dialogue . . . with the broader philosophical community." Seeing philosophy as, in the words of one of her students, "just like one big conversation," she enacts the primacy of dialogue within, between, and among the disciplines that lies at the heart of what the Knight Institute is about. Exploring her field's "distinctive 'disciplinary culture,'" she concludes by affirming that "philosophy, perhaps more than any other discipline, is fundamentally dialectical." Drawing, interestingly, on terms that have a complex (inter)disciplinary pedigree, she wants her students to become "participants and not simply observers," acutely aware of issues of disciplinary positioning.

Such positioning is a source of rich reflection in Romance studies professor Marilyn Migiel's "Writing (Not Drawing) a Blank," which begins by recalling a student's pointed question about her own disciplinary identity: "'What *are* you?'" the student asked. Echoing again the resistance to disciplinary confinement so prevalent among the volume's contributors, she answers: "I would prefer to escape . . . a restrictive notion of what it means to immerse oneself in the study of a foreign language and culture" (in this case Italian studies). Having come to feel less comfortable after her first decade in the profession, Migiel credits her First-Year Writing Seminar with moving her toward "a massive paradigm shift: teaching centered not on what I knew but what somebody else needed to know." Like such colleagues as Isbell and Sawyer in this respect, she wants to offer students the possibility of reclaiming their language. Focusing on the topic of her current research, the *Decameron*, because it "takes as its subject language itself," her course syllabus documents "two crucial shifts in my pedagogical approach: one in the sequence of assignments, the other in use of writing assignments that are personal and creative rather than traditionally 'analytic.'" To illustrate the possible consequences for students of her desire to "mirror the nonlinear processes of composing, revising, and rewriting," Migiel includes in her appendix a paper by Jessi King, the very student who asked her who (or rather "what") she is. What both Migiel and her student share in the end, what the First-Year Writing Seminar allows both teacher and student to explore with each other, are their interdisciplinary interests, their resistance to disciplinary confinement. While Migiel resists this confinement by teaching a First-Year Writing Seminar in her area of professional expertise, the student does so by entering Cornell's College Scholar Program. Migiel's course thus becomes the place where a student interested in "philosophy, government, and psychology" can learn to integrate "the various languages and modes of argument" in these various disciplines, a path "outside rigid disciplinary boundaries" perhaps too seldom found in today's multiversity, even one such as Cornell, where "any person can pursue any study." Offering an occasion for the student to discover "that the acquisition of knowledge . . . is not limited to a single discipline . . . the presence of multiple answers is not proof of no answer," her First-Year Writing Seminar exemplifies the function of writing courses not to settle on a premature "thesis," as if such a thesis were a final resting place, but to explore question after open-ended question.

## Writing in the Social Sciences

In 1997, the Park Foundation awarded a five-year grant targeting the development of Writing in the Majors at Cornell, specifically in the social sciences. Thanks in part to this grant, the past five years have yielded an impressive array of courses in two areas that are represented with particular strength in the present volume, anthropology and government. As anyone with a Ph.D. in virtually any field understands, the sometimes monolithic appearance a discipline may have to those outside the discipline can be wildly misleading. Colleagues in the same field may look more like colleagues in another field, as government professor Matthew Evangelista observes of his political scientist colleagues, than like each other. In including chapters by several colleagues in the same field, *Local Knowledges, Local Practices* offers students and faculty alike a chance to explore what members of a disciplinary culture have or don't have in common in their writing practices, not only with colleagues from other disciplines, but among themselves. The process of observing differences within, among, and between disciplines may be one of the more liberating, if also one of the more vexing, experiences university students (and faculty) may encounter.

Noting the recent crisis in anthropology as a discipline that has arisen through acute self-consciousness about "the role of writing in its intellectual project," Jane Fajans understands her First-Year Writing Seminars and Writing in the Majors courses as occasions to exoticize the familiar and familiarize the exotic through a focus on food. Seeking to help students become more analytical and less descriptive than they tend to be in first drafts, she wants to improve students' "conceptual and communicative skills," help them understand the "correspondence between thinking and writing," and gain an understanding of anthropological writing as a "complex genre of research and analysis." Like English colleague Paul Sawyer, Billie Jean Isbell sees her First-Year Writing Seminar in anthropology as an occasion, above all, to think about "the kind of citizens we are producing in an increasingly interconnected global environment." Focusing on materials from three Latin American countries: Guatemala, Chile, and Argentina, she wants her students to focus on issues of "difference and equality" and "the imperatives of freedom and justice" and wonders whether students remain "isolated from world events across the disciplines as they complete their degrees." Isbell questions what role disciplines play in encouraging global citizenship from the perspective of the intensely interdisciplinary mix of students in her class, who typically come from the College of Agriculture and Life Sciences, the College of Engineering, as well as the College of Arts and Sciences; as part of this exploration, she asks her students to pretend that they are members of an international organization of global managers meeting to discuss common issues. Constructing writing assignments that situate her students in contexts beyond the academy, she asks them to write about the effects of their decisions as engineers on corporate policies. Such concerns are, for her, a pervasive reason for faculty participation in First-Year Writing Seminars and Writing in the Majors. Like Sawyer and Whitman, Isbell encourages her students to explore various genres as preparation for real-world engagement after the university. One powerful example of her work in this way is her attention to the genre of the "testimonio," which raises questions of the relationship between individual and collective authorship, culture, and authority, in ways that open onto broader contexts. In asking her students to follow the Rigoberta Menchú controversy through *Active Voices,* the on-line journal of *Cultural Survival,* Isbell brings her students to think about the relationship between writing and culture with a particular sense of urgency. In following the popular press and journals, her students gain a sophisticated sense of questions of genre and audience, reading, writing, politics, and mass media. Her focus on the testimonial as a literary genre and its relation to anthropological writing allows her students to explore "collective autobiographical witnessing" and "co-authored texts," to ask who has the authority to create a narrative or a history, and engage the complex disciplinary questions of a "postmodernist anthropology" through a matter as apparently "simple" as pronoun usage.

As Kathryn S. March makes clear in "Writing from (Field) Experience," writing is "pivotal" to learning in all her upper-division classes. Typically cross-listed with anthropology, women's studies, and Asian studies, March's courses seek to move students away from the conventional term-research paper toward a more complex understanding of the processes of writing as "entangled in every stage of the enterprise, from observing to recording, testing to verifying, disseminating and critiquing, revising and finalizing." In emphasizing these more "interstitial moments, where writing is integral to the larger tasks of seeing, recording, understanding, and communicating the world around us," she, like Isbell, wants to move her students "beyond textual learning into the practical world." Joining "the recent anthropological call for a better understanding of disciplinary practice" with her understanding of writing as the cornerstone of "enhanced critical awareness," she works with her students to unlock the "paralysis that this new critical awareness seems to produce." In examining the limits of disciplinary self-critique, the ways "knowledge is inherently adverbial," her readings range from the feminist critique of anthropology, to history of science and "the fundamental relativity of scientific truth(s)," to "feminism and the problematics of ethnographic authority," including the "tangible practices in writing"—such as uses of quotation marks, qualifying phrases, point of view, passive voice—with which these issues articulate themselves.

The government department's three contributions offer a particularly thought-provoking set of examples and perspectives on disciplinary writing practices within the same discipline. Noting that political science or government includes "people who act very much like economists or sociologists, statisticians or historians," as is true also in his own subfield, international relations, Matthew Evangelista affirms the value of his Writing in the Majors course for exploring interdisciplinary identities. Given this complex makeup of his field, he wants to expose students to an "extensive range of writing styles," including those of game theorists, statisticians, and postmodern scholars. Charting "a middle course" among various options, he argues that despite their differences, political scientists are united by their shared desire to "account for some political behavior . . . by developing competing explanations and evaluating the evidence." Writing "short opinion pieces on topical issues, or even letters to the editor," as well as pieces in other genres, Evangelista's students unlearn high school lessons concerning outlines, first person, and passive constructions, and learn to think of writing as an integral disciplinary concern. Maintaining an editor's emphasis on "clarity, consistency, and organization," he attempts to balance portability and professionalization, encouraging students to reconcile "redundancies and contradictions" and deal with "problematic evidence and alternative explanations." While he admits to a bit of a "cookbook quality" in his writing guidelines, he has thought carefully about them. His self-avowedly formulaic approach, concerning, for example, introductions and conclusions, contrasts with the approach of his government department colleague, Mary Katzenstein, whose sense of what constitutes good writing tends to emphasize a more exploratory and aleatory approach. Stressing "clear presentation and coherent argumentation," Evangelista understands that the purpose of Writing in the Majors is "to integrate the teaching of writing with the substantive study of an academic discipline." In this vein, he offers his students opportunities to use "primary sources, such as newspapers; secondary historical accounts; and theoretical discussions," and argues, like sociologist Michael Macy, that learning to read critically is an important way to improve one's writing skills. Since in fields "as varied as political science or international relations, what qualifies as good writing may be a matter of dispute," he exposes students to theoretical abstractions, but also "real-world politics." Evangelista shares with many contributors, including, for example, Jennifer Whiting in philosophy and Mary Katzenstein, a concern to make his teaching of writing at once discipline-specific and portable to other disciplines. To do so, he stresses "clear organization and exposition; relating evidence to arguments; and evaluating competing explanations" as "the necessary core of good writing practices in the discipline."

Mary Fainsod Katzenstein's "Writing Political Science: Asking a Question then (Actually) Answering It" questions what we are training students to write *for*. Are faculty within her discipline training students to be "bonsai political science professors (diminutive replicas of ourselves)"? She understands her First-Year Writing Seminars and Writing in the Majors courses in government, as Migiel understands hers in Romance studies, as places to ask hard questions about disciplinary identity and belonging. Preferring to err on the side of the "indisciplined," she emphasizes "open-ended assignments," abandoning sequencing questions, and encouraging students to find their own way. Recalling that the first essay she ever wrote as an undergraduate of which she felt real ownership was one she wrote in her junior year comparing and contrasting two authors on the issue of community and individualism, she wants her students to feel, as Whiting also emphasizes, "a personal stake . . . in a collective conversation." In this regard, she sees a clear difference in the writing of first-year and upper-division students. Where the latter find it harder "to come up with 'the' question, but easier to make it interesting once they do," first-year students find it "easier to define the question, but harder to get beyond the prosaic." Concluding with two opening paragraphs from a freshman essay, Katzenstein echoes Whiting's call (and Sherman's, and Schwarz's), for writing to open onto a "perpetual dialogue." Like Sherman and Evangelista, she emphasizes the importance of falsifiable queries and of the ability to account for "possible alternatives" as a hallmark of the capacity to distinguish a good from a bad question.

In "The Politics of Writing," government colleague Rose McDermott is concerned first and foremost with the challenges involved in integrating scholarship and teaching and distinguishing the needs of different levels of students. Including sections of her course syllabi, writing assignments, and student work, she argues that First-Year Writing Seminars offer a rare opportunity for faculty to explore the relationship between research and teaching in ways that "reconnect with what they originally found compelling and engaging in their own field," including current events. With undergraduates, she writes, "the wedge into consciousness is not the door of abstract theory, but the window of these concrete events and circumstances from which the academic discipline also extracts facts, evidence, and arguments." Wanting to emphasize "questions and problems in the world," she sees her First-Year Writing Seminar as a place for teachers to "discover ways to reformulate abstract theoretical constructs into more accessible, useful, and interesting arguments." The First-Year Writing Seminar is, for her, a hinge between the culture(s) of a discipline and the broader culture, an opportunity for faculty both to "have an immediate impact on student understanding and to refine and extend the meaning and value of their more abstract work in their own writing." Exposing her students to "several kinds of political writing," including journalism, reporting and analyzing, professional political science writing, and political journalism, she hopes, like Isbell and other colleagues from across the disciplines, to create "sophisticated and active members of a democratic civil society." The First-Year Writing Seminar offers a rare opportunity, she writes, to work against those "academic incentives" that "reward the theoretical, not the political." Attentive to "the disciplinary argot of political science," she nevertheless wants to widen "the scope of how we define our discipline." Convinced that "truly great writing surpasses disciplinary boundaries," she wants to offer, like Evangelista, Sherman, and others, alternative explanations and a variety of disciplinary perspectives.

Like Brann in Near Eastern studies, but from the perspective of a professor in city and regional planning with a focus on North American cities, William Goldsmith takes cultural difference as the topic of his First-Year Writing Seminar. Like Sherman, Whiting, and others, Goldsmith credits his seminar in his chapter, "The Invisible City of Color, or 'I Thought This Was a Course on Writing!'" with transforming his teaching at all levels of the curriculum. Using "fiction, essays, and journalism on race, inequality, 'invisibility,' and the city," he works to help each student learn to "write for the public" within a field that is broadly interdisciplinary.

In his Writing in the Majors course called "Group Solidarity," sociologist Michael Macy values the opportunity to work against the anonymity of the lecture class to create the kind of interaction English colleague Schwarz calls a "community of inquiry," an emphasis that will be integral in years to come to the development of the Knight Institute's Sophomore Seminars, with their limited enrollment of only fifteen students per course. Like John Whitman's chapter on teaching writing in the foreign language classroom, Macy's piece is striking in its use of the terminology of his own discipline to talk about the teaching of writing, as in his helpful distinction between "instructionist" and "constructionist" approaches to learning and his application of "game theory" to the pedagogy of writing instruction. Articulating an appreciation of reading and the teaching of writing from within a sociologist's frame of reference and with a sociologist's terminological tools, Macy demonstrates a keen interest in the construction of multiple meanings and the usefulness of writing to guide, rather than stifle, critical inquiry. Of a piece in this sense with the similar emphases and different tactics of Katzenstein and Evangelista in asking and answering good questions, Macy's chapter proposes that the purpose of a "carefully structured writing exercise" in a Writing in the Majors course is "not to teach writing but to teach sociology." Accordingly, he uses writing in Group Solidarity to move more effectively between "highly theoretical accounts" and "empirically grounded case studies." Requiring a short paper every three weeks, he asks students to take on the author's voice, rhetoric, and style, and criticize a previous reading assignment. Whether exploring point of view, as in Schwarz's English course, or issues of authority, as in Isbell's and Migiel's, Macy understands frequent feedback as a crucial feature of Knight Institute–sponsored courses at all levels of the curriculum, one that helps students move "beyond rote exegesis," linking social science to science. Macy shares Evangelista's emphasis on asking students "to read not as a reader but as a writer," and appreciates Migiel's focus on the interpenetration of reading and writing skills as students explore nonlinearity in the *Decameron*. In writing of a text as a "toy," and asking his students to engage in playful disassembly and reassembly, as for example from the point of view of a game theorist, Macy comes close to Whiting's and Katzenstein's emphases on open-ended questions. At the same time, the "concise but highly effective argument" and use of sociological terminology documented in the student paper excerpts he has included recall Evangelista's similar point. Macy writes, "I am not trying to teach students to write, or for that matter, to write like a sociologist. I save that for graduate seminars. Here, I am using writing exercises to teach students to *read* like a sociologist. . . . Real learning begins when students are able to reconstruct what they read, and to that end, writing can be an effective tool." Allowing multiple iterations for students to learn and improve, the short writing exercises he assigns indicate how seriously he takes the issue of student writing as part of the learning process. At the same time, encouraging an awareness of outcomes and meaningful evaluation, his longer assignments ask students to apply theories, like Migiel and McDermott, in ways that reinforce reading and writing as complementary skills.

In offering these brief accounts of some of the more striking particulars of the wide-ranging chapters that follow, I have attempted to give some sense of the variability of response they may engender in accordance with the three major traditional divisions of academic knowledge and practice. Taken together, the chapters clearly resonate with one another in ways that resist overly narrow disciplinary appropriations. As productive as it may be to compare and contrast approaches to the teaching of writing within a discipline, as in the examples from anthropology and government, or from discipline to discipline, as between, say, city and regional planning and Near Eastern studies, it may be equally fruitful to juxtapose essays moving within the same level of the curriculum, or from a First-Year Writing Seminar to a Writing in the Majors course. The chapters contained herein attest to the endless possibilities every undergraduate, every graduate student, and every faculty member encounters—at least potentially—every day within a university's curriculum, possibilities that call us back to the fundamentally open-ended richness and variety of each discipline's local knowledges and local practices.

# TAs and the Teaching of Writing at Cornell

## *A Historical Perspective*

---

KATHERINE GOTTSCHALK

Director, First-Year Writing Seminars,
Knight Institute

*CP* Most research universities, Cornell among them, rely on graduate students as teachers. Some feel guilty about this use: graduate students are paid too little; they are given too many courses to teach; they teach upper-level courses for which faculty should be responsible; too few full-time faculty are employed because TAs are over-employed; and so on. The complaints are well known; in fact, some have argued that ideally graduate students should teach very little, if at all. I have myself so claimed. Nonetheless, I have come to realize that the preparation and use of graduate students as instructors of First-Year Writing Seminars provides a crucial means to success for Cornell's Knight Institute and can act likewise for writing programs at other research universities. This may be particularly true if TAs are drawn from many departments in addition to English, and if graduate students are given opportunities to teach writing seminars on topics within their own disciplines.[1]

At Cornell, certainly, graduate students are a wellspring of the Knight Institute's vitality. From the most local point of view, using well-trained TAs means that the First-Year Writing Seminars are generally excellent, probably better (for reasons I'll discuss later) than if only faculty taught them. Institutionally, training TAs means affecting faculty connected with them, and thus affecting faculty attitudes across the curriculum about the place and uses of writing in their departments. More broadly yet, training TAs means training not just teachers of writing at Cornell but future teachers in many disciplines at many institutions.

22

My formulation of these claims emerges from years of experience in Cornell's remarkable system of teaching writing, one that has developed from seeds planted more than a century ago. That first-year students may now select First-Year Writing Seminars offered by over thirty departments and programs in over one hundred different subjects, and that over one-third of them are taught by faculty, speaks to the long commitment of faculty in disciplines across the curriculum to the teaching of writing. The current intensive developmental programs for TAs speak to the university's long belief in the centrality of the teaching of writing.

## A Brief History of Writing Programs at Cornell

Remarkably, most changes in the teaching of writing at Cornell appear to have come about in association with a tenacious conviction that studying writing means not just the study of form and grammar but also the development of ideas and inquiry through writing. This belief remains crucial today; it makes possible the effective use of TAs to teach writing within their disciplines.

Early faculty at Cornell University nourished the belief that the teaching of writing should be integrated with the study of material about which faculty were (and students would become) knowledgeable. Reacting to Harvard University's famous "theme a day on any subject" approach, considered by some to favor form over substance, Cornell English professor Lane Cooper in 1910 enjoined: "Some portion, or phase, of this subject which [the instructor] loves is the thing about which he may ask his students to write; and not in helter-skelter fashion, as if it made no difference where one began . . ." (Brereton 1995, 257). Cooper's colleague, Professor James Morgan Hart, likewise was noted in his day as emphasizing content over form and grammar: "Our Cornell experience is that the most difficult thing to overcome is the lack of thought. Most of our freshmen seem to believe that anything patched up in grammatical shape will pass for writing . . . " (Brereton 1995, 289–90). The belief that sound writing means sound thought about substantial matters was and remains a crucial one.

## Freshman English: Teaching Writing as Teaching English

Cornell established its writing courses early, with faculty even publishing in the field: by 1895 James Morgan Hart had written *A Handbook of English Composition* (Brereton 1995, 450). For many years, the writing classes were offered only by the Department of English, in courses firmly rooted in the study of literature. This early program has some claim to fame through association with William Strunk, who in 1918 wrote a handy little book, then titled *The El-*

*ements of Composition,* for use in his classes; of course, the little book, later re-vised by E. B. White, became a classic as *The Elements of Style.*[2]

A challenge for the program was that while freshman English was taught only by the Department of English, located in the College of Arts and Sciences, the course nevertheless served students in all seven colleges.[3] Unrest was bound to develop. According to faculty who taught in the 1950s and 1960s, freshman English, when led by William Sale, required that (on the model of a course at his alma mater, Yale) a paper be written for each of the three weekly class meetings. Further, in the fall semester, all instructors taught from the same volume of es-says; only in the spring could they shape the course more to their tastes. One distinguished professor, Scott Elledge, recalled that while those who taught the course cared about *how* things were written, they also frequently voiced concern over whether it was *about* anything. Edgar Rosenberg (then associate professor of English), when later commenting on the weaknesses of freshman English, noted the boredom shared by students and instructors in the homogenous course: "I'd rather teach cooking," Rosenberg reported one instructor as saying (Rosenberg 1966, 3).

Outside the Department of English, other faculty were dissatisfied with the emphasis placed on writing skills—students, they believed, should concen-trate on writing that emphasized reading and thinking. Also prevalent was the concern that in order to staff the courses, the English department was hiring many adjunct and junior faculty who had no hope of being hired permanently and that too many TAs worked without adequate supervision and preparation. The teaching of writing therefore received attention in a 1965 "Report of the Faculty Committee on the Quality of Undergraduate Instruction." In agree-ment with an even earlier study, the report recommended that writing seminars become the responsibility of many departments, not just of English. The idea received enthusiastic support from departments such as history of art and phi-losophy, which, while they saw writing seminars as excellent forums in which to target future majors, also saw writing as integral parts of their own disci-plines. They wanted to share the program with English, in a redistribution that would revitalize the content of the seminars; provide additional faculty-taught seminars; increase financial support for their TAs; improve TA teaching op-portunities; and ensure faculty supervision and preparation of graduate student instructors.

## Freshman Humanities: Teaching Writing in the Disciplines

In 1966, therefore, the new Freshman Humanities Program began, with seminars in thirty subjects offered by nine departments: comparative literature,

English, German studies, government, history, history of art, philosophy, Romance studies, and speech and drama. The brochure introducing the new humanities seminars reviewed the plan for faculty participation in teaching and in supervising TAs, in seminars based on disciplinary topics:

> [T]he staff of each course will be working in close rapport. . . .
> Since each of the colloquia reflects . . . the instructor's particular
> field of interest and expertise, we may expect the caliber of the
> instruction to be uncommonly high. . . . [T]he Cornell freshmen
> colloquia will be taught largely by faculty members and only the
> very ablest assistants. But the essential aim of the program (and the
> most urgent reason for its institution) is to respect, as nearly as
> possible, the intellectual proclivities which the freshman brings
> with him to Cornell, and to give him a reasonably wide choice of
> courses from the start. (Fall 1966, Freshman Humanities Courses
> brochure)

Aside from the shock that instructors in fields such as history of art experienced when they first read essays written by students who didn't intend to major in their fields, who were even intending to be engineers or dairy farmers, things seem to have gone smoothly for awhile. New courses and programs began: in 1972 a small bequest established a tutorial service, which later developed into a special tutorial writing course and a writing center, now the Writing Workshop. TAs in some departments benefited from working closely with faculty, and in the spring of 1975, the English department's Robert Farrell developed a voluntary summer training and apprenticeship program for TAs called Emphasis on Writing (EOW). Students and instructors alike appreciated the choices available and the intellectual stimulation of working within their chosen fields.

Of the complaints recorded in 1967 by the new director, Edgar Rosenberg, on the then nine-month-old program, one is, interestingly, that the engineering students and faculty wanted to see still *more* choice of courses, preferably in fields such as government. Rosenberg did report that one chair "who expresses . . . complete satisfaction with the program nevertheless subjoins her fear 'that over the years the concerns of exposition will disappear altogether in favor of a completely literary (or, say, historical, anyhow professional) approach'" (Rosenberg 1967). The problems that this chair anticipated were soon to develop. By 1972 the courses were arousing a variety of anxieties, including concern that little attention was given to teaching writing (Elias 1976, 1). When, in 1974, David Connor took over the directorship of the program, now called the Freshman Seminar Program (FSP), he acted to intensify attention to writing and improve supervision of the instructors; a slim handbook he wrote for their use remains in the program's files. Nevertheless, the crisis continued to grow. The problem appears to have been caused by more than a weak emphasis on writing (according to a 1977 student survey, most seminars at least required seven to nine essays). Rather, there seems also to have been a growing hostility emanating toward and from the Freshman Seminar Program. Why?

### Problems with Administration: The Need for a Decentralized Center

A major source of aggravation seems to have been inadequate recognition of the complex administrative problems that would arise and require close, full-time handling now that the Freshman Humanities Program included writing courses taught by faculty and TAs in many departments. The seminars historically had been both taught and administered by just one department, English. English still provided the director, in a rotating, part-time faculty position; but many departments now offered the seminars. Insularity was likely, and insularity is hazardous, as a current, experienced writing program administrator, David E. Schwalm, has commented tellingly:

> [A]s a regular faculty member I had absolutely no concept of my university beyond my department. . . . The nearly catastrophic mistakes I made as a WPA [writing program administrator] . . . mostly were a result of not yet having developed an institutional perspective that allowed me to locate the writing program in the overall institutional picture. Does this resemble the experience of others . . . ? (Schwalm 1996)

Indeed! The need for perspective ranges from awareness of university-wide politics to awareness of the diverse roles of writing throughout the university. The first professor to take on the directorship, Edgar Rosenberg, admitted to inexperience that led to initial missteps: "The truth of the matter is that when I was asked to take on this term-appointment as freshman impresario a mere three months after I joined the Cornell faculty, I had only the dimmest awareness of anything beyond Goldwin Smith [Hall]" (Rosenberg 1967, 5). A similarly dim awareness of life outside the College of Arts and Sciences or even the Department of English was bound to persist with new directors, causing problems of communication and cooperation with the many newly participating departments and the six client colleges.

Among the collaborative problems facing the program's directors were those of ownership. Registration into the seminars, for example, became much more problematic in the 1970s than in the old one-course, one-department days.

Departments wanted to see big enrollments in their own seminars, not just in well-known English department offerings. Students, they pointed out, equated writing with "English": did the Freshman Seminar Program sufficiently encourage students to broaden their views? Evidently not–fully 40 percent of students one year asked for "Writing from Experience" or "Practical Prose Composition," and sections were added whenever possible in response to demand. To achieve fair placement of students into courses, quotas were set up to save places in each seminar for students from each of the seven colleges. Unfortunately, these quotas seem instead to have created, or more likely fortified, the notion that students from the College of Arts and Sciences were favored and that students from the Colleges of Agriculture and Life Sciences (CALS) and Engineering, among others, were discriminated against, by teachers as well as by the registration process. Surveys run by CALS itself in 1979 did not strongly support this view, but dissatisfaction was deeply entrenched, culminating in a 1981 submission from CALS to the university's provost of a "Resolution on Writing Skills" that asked for improved attention to writing. CALS was not alone in its discontent. In May 1978, the Hotel School had withdrawn from the Freshman Seminar Program and established its own writing faculty, and "in June 1980 the committee evaluating the Core Curriculum of the College of Engineering expressed reservations about the quality of writing instruction offered in the FSP" ("Report of the Provost's Commission" 1981, 9).

Difficulties with the colleges and with faculty in departments such as history were not easily solved. There are signs that the staff of the Freshman Seminar Program felt and acted beleaguered and insular. For example, in 1977, the author of a generally positive report summing up a student survey began her concluding remarks thus: "What I regret is that a few instructors, including all those in the German department, refused to have anything to do with the questionnaire . . ." (Johnson 1977, 72). This observation in a publicly circulated report surely did not improve collegial relations. The writer also noted using, in her writing of the survey, "more than a touch of that wryness for which those who have taught college composition for many years are noted—and sometimes criticized." The writing program had become a separate, separated group, separated from the very departments and faculty who actually comprised it.

In late 1980, therefore, the university's provost established a Commission on Writing composed of fourteen faculty members drawn from across the university; the commission worked intensively for nearly a year. Its year of investigations along with a 1981 large-scale survey administered to faculty, seminar faculty, and students provided the commission with observations that led to large-scale suggestions for changes in the university's approach to teaching writing. These recommendations were presented in October 1981 in a "Report of the Provost's Commission on Writing," commonly known as the Holmes Report after its chair, professor Clive Holmes, Department of History.

The Holmes Report, along with the College of Arts and Sciences' response ("Report of the College Writing Committee" 1982), are important documents in the history of the teaching of writing at Cornell; they voice perceptions as worthy of note today as they were then.

Significantly, the Holmes Report did not focus only on the teaching of writing in the freshman year: many of its conclusions and recommendations addressed the need for continued attention to writing throughout a student's years at the university. In terms of the Freshman Seminar Program, it criticized less its substance than its administration:

> The Freshman Seminar Program (FSP) is well thought of by students, but, as the one University-wide program which explicitly purports to develop students' writing skills, it has borne the brunt of the criticism of a faculty troubled by undergraduates' writing deficiencies. Some of the criticism seems misplaced. It is based on [a] misapprehension . . . the comfortable assumption that the Freshman Writing Program is uniquely responsible for students' writing skills. Other criticisms are concerned less with the substance of the program than with poor communications between the "consumer" colleges and the Director of the FSP. (25)

All those failures in administration that could be expected in a huge program run by a part-time English department faculty director had become fully evident, with much criticism concentrated on TA-taught courses and TA training, where the lack of communication and collaboration was particularly harmful. The commission discovered that "there has been virtually no coordination between the Directors of the FSP and of EOW [the program that included summer internship and training for TAs] . . ." It found that even "faculty actively involved both as teachers and administrators in the FSP had 'only vague knowledge' about the activities of EOW" ("Report of the Provost's Commission" 28). It found also that no attempt had been made to ensure training of TAs (29); and that some were trained who never taught (29)—more failure in coordination. Most damagingly, in terms of administration and the use and training of TAs, the commission concluded that "The current [title of] 'Director" seems a misnomer: he *directs* very little. The director is scarcely involved in the activities of the EOW program or of the Writing Workshop: both are, in effect, independent agencies. The director is hostage to the department for the provision of seminars: who teaches and what is taught are matters about which he can do essentially nothing" (37).

These were the administrative difficulties of a too-isolated center that had too little contact with its teachers, especially with its TAs, leading to the much-noted problem that a substantial number of the writing seminars failed to follow program's guidelines: Clive Holmes, the chair of the Provost's Commission, reported in an Arts College faculty meeting that "students are sometimes asked for only three or four large papers; they are seldom given the opportunity to rewrite their papers, and grading is often inadequate or untimely. These conditions are the result of administrative weakness, due to the departments' independence and the lack of supervision of the graduate students teaching the courses" (Faculty Meeting Minutes, College of Arts and Sciences, 3 November 1981).

Despite having found the program's administration to be largely at fault, the commission, in a move still unfortunately common, nevertheless proposed a "back to basics" retreat, with seminars in the first semester that "would concentrate on principles of sentence and paragraph structure" in courses taught predominantly by English department faculty. ("Report of the Provost's Commission" 39) In the second semester, the writing of "substantial expository essays" (14) on subjects in the expressive arts, humanities, or social sciences (39) could return. Fortunately, the problems with this revisionist approach were firmly noted. Jonathan Bishop, professor of English and then-director of the Freshman Seminar Program, argued in a 1981 faculty meeting that continuing to house the writing program in the Department of English would mean perpetuating its problems:

> [T]he recommendation that the program be moved back to one
> department seems to be in conflict with the desire for strong
> administration. To fulfill that aim, an independent program,
> separately funded, answerable to the Provost, would be indicated;
> instead, the [present] proposal would reinforce the director's role as
> a servant of the English department, and at the same time do away
> with a program that has been moderately successful. (3 November
> 1981 minutes)

Ultimately, after well-attended, passionately-argued faculty meetings, the College of Arts and Sciences responded by approving a 1982 follow-up "Report of the College Writing Committee," which pointed out that "the commission's report nowhere explicitly addresses the crucial question of whether writing has been taught well in courses which do adhere to the current guidelines" (6) and successfully argued that instead new procedures for ensuring good teaching and good administration be instituted. The recommendations of the College Writing Committee's report accordingly became the primary basis of the current Knight Institute.

The solution to ensuring that lines of communication and cooperation were working between administrators, faculty, and colleges lay in "decentralized centralization."[4] Departments continued their financial and professorial commitments to the program (funding graduate student and faculty-taught seminars, maintaining faculty mentorship of graduate students, designing seminars), while the writing program gained authority and perspective. It disengaged allegiance to one department and its course(s) and became an independently situated program that reported directly to the dean of the college and consulted regularly with a university-wide committee. The program was given its own substantial financial base (which has since been improved with endowments). Most important in the financial base were funds with which to pay for TA-taught seminars in participating departments and funds for TA training. At last the writing program would have a centralized and effective approach to the decentralized seminars, an approach that built on the funding and training of TAs as a means to many ends.

## *The John S. Knight Institute: TAs and the Decentralized Center*

The new writing program began, then, in 1982.[5] Its first director was Fredric V. Bogel; I began my association with the program at the same time, as the associate director. While both Rick Bogel and I were members of the Department of English, future directors could be drawn from other participating departments. In fact, the Knight Institute's current director, Jonathan Monroe, is a member of the Department of Comparative Literature, an appropriate choice for an interdisciplinary writing program. As had been made clear, much of the future success of the writing program would depend on the involvement of the directorship with other colleges and with departments across the curriculum; this involvement would be made possible and effective through improved contact with TAs. Starting in 1982, then, what directions did the new center for a decentralized program take?

A pressing task for a writing program with seminars and teachers scattered across the curriculum is to provide effective means of collaboration and coordination, to be sure that participants, whether instructors or students, and onlookers, whether faculty or administration, actively share the commitment to the teaching of writing. We wanted, of course, to work with the principles and practices of faculty across the university. What we had immediate access to were TAs. In the end, this was our good fortune. While TA-taught seminars had been criticized as a source of weakness in the past at Cornell, they became a major source of strength, both for better-taught writing seminars and for increasing the understanding and uses of writing in the disciplines.

There are a number of reasons that working with TAs can be an effective means of developing collaboration and coordination between departments. TAs are many and accessible; they are not as elusive and independent as faculty. They still see themselves as students. They are more comfortable acknowledging that they don't already know how to teach than are new faculty. Because they haven't taught before, they haven't developed fixed ideas about pedagogy. Not having tenure, they often, in fact, bring considerable eagerness and openness to training. One can reach TAs, in other words, because they are at an accessible stage of their careers, and one should indeed reach them, because they are at turning points in their work as teachers. Furthermore, departments will often support training and teaching opportunities for their graduate students. Most faculty agree that TAs can benefit from various kinds of training; at the least, they want the financial support for their TAs that comes from teaching: naturally departments are pleased if financial support can be provided by someone other than themselves.

A successful strategy for reaching TAs and their departments developed quickly once the new Knight Writing Program was underway: The program was given control of financial support for TAs who teach a seminar for a semester or a year. It can distribute this funding to whatever departments it wishes. This strategy provides an easy way to remind departments to remain attentive to their involvement in the teaching of writing. For instance, the writing program much prefers to fund TA-taught seminars in departments where a regular number of faculty teach seminars and where these faculty conscientiously fulfill their role as mentors for TAs. Naturally, it also prefers to fund seminars in departments where the TA-taught seminars are indeed excellent, as indicated by required end-of-semester evaluations (administered by the writing program) among other measures. Further, the writing program prefers to award additional TA monies, when available, to departments that offer additional faculty-taught writing seminars or that engage in outstanding mentoring of TAs. The writing program's financial support for TAs should be, and has been, decreased if TAs receive inadequate faculty mentoring or if departments decrease their numbers of faculty-taught (and TA-taught) seminars or if TA-taught seminars are poor.

When a writing program holds the reins that control a few stout financial horses, the cart can move forward (the program may even buy a carriage). The strategy is a financial means to an altruistic end. Because of it, participating faculty and departments are reminded each semester, and each year, that the university's faculty members committed themselves to teaching seminars and to assisting graduate students; all remain conscious that faculty participation is the bedrock of a program based on the belief that writing is embedded in the disciplines; faculty participation provides a foundation for the development of graduate students, who look to faculty as exemplars of academic life and for support in their teaching work.

## Preparatory Programs and Mentoring of TAs

A writing program can acquire financial control of teaching assistantships quickly, given the university's support, but long-term results occur only gradually. Attitudes toward training of TAs do not change overnight, even when, officially, the programs have been approved. At Cornell, prior to 1982, preparatory programs had not been required, and many departments thought of their TAs as superior teachers who required no help. Or departments didn't want graduate students to "waste" their valuable research and course time on a required pedagogy and composition theory seminar. Converting resistance into normal expectation is a matter of operating as if everyone agreed. One must, daily and yearly, insist on the value of training; just as important, one must ensure that the training provided is indeed valuable. Clearly, no amount of insistence on training works if a department does not find its own best interests served: graduate students must benefit, immediately and in the long term, from learning how to teach and from developing their own seminars. Faculty must be made aware of those benefits, of which TAs are often more aware than are faculty.

Concentrating on the supervision and official preparation of TAs for teaching provided the writing program with excellent possibilities for working with departments, then, as well as for improving the quality of teaching. But what kind of preparatory program would make sense, given that our TAs come from a wide variety of disciplines?

The approach we have developed is many layered. One level had been in place since 1966, when the brochure for the first humanities seminars announced, "staff of each course will be working in close rapport." This rapport had translated into the provision of close faculty supervision for graduate students by "course leaders," or faculty mentors who also teach first-year writing seminars in the TAs' departments. Mentors may help TAs plan syllabi, consult on the selection of readings and development of assignments (or share syllabi for an established seminar), call meetings for discussion of teaching, visit classes, and examine essays to which TAs have responded. The writing program's role since 1982 has been to ensure that each department appoints a faculty mentor for each TA. What happens after the appointment, alas, remains less certain, despite the writing program's efforts. The Department of English, perhaps because of its early and central role in the teaching of writing, does excellent work, especially with TAs teaching for the first time. Other departments have also provided excellent faculty mentoring, as, for instance, the Department of German Studies, where many members of the faculty have long known what it means to do a good job. As in so much of academic work, much can depend on a few invested people. Much also, unfortunately, can depend on tradition, and traditions are difficult to change. If departments remain interested in their graduate students' research and not their teaching, course leaders will be present only nominally. In such cases, the writing program tries to provide the support lacking in the departments themselves.

Interestingly, even departments that have been slow to take an interest in their graduate students' teaching have begun to think differently. Some of this change is due to the writing program's continuing efforts to involve faculty across the curriculum in the Faculty Seminar in Writing Instruction (described elsewhere in this volume) and in the mandatory preparatory seminar, Teaching Writing, which is required of TAs. Participation in Teaching Writing can be especially valuable. Recently, for example, a senior member of the anthropology faculty agreed to sit in on Teaching Writing and respond to the work of the TAs from his department. As a result of his experience (he did all the readings and attended every meeting), he altered the way graduate students would be mentored in his department, decided to make major revisions in his "non-writing" courses, and provided a wonderful model to the appreciative TAs. Involvement of faculty with their TAs in the very successful Writing in the Majors program (also described elsewhere in this volume) has had similar positive effects. In other words, if faculty become involved with the teaching of writing and with training teachers, not surprisingly, the culture surrounding the teaching of writing gradually changes.

The Teaching Writing seminar developed because a centralized, required preparatory course for TAs seemed imperative for a program previously troubled due to its lack of coordinated preparation. As indicated earlier, failures in preparation had led to problems such as instructors' giving no attention to the process of writing; inadequate preparation had led to departments not sharing a common understanding of the methods and purposes of the First-Year Writing Seminars. All three directors of the Knight Institute and I, with the invaluable assistance of James Slevin (Department of English, Georgetown), have therefore devoted maximum attention to the development of the six-week required course. It is now taken by some eighty new TAs each year. Further, in a regularization and expansion of an earlier program, thirty of these new TAs also work as interns with a faculty mentor in a six-week summer session writing course—an activity much sweetened by the summer stipend provided through the Knight Writing Program and graduate school.

It is worth looking at the historical evolution of the Teaching Writing course to examine the shifts that came about with the three changes in directorship—a directorship in the hands of faculty *not* trained in composition—and with continuing shifts in institutional attitudes toward the place of writing instruction in the institution.

Where did we start in 1982? The first director, Rick Bogel, and I began where we could, with what we could accomplish then. We required the training course of all graduate students who had not taught a writing seminar, an easy move, since that was what the institution wanted, and we offered optional internships during the summer. The course itself was offered during both the summer and fall semesters. Credit? No. We argued for it, but failed, although the participants read extensively in composition theory and wrote several papers. Note, of course, the standard format of the course: lecture, discussion, two papers. From today's perspective the format looks impoverished, but it was acceptable, even comforting, to those required to take the seminar. It did not push the boundaries of how a "normal" course should run. All were on familiar territory: lots of readings, not much writing, and regular discussion.[6]

Two papers and reading assignments, however, do not an instructor of writing make. To some, the course felt like make-work; it required a lot of reading, but didn't seem to provide the help instructors actually wanted—theory without the application to practice. When Harry Shaw followed Rick Bogel as director in 1985, he had heard the grumblings of graduate students and decided to institute immediate changes.[7] First, he brought James Slevin into association with the program. After intensive discussion, Shaw and Slevin emerged with a new plan for Teaching Writing. The formal and often ineffective papers were abandoned, as was the twelve-week sequence on isolated topics such as grammar and invention. Instead, the course worked from a theoretically unified approach with a sequence that allowed participants to read, think, and write about the intertwined relationships of writing and writing in a discipline. Topics were: Thinking through Writing; Writing to Read; Reading to Write: Readings as Matter, Readings as Models; Commentary on Student Writing; Style: Prose and the Disciplines; and, finally, [Assignment] Sequences. These topics suggest the familiar underlying principle of the writing program, namely that writing is best addressed by teachers as part of the intellectual journeys upon which students embark; writing is not simply a skill.

At last the writing in Teaching Writing began to follow the same principle. Participants each week did not produce isolated essays: they produced six assignments—assignment sequences—for their students, along with the rationales for those assignments. They produced these assignments with no complaints about the increased work, because the writing was part of their work as teachers. Designing the assignments helped the instructors take intellectual journeys of their own, in that the well-planned assignment sequence guides students into increasing understanding of writing and of a discipline; it takes students through systematically planned experiences with uses of language and the development of essays. Because designing such sequences is difficult, we quickly realized that we should provide additional incentives. We therefore began giving a handsome prize for outstanding sequences each semester. Thanks to that award, we have been able to collect excellent examples of what the writing sequence can do, two of which I will discuss later.

A third shift in Teaching Writing took place when in 1992 Jonathan Monroe replaced Harry Shaw as director. With the perspective of a comparativist, Monroe moved to bring in voices from other institutions. As a result, in addition to James Slevin, guest speakers have now included Nancy Sommers (Director of Expository Writing, Harvard University) and David Bartholomae (Department of English, University of Pittsburgh); others have followed. Working still as a comparatist, and realizing that the course no longer served those most active in its teaching, Monroe also decided to involve more people in the planning and teaching of Teaching Writing, namely staff from the Writing Workshop. With these new perspectives, the topics moved from a fairly narrow focus on the assignment sequence to include interest in students and in the TAs as novice teachers, with such subjects as "What is a First-Year Writing Seminar?" Further, realizing that we should practice what we preach, we integrated informal writing into the seminar, treating assignments submitted by the TAs as drafts. We removed readings, put new ones in place—and the process of regular change was instituted. Yearly reinspection of our methods, our assignments, and our readings is now the norm. The constant process of change serves well our wish to help instructors think about the teaching of writing not just as a paid task but as a national issue that sweeps through disciplinary boundaries. Could this be, perhaps, a sign of the success of the course, and of changing attitudes? We renewed our request to the College of Arts and Sciences that Teaching Writing receive credit, and the recommendation went through without comment or challenge.

An ongoing issue for any writing program is, of course, how to support its instructors after they have participated in the required preparatory course or program. Experience with offering supplemental workshops can be discouraging: everyone wants to see that they are available; virtually no one wants to attend except the already converted. Workshops developed for specific groups, at their request, with attendance ensured, are satisfactory. But we have found other ways to continue conversations about teaching. The best of these has been the Peer Collaboration Program, developed by Jonathan Monroe. For a nominal stipend, we discovered, many TAs gladly develop collaborative projects on which they work over the course of a semester. Some typical activities include visiting each other's classes, grading sets of papers collaboratively, or designing writing assignments. The formality of providing an initial proposal and then a final written report, all of which must be approved by the faculty mentor and by the writing program, seems to provide just the right amount of institutional structure and encouragement. A less used program is one in which instructors of First-Year Writing Seminars submit a set of "marked" essays to a "walk-in" service tutor. These tutors, having seen hundreds of marked essays and assignments along with the responses of the student, are in an excellent position to critique the strengths and weaknesses of instructors' commentary (and often of their essay assignments). Those who participate are very enthusiastic about the program.

The Knight Institute encourages participation in these developmental activities, as well as others provided by the university's Office of Instructional Support, with its yearly Recognition of Achievement in Teaching award, which reviews an instructor's participation in professional development programs and teaching. It also gives once-yearly awards for the development of outstanding teaching portfolios (documentation of teaching). Interestingly, but not surprisingly, initial resistance to the idea of teaching portfolios came not from TAs but from faculty. TAs face realities of the job market that their faculty mentors may have been able to ignore. It was because of the continued encouragement of TAs, in fact, that workshops and materials on teaching portfolios are now provided.

## TAs at the Center

We believe, in other words, that attractive, ongoing programs which help TAs to improve their teaching are important—all the more so because they reach TAs in so many disciplines. TAs' experience learning to teach writing in their disciplines can influence what kind of teachers they will become when they no longer teach a "writing course," because in the seminars, writing is part of their disciplines and of students' learning. With their experience as teachers of writing in their own disciplines, we hope they will become the faculty at other institutions who assume their share of responsibility for their students' writing, and who do not consider a required first-year composition course on the sentence and paragraph to be the answer to "the writing problem."

Let's look at what can happen when a fledgling teacher first teaches a writing seminar in the discipline of his or her own design, with its development supported through an intensive preparatory seminar. Richard Will was a Ph.D. candidate in the music department when he took Teaching Writing; he does research on symphonies of the late eighteenth and early nineteenth centuries, as well as on contemporary pop music. Paul Doremus was a Ph.D. candidate in the government department. Teaching writing courses deeply rooted in their own fields served the writing program's goals at the same time that it admirably served their own purposes. For Will, writing formed a necessary part of learning in a field that would remain a major part of many students' lives—popular music. For Doremus, writing meant students learning how to think critically and being able to enter into major policy discussions.

Will's First-Year Writing Seminar was called Music 117: Popular Music since 1950. It was open to students from any college or major. Here are Will's goals as he stated them:

> My aim . . . is twofold: first, to introduce students to techniques appropriate for the analysis of popular music; second, to encourage them to evaluate critically what they read about pop. I pursue both of these goals through writing. In studying analysis we examine what musical parameters respond best to verbal description. This involves teaching the students some music-theoretical terminology, but I also encourage them to imagine their own "discourses"; the interaction of music with prose remains highly problematic even in professional musicology, and new "solutions" are offered frequently. I ask the students to engage critical writing on two levels. First, they practice adopting various common languages—the hyperbole of the rock critic, the objectivity of the historian, the density of the sociologist; I find this sensitizes them immediately to the advantages and disadvantages of each style. Second, they write "metacritical" reviews, in which they take a stance on selected methodologies and styles.
>
> Both of these components ultimately work for a common purpose: to help students find a "voice" for writing—and thinking—about popular music. This goal has repercussions beyond the seminar room; as both liberal and conservative critics are quick to point out, pop music forms a potent "subtext" to undergraduate life. . . . Pop is a primary topic of conversation for casual fans as well as *aficionados*, and its lyrics serve as a fund of social philosophy for dealing with daily life. I believe that awakening students to the nature of this phenomenon—to the effects of both its music and its attendant criticism (which is likewise highly popular)—provides them with a first step toward understanding their place in our media-saturated society. It is upon structures of production and reception developed in pop that those of other mass-media forms

(television, advertising) are based; even a rudimentary understanding of their function will encourage students to approach the discourse of media more critically.

We see in Will's statement of goals not just concern for teaching musicology—he knows that for his students this is their first and probably last course in the subject—but for teaching them about what it means to be communicators in a mass/multi-media culture. He is concerned about students' self-awareness, authority, and voice. Students are to "imagine their own 'discourses'" and "find a 'voice' for writing—and thinking." All Will's assignments are designed to help students understand the voices of the texts they read and then to enter into a conversation with them. That's learning to write, to learn, and to think. His eighth and final essay assignment therefore asked students to compile a discography and bibliography for one artist or musical group, and then to write an interpretation of that artist or group suitable for inclusion in an informal reference book of the type students had been using for the course. With an essay requiring extensive use of secondary material and quotations and preparatory work that helped students to critique sociological prose and criticism itself, Will wanted to provide "a final and valuable lesson on the students' relationship to pop writing" and on "their tendency to let the critics speak for them. . . . It is an understanding of this authority, and a knowledge of how to appropriate it for themselves, that I would hope the students to have gained from the course. It is a first step towards participating in, rather than simply absorbing, their popular culture." It is difficult to imagine Will not teaching writing similarly in future courses, even if they are not writing courses.

Paul Doremus was a TA in government when he taught the First-Year Writing Seminar, "Containment and Hegemony: The Politics of Imperial Decline." His goals for students as writers, like Will's, were part and parcel of his goals for their experience with his discipline, as is very clear from the rationale he wrote to accompany the description of his essay assignments:

> As is appropriate for a course in government, my seminar focused on persuasive argumentation. Early writings emphasized description and analysis of international relations and foreign policy theories; students then practiced applying theories to particular documents and historical periods. After these two stages, the assignments involved taking policy positions and then integrating those positions with theoretically informed long-range strategies. The progression of assignments corresponded with the four-part organization of the course: The first covered international

relations theories about declining hegemony; the second covered the history of the Cold War, with containment as the organizing theme; the third covered the competing foreign policy strategies of Carter and Reagan; and the fourth returned to the systemic, long-term considerations that were introduced in the first part.

Doremus's assignments resemble Will's in leading students through staged experience with materials and methods in the discipline; at every stage, interest in voice, style, and engagement in dialogue informs Doremus's approach to his students' learning. Like Will, Doremus provides a final project in which students' own voices can definitively emerge: Doremus's students draw directly on their earlier work as well as on additional research in order to write an extended policy position paper in which they describe "the major challenges that the U.S. will face during the rest of this century, and from this picture derive a conception of what long-term strategy America should pursue." Students are asked to incorporate material from a previous essay assignment in which they were to "take one of their recent policy positions and explain how it fits into a large strategy"; they also draw on earlier assignments in which they described and analyzed materials that serve now as the basis for their own formation of positions. Students in both Will's and Doremus's seminars should emerge sensing the significance of the fields in which they worked for a semester, with an appreciation for the complex role of writing in those fields, and with, one hopes, an increased understanding of the complex responsibilities of intellectual engagement, whatever the subject.

In my experience, TAs do not value mechanical replication of ideas; they hope for their students' genuine intellectual involvement. As a consequence, when given an opportunity to teach First-Year Writing Seminars, and required to participate in the preparatory seminar, graduate students typically produce sequences of essay assignments and preparatory writing that ask students to explore a subject and gradually become more and more involved in the conversation. TAs understand that helping students take part in their disciplines means actually teaching them to write in those disciplines.

It is gratifying, but not surprising, to learn that many TAs value the opportunity to teach First-Year Writing Seminars. In fields as remote from "composition" as archeology, TAs have chosen Cornell for graduate study because they sought a genuine opportunity to teach courses of their own, an opportunity available in the form of First-Year Writing Seminars. Others come to appreciate the experience during their time here: TAs regularly claim that teaching a First-Year Writing Seminar has been one of their most valuable experiences, especially because of the required preparatory seminar and because of the integration of the teaching of writing with a subject of their own choosing. They find in the First-Year Writing Seminars a place where teaching is valued, and where they can develop their own teaching values.

I began my review of the Cornell Knight Institute for Writing in the Disciplines and its use of TAs with the recollection that I once disapproved of having graduate students teach. For reasons that should now be clear, I have come to see them as a major source of strength in the program, and the writing program as a source of strength for them. As I have frequently pointed out, in a deep sense, the graduate students, like faculty across the curriculum, *are* the writing program.[8] I hope they remain so for the rest of their teaching careers.

# Writing without Friction

KEITH HJORTSHOJ

Director, Writing in the Majors,
Knight Institute

*15 May 1997*

Doctor Harrison,

I am writing to you on behalf of the newly formed Biology
Student Curriculum Council, of which I am the vice president and
elected representative to the Divisional Biology Curriculum
Committee. As I am also an ecology and systematics concentrator, I
was chosen to submit this petition for your perusal.

In short, it is the unanimous opinion of the sixty-member
student council that BioES 278, Evolutionary Biology, does not offer
enough students the opportunity to participate in the four-credit
option if only one such section is taught. It is our feeling that all
students who wish to broaden their understanding of evolution by
electing additional coursework should be able to do so.

To that end, we petition the section of ecology and systematics
to provide a minimum of forty students per semester the opportunity to take BioES 278 for four credits. This could easily be accomplished by offering two four-credit sections of twenty students
apiece. We estimate that this will meet the current demand.

☞ In this letter and petition to Richard Harrison, the chair of the ecology and
systematics section of the Division of Biological Sciences, representatives of
nearly two thousand biology majors at Cornell in 1997 demand more sections of
an experimental, interactive version of Evolutionary Biology, a core require-

ment for all majors in the field. Students enrolled in these optional, extra-credit sections—known as "track two" within the division—attend lectures and complete readings in the course at large, but they do not take formal exams. Instead, they meet twice each week in classes of twenty, where they discuss the course material in depth, explore new directions in the field, write and revise several papers, and keep reflective journals on the lectures and readings. With doubts that many biology majors would make this choice, ecology and systematics first offered the track two option in 1992 in collaboration with Writing in the Majors, which helps to support and train the biology graduate students who lead the four-credit sections.

In a small way, this student petition for additional track two sections of Evolutionary Biology fulfills all of the goals Harry Shaw and I had in mind when we initiated Writing in the Majors in 1988, along with objectives and limitations we had not yet envisioned.

The demand for more of these writing-intensive sections of BioES 278 came initially from the undergraduate majors who take the course, not from administrators of the university, the biology division, or the writing program. And this demand was actually much greater than the letter suggests. In the spring of 1997, more than eighty students (in a class of about two hundred) had requested enrollment in the extra-credit section. The following semester, when we had met the demand for two sections that reduced scheduling conflicts, the requests rose to one hundred.

The students who take this course, like most of the others affiliated with Writing in the Majors, obviously think of this option as an enriched way of learning the subject, to "broaden their understanding of evolution." They do not view it as a writing component, distinguished from the biological "content" of the course. Although the attention to writing and revision in these sections would satisfy guidelines for any WAC (writing across the curriculum) program in the country, this request does not mention "writing" or Writing in the Majors, and it was sent to the chair of ecology and systematics, not to us.

The content and direction of the request indicates that responsibility for the design, administration, and success of the course lies primarily with the biologists who teach it, not with Writing in the Majors or the Knight Institute. Responsibility for failure would fall in the same direction.

Like other Writing in the Majors courses, BioES 278 offers graduate students excellent training as college teachers and strong credentials for teaching positions. Those who lead track two sections collaborate closely with biology faculty, with one another, and with Writing in the Majors staff. They have developed innovative methods that influence teaching practices in the division at large, and several have carried these ideas to biology programs at other institutions.

BioES 278 and its track two sections are not in any way marginalized components of the curriculum, and they do not marginalize writing in the minds of biology students and teachers. Evolutionary Biology is one of only three core requirements within biology for all majors, in a curriculum of nearly two hundred undergraduate courses. Within this required course, as in two other large courses for majors (Ecology and Environment and Introduction to Behavior), students view the writing-intensive sections as a privilege, not as a burden.

Privileges, however, are also exclusive. Although we initiated the track two option with the concern that few biology majors would choose it, we are now unable to meet the full demand for these sections. This shortfall in BioES 278 applies to the dimensions of Writing in the Majors within the curriculum at large. Since the second year of the program, we have not been able to satisfy the demand for these projects, much less to meet the goal of providing enriched language and learning courses for all majors in all fields.

The four-credit sections of Evolutionary Biology have become increasingly popular because they address the needs of students and teachers in this course and discipline, not because they conform to general standards for writing and teaching across the curriculum. Writing in the Majors courses in other fields, even within biology, have very different designs, and they work in very different ways for specific purposes. In collaboration with Writing in the Majors, the Department of Astronomy developed a small course called Astronomy 233, Topics in Astrophysics, when it created an undergraduate major in the field. Potential astronomy majors had already learned to accumulate knowledge and complete problem sets in physics and mathematics. The department designed Astronomy 233 to teach these students scientific intuition, creative and critical thinking, and communication. As a consequence, there are no exams or problem sets in this course, and in its first version, developed by Steve Beckwith and Steve Squyres, students wrote and revised six papers. Although the design of Astronomy 233 departed radically from the typical lecture/exam/problem set format of upper-level science courses, students never questioned the relevance of this work to the study of astrophysics. How could they, while completing assignments such as this?

> Pick two subtopics in the study of dark matter. . . . Compare our knowledge or thinking about each of these two subtopics between 1979 (Faber and Gallagher article) and 1987 (Trimble article).
> If possible, choose one topic where you believe our knowledge has progressed toward the solution of the problem or ultimate

answer and one topic where you believe we are actually farther
from the answer than we believed in 1979.

Condensed here from a full page of discussion, this assignment asks students to explore one of the most fundamental, unresolved problems in astrophysics and skillfully disrupts linear assumptions about the development of scientific knowledge. Professor Martha Haynes, who later taught Topics in Astrophysics and developed another Writing in the Majors course in astronomy, created assignments addressed to a wide range of audiences, included formal peer review of student papers, designed computer lab programs that simulate observational data for writing, and organized topical symposia in which students present reviewed papers that are then published in symposium "proceedings."

Topics in Astrophysics, however, is no more a "typical" Writing in the Majors course than Evolutionary Biology. Nor was Government 353, Feminist Movements and the State. With Writing in the Majors support, Mary Katzenstein completely restructured Government 353 because she felt cut off, as a lecturer, from the sixty students who enrolled in the course. When we agreed to support a second graduate teaching assistant, Professor Katzenstein divided the central nine weeks of the course into three, three-week modules on specific themes, each taught by one of the three "instructors" (as they were all listed on the syllabus) in her area of expertise. Following introductory lectures, the sixty students rotated through these modules in groups of twenty, all receiving the advantage of lively discussions in topical seminars with three skillful teachers. In each module they wrote and revised position papers, and each student developed an independent research project under the guidance of one of the instructors. The two graduate teaching assistants, who also gave lectures at the beginning and end of the semester, felt that this course offered the most valuable teacher training they could imagine.

Since 1988, Writing in the Majors has directly supported changes in sixty-five other courses, offered among twenty-two departments, and has consulted with faculty and teaching assistants in many others. Enrollments in these courses have ranged from ten students to more than three hundred, and their designs and functions have varied just as radically. All of them include writing assignments, usually with revision, but the proportions of writing to other uses of language differ considerably. In Human Genetics and Society, a course for senior biology majors, students write and revise research-based position papers on the social, ethical, or legal implications of new developments in genetics and reproductive technology. Equally important, however, are collaborative presentations to the class, lively discussion of these presentations, peer reviews, visits from guest speakers, and a general emphasis on critical thinking. Other Writing in the Majors courses have included individual and collaborative research projects, collaborative writing, oral presentations, group oral exams, field studies, authentic laboratory experiments, debates, reading exercises, topical symposia, conversation groups, student-led discussions, poster sessions, and many kinds of informal writing, including on-line exchanges.

All of these courses are continually works in progress, and their great variety results from the absence of program-wide guidelines. Such guidelines are unnecessary, in turn, because courses affiliated with the program do not constitute a designated category of instruction. They are not labeled "W" (writing) or "WI" (writing intensive) in the course catalogue, and although most of them complete requirements for majors, they do not satisfy any formal writing requirements. Because writing assignments and other features are included in course descriptions and syllabi, students who enroll in these courses know what they are getting into, but they are often unaware that a course is affiliated with Writing in the Majors. As much as possible, we have tried to put work with language into solution with learning, so that writing becomes, as Martha Haynes noted in her syllabus for Astronomy 201, "a natural consequence of trying to understand *any* subject." If students protest that so much writing, peer review, and revision is an unreasonable burden in a science course, Haynes does not attribute this burden to the demands of the writing program. She tells them, instead, "I won't ask you to do anything I don't have to do myself."

Faculty responsibility for the design, success, or failure of these initiatives results from entirely voluntary participation. There are no institutional mandates for departmental or faculty involvement in Writing in the Majors. None of the more than one hundred faculty members who have collaborated with us since 1988 were obliged to do so, and all of them have been free to discontinue projects for any reason, including time constraints and dissatisfaction with the program. The opposite is true as well. Because we do not rely on requirements or quotas of any kind, we do not try to persuade professors and departments that they should work with us, or that they should make changes in their courses according to our objectives. Nor are we obliged to collaborate with everyone who requests support from the program or to continue projects we consider unsuccessful. Over the years, five or six professors have abandoned projects as a result of dissatisfaction or disinterest, and we have discontinued about four initiatives for comparable reasons. Other fluctuations have resulted from routine changes of faculty and teaching assignments within departments.

I am not suggesting that Writing in the Majors courses (or the program at large) run like well-oiled machines, without design flaws and disorders. Problems arise continually. Particular assignments and teaching strategies fail; courses sometimes become overstructured, or their components become uncoordinated; workloads become too heavy; changing enrollments undermine course designs that worked well in the past. Innovation usually creates a certain amount of disruption, along with disconcerting revelations. It is easy to assume that students are getting what you want them to get out of a lecture, for example, as long as you don't ask them what they got. When a professor of government told students to summarize the past three weeks of lectures, therefore, she was disturbed to find the cohesive fabric of her teaching chopped into lists of disconnected "points." New teaching strategies yield new kinds of satisfaction *and* dissatisfaction. "Things fall apart," especially when we are trying to rebuild them.

Frustrating as they can be, the kinds of problems that send us back to the drawing board still differ from the types of *resistance* that led WAC program directors at large universities to call their panel at the 1991 CCCC meetings "Trials of the '90s." All of these WPAs (writing program administrators) ran institutionally mandated programs with broad guidelines for designated courses that satisfied undergraduate writing requirements, and in the process of implementing mandates they had encountered resistance from everyone involved: from university administrators who had pledged support for the programs, from departments required to offer designated writing courses, from faculty members assigned to teach these courses, and from students required to take them. Their tales of administrative struggle and betrayal were versions of the children's story, "The Little Red Hen," in which the title character couldn't get anyone to help her make the bread everyone wanted to eat. Everyone in the university seemed to acknowledge the importance of writing and the potential benefits of writing instruction across the curriculum. Funding this instruction, taking real responsibility for providing it, and taking it seriously as an integral part of undergraduate education were different matters.

In contrast with the long, evolutionary history of Cornell's writing programs, these were young programs established by decree, still negotiating the contradictions between the premises of WAC and the traditional divisions of labor established in their institutions. Since 1991 these negotiations have progressed at many universities, and the identification of writing instruction with freshman English has proportionally weakened. Writing program administrators, typically educated in English and in related fields, have also developed better strategies for collaborating with scholars and assessing the needs of student writers in other areas, and, as a consequence, mandated WAC programs are often better integrated with other dimensions of teaching and learning than they were a decade ago. The shift that Charles Bazerman described in 1991 as a "second stage" of WAC—through attachment "to the lifeblood of communication by means of which disciplines and professions organize themselves" (210)—reduced some kinds of resistance to the goals and methods of interdisciplinary writing programs.

To some extent, however, program-wide guidelines, designations, and requirements will always make "writing" a distinct category of instruction and thus offer something to resist, perhaps even for good reasons. Anyone in charge of such a program must assume some responsibility for determining what writing is, what students need to learn about it, and what will or will not "count" as real writing instruction. Even for the purpose of attaching "itself to the lifeblood of communication" in a discipline, WAC must be an "it," somehow distinct from communication, teaching, and learning already established in that discipline. Certified "writing" courses must differ in some way from other courses, other kinds of learning offered in a department. And to the extent that WAC programs are part of a larger "movement," as Barbara Walvoord and others have described such programs nationally, this movement must convey something across the curriculum that was not already there—something that teachers and students in the disciplines might accept or resist.

I don't intend to assess the ways in which this substance of WAC has been construed, or to argue that interdisciplinary writing programs across the country should abandon all requirements, designations, and guidelines. Because these features of writing programs have both advantages and disadvantages that vary considerably from one institution to another, I don't propose that Writing in the Majors should serve as a model for other upper-level programs. At this large research university we have addressed problems and utilized resources that do not exist at many other schools. Some of the features of Writing in the Majors also emerge from the long, somewhat peculiar history of interdisciplinary writing programs at Cornell, described in other chapters of this book.

The evolution of WAC to a "second stage," however, presupposes a first—one that was "driven," Bazerman says, "by the missionary zeal of composition and the institutional designs of administrators looking for broad structural fixes . . ." (209). Writing in the Majors is most useful, perhaps, as an example of an "unstaged" program that began without a legacy of missionary zeal, administrative mandates, or prior assumptions about the forms writing instruction should take among the disciplines. For programs and institutions of all kinds, the results of this experiment demonstrate some of the ways in which teachers in the disciplines invent writing and other forms of language instruction without external constraints, in accordance with their own concerns, motivations, and conceptions of writing itself. These developments have revealed great variation in the roles of written language among disciplines and levels of instruction, but they have also revealed striking patterns across the curriculum—patterns obscured by the assumption that academic disciplines or clusters of disciplines represent separate realms of discourse.

## *("Writing") in the Majors*

In the chapter on his term as director of the Knight Writing Program, Harry Shaw discusses the values and concerns underlying the inductive, experimental design of Writing in the Majors. Because "the devil really is in the details," as he notes, I'll simply provide some illustrations of implementation and outcome.

One of Shaw's guiding principles, as he says, was that of "helping capable people deal with real problems in ways they made their own." As we tried to imagine the task of integrating writing instruction with learning in highly specialized courses, this principle was reinforced by a deep reluctance to assume prior knowledge of the links between language and learning in fields of study we knew little about. At the freshman level, it is easier to maintain the notion that terms such as *writing, reading, authorship, clarity, organization, thesis, citation, argument,* and *evidence* have general meanings, and that they are linked with general "skills" that remain stable among the disciplines. As students move from introductory courses into specialized branches of departmental curricula, uses of language also divide and subdivide in complex, largely uncharted, unpredictable directions and intersections, like rivers converging in deltas.

Mapping these channels would be easier if disciplines only subdivided into separate areas of specialization. But *specialization* does not always mean *separation.* At advanced levels, biology both divides and intersects with branches of chemistry, physics, psychology, anthropology, and history. Branches of literary studies overlap with social philosophy, linguistics, and cultural history. New disciplines such as biophysics, neuroscience, cognitive studies, environmental studies, and cultural studies include scholars from disciplines that were traditionally separate. At the highest levels of the curriculum, the boundaries of "discourse communities" do not reliably correspond with the boundaries of academic departments. What would terms such as "writing," "reading," and "authorship" mean in conjunction with learning in a physical chemistry lab course, a seminar in astrophysics, a lecture course on the history of American foreign policy, or one on economic policies in China?

We really had no idea.

Because the potential functions of writing in such courses remained unknown, we tried initially to put this term in parentheses, so that generalized assumptions about the goals of a writing program would not undermine the investigative task of finding out what the term could mean. In other words, we began not by asking about the roles writing might play in a course, but about the design and functions of the course itself, the goals of teachers, and their dissatisfactions with student learning. If these conversations led to projects, they did so because writing and other uses of language fell into place, eventually, as specific solutions to specific problems we could not predict in advance.

In my first conversation with the physicist Persis Drell, for example, I asked her about the roles of her particle physics course in the undergraduate curriculum for physics majors. She explained that Physics 444, Nuclear and High Energy Particle Physics, gave senior majors a "first exposure" to the "phenomenology" of real experimental physics. Moving beyond basic knowledge and theory, she said, the course addressed the question "What is nature telling you when you do experiments?" As a consequence, this course and a couple of others in the department served as transitions between undergraduate and graduate studies, between textbook instruction and primary literature, and between established knowledge and current issues in the field.

This explanation led us immediately to the main problems Physics 444 posed, both for Professor Drell and for her students. Accustomed to learning physics through textbooks, lectures, and problem sets, these students had little experience locating, reading, analyzing, or synthesizing professional literature in the field. Nor had they faced the uncertainties of research and debate at the frontiers of physics, where the "right answer" (perhaps even the right question) is still in doubt. A topical research paper based on primary resources, Drell suggested, might engage students with these unfamiliar dimensions of experimental physics. Over the following weeks and in collaboration with Adrian Cho, an advanced graduate student in physics, we designed a research paper project, in stages, on "a problem crucial to the development of high energy physics in the past fifteen years." The research project would replace the final exam, and at the end of the term students would give oral presentations on their research—another neglected skill they would need in graduate programs and professions. Early in the term Drell would ask students to locate and summarize research articles on particular topics, to give them some practice.

This is how one of our first projects began. Initial experiments in Professor Drell's course, as in most of the others, underscored the need for this kind of work, raised new issues, and led to further revisions. When Drell asked her students to locate and summarize a research article, for example, two of them copied large sections verbatim without quotation, and without any awareness that this was plagiarism. Another student simply photocopied the article, as though the assignment were a treasure hunt. A professional article, from their perspective, was a perfectly intact, unalterable representation of knowledge; having that knowledge was simply a matter of finding it. For similar reasons, students were initially reluctant to discuss issues in class, because admitting uncertainty or confusion seemed to reveal weakness. Adrian Cho, the graduate teaching assistant, helped to solve this problem by sitting among the students, stimulating discussion by admitting his own confusion, and raising questions.

"First exposure" to real research accurately described the functions of many other 400-level science courses, but individual teachers devised different strategies to help students make this transition. Biochemist David Shalloway described Oncogenes and Cancer Viruses as a course "on reading the research literature," and for this purpose the writing assignments he and his teaching assistant created were also reading exercises, culminating in an extremely difficult project. In the final weeks of the term, the senior biology majors and first-year graduate students in the course were given only the data tables from published research and were asked to write a professional article based on this data. In Solid-State Physics, another 400-level course, Geoffrey Chester and his teaching assistant, Chris O'Neill, designed a series of encounters with research literature to encourage critical reading and deeper understanding of the way knowledge progresses. One of these exercises asked students to evaluate, in a four-page paper, the "fit" between Debye's "Theory of Specific Heats," first published in 1912, and data from recent research on the specific heats of aluminum and silver. This assignment demonstrated that theories in physics are not simply true or false. Their validity and usefulness often change gradually with new sources of information.

When we began by asking teachers to describe learning issues in their courses, both the problems they identified and the solutions they proposed greatly expanded our prior understanding of writing, its potential roles in the curriculum, and its connections with other uses of language. Barry Carpenter, who taught an organic chemistry lecture course at the 300 level, also hoped to move students beyond what he called "the myth of certainty": to encourage them to ask of chemists "not only *What do you know?* but *How do you know this?* and *What else do we need to figure out?*" How could we include these kinds of thinking in a densely structured lecture course for sixty science majors?

If I had begun by suggesting that Professor Carpenter should add writing assignments to Organic Chemistry or convert it to a writing-intensive course to improve his students' writing skills, our conversation would have ended abruptly and these questions would not have arisen. Once he had raised them on his own as learning issues, however, Carpenter began to think of possible solutions, and by the beginning of the semester he had devised what he called "the even-numbered problem sets," described in this passage from the syllabus:

Problem sets 2, 4, 6, and 8 are intended to introduce you to the processes of development and communication of scientific thought. You will be given a set of facts that you can imagine might have been acquired in your own laboratory. You will be requested to formulate some theory about these facts and to communicate both the facts and your ideas about their significance to the editor of a scientific journal in a brief article (limited to one thousand words, according to the rules taken from *The Journal of the American Chemical Society* for communications to the editor, on the attached page). . . . You may work in groups on these (even-numbered) problem sets. If you do, then each article should bear the names of all members of the participating group. . . . Groups can change from one problem set to another. You will have to decide whether a given individual has contributed enough to the thought process and production to have his or her name included. For these problem sets there need not be a single "right" answer. You will be graded on the quality of your thought process and your ability to communicate clearly within the limits of the journal requirements.

Complex and intensely difficult, these problem sets simulated many aspects of scientific research and writing: real laboratory research problems, enigmatic results, irregular data tables, and the challenges of working and writing with others. Problem set 6 begins:

One of the problems with scientific research is that one frequently doesn't know which of the many pieces of data that can be gathered are really relevant to the problem at hand. Here is a case in point:

You are working for a chemical company that has isolated a mixture of a couple of organic compounds from a Norwegian tree bark . . .

Many mysteries arise in the two pages of experimental procedures that follow. And while there are various ways of solving these mysteries, neither the methods nor the solutions appear obvious in the lectures and textbook for the course. Due to the difficulty and value of these problems, in final evaluations the same students occasionally listed them both as the best and the worst part of the course. "It was confusing and frustrating most of the time," one student commented, "but the feeling of having something work out was . . . ahh . . . superb." The great majority recognized the authenticity of these struggles, and in spite of the strict professional standards for communications imposed on the finished products, no one complained that writing assignments do not belong in an organic chemistry course.

A couple of early strategic blunders taught us that certain kinds of explicit emphasis on writing can obscure its actual roles and values in the disciplines. In one of our first projects, economist Robert Frank was teaching a new course for economics majors called Departures from Rational Choice. He wanted to include writing assignments based on forms of analysis and explanation he had developed in a book that was going to press at the time, *Passions Within Reason: The Strategic Role of the Emotions*. Because these methods of analysis borrowed heavily from the behavioral sciences, Frank wanted students to write and revise case studies of economic phenomena they observed as "economic naturalists," using traditional and nontraditional methods of analysis.

These assignments were vitally relevant to the substance of the course. To emphasize their importance, however, Frank announced in the first class that the course was affiliated with the Knight Writing Program and that his teaching assistant, an advanced graduate student in economics, had been specially trained to help them with their writing. In the minds of the students, this explicit emphasis on writing had the unintended effect of isolating the writing assignments and the graduate teaching assistant from the core content of the course. In discussion sections, the teaching assistant found it difficult to link work on students' papers with the study of economics, and felt generally marginalized in the role of the "writing TA." Final evaluations indicated that although most of the students appreciated his comments on their papers and acknowledged the general importance of writing and revision, they did not see connections between writing and learning in this course or in the field of economics at large.

The following year, Frank taught Departures from Rational Choice with the same assignments, but with a larger proportion of the grade attached to revisions and required conferences between drafts. The second year the same teaching assistant gave a couple of lectures in the course, establishing his credentials as an economist. The other main change was that Frank gave students no indication that the writing assignments were distinct from other features of the course, or affiliated with Writing in the Majors. This small change had rather dramatic effects. Attendance in discussion sections increased, the instructors saw more substantial improvement in the finished papers, and students accepted the written work as a natural dimension of an economics course. Asked in the numerical evaluations "How well did the writing assignments contribute to your understanding of the course material?" the mean response was 4.3 on a scale of 1 to 5.

Changes of this kind occurred in the opposite direction several years later in a physical chemistry lab course for junior majors. In collaboration with the professor in the course, an advanced graduate student in physical chemistry had developed successful exercises in reading professional articles, writing experimental abstracts, and revising lab reports. Students appreciated the value of these exercises, which dissolved some of the mysteries of writing and reading in their field. The following year, the same graduate student became an overly zealous convert to writing instruction, designated herself the "writing TA," and began to give students "writing comments" on their lab reports, in addition to the ones they received from the teaching assistants who supervised their experiments. In practice, however, there were no clear boundaries between the writing and the chemistry or, for that matter, between the "writing TA," who was a fine chemist, and the other teaching assistants in the course who were broadly concerned with the qualities of lab reports. Students often received conflicting advice, and the resulting confusion led to substantial criticism in the final evaluations.

By the end of our third year, "Departures from Rational Choice" might have become the motto for Writing in the Majors, and in an inverted, counter-intuitive resistance had become an important feature of the program. Because uses of language are essential to learning in every field of study at every level, resistance meant that attention to language had become disconnected from learning, in the minds of teachers and students or in the structure of the course. Writing had come to represent something *other* than learning economics, physical chemistry, anthropology, or history. The appropriate response, therefore, was not to struggle against this resistance but to examine its causes, and work toward the reintegration of language and learning.

In turn, we found that we needed to resist abstract, generalized, narrow, or pedantic assumptions about writing, writing instruction, and writing skills. We did not presume that we could eliminate these ideas, but we could make sure that our program did not represent or support them. On the assumption that we simply advocated *more writing*, for example, professors sometimes requested support for courses that already included writing assignments used essentially as examinations, or for the simple addition of assigned papers to courses that would remain otherwise unchanged, as though assigning writing were in itself a virtue, deserving of a teaching assistant to "do the grading." These proposals often conformed to the quantitative guidelines of mandated programs, in which they would have been hard to resist, and they came most often from teachers in the humanities.

## Inversions

In this respect our assumption that Writing in the Majors would develop most easily in the humanities was correct. It would have been easy to enlist humanities professors who were willing to assign writing. It would have been easy to let writing hold unchanged meanings and roles within the curriculum, and work only toward greater volume. But such work would not have been very interesting, and as we listened to this kind of proposal we learned to let our lack of interest show. We also learned that when teachers are satisfied with their courses, persuading them to try something new is a lost cause. Descriptions of some of the more ambitious changes we did support usually ended these conversations, and both Harry Shaw and I had to remind ourselves that this outcome was completely acceptable, unavoidable, even necessary. Because we couldn't work with everyone, using our resources well meant that we should support changes that offered the greatest potential benefits, primarily to undergraduates but also to their professors and graduate teaching assistants.

Yet the distribution of these benefits was very uneven. In 1992, more than 75 percent of our projects were in astronomy, biology, chemistry, and physics, and colleagues in mathematics were experimenting with related uses of writing without our support. Against all of our expectations, and against the current of expansion in most interdisciplinary writing programs, Writing in the Majors was in danger of becoming an upper-level science program.

While they had initially encouraged and appreciated our work in the sciences, the deans in the College of Arts and Sciences urged us to move in the opposite direction: toward the humanities. We took this advice to heart, and new support from the Knight and Park Foundations has allowed us to expand projects in the social sciences and humanities to half of the thirty courses now affiliated with the program each year. The humanities still represent the smallest category of projects, however, and the peculiar direction of the program deserves some further discussion.

As I noted previously, the inductive, experimental nature of Writing in the Majors partly explains its reception in advanced science courses, at the opposite corner of the curriculum from the traditional domain of writing instruction: freshman English. But there are some other, related reasons that also made it difficult, for some time, to develop comparable projects in the humanities and social sciences. Harry Shaw and I often had to remind department chairs and faculty that we did not support "business as usual"—forms of teaching and learning or roles for graduate teaching assistants that had already become routine. In the humanities and in some of the social sciences, certain kinds of writing—such as formal essays, term papers, and essay exams—*were* "business as usual," and regardless of their value we saw no point in using scarce resources to support established practices.

In science curricula, however, there were no conventional forms of undergraduate writing apart from lab reports and "word problems," and even "discussion" was an ambiguous category of instruction, often limited to question/answer exchanges in review sessions. (An astronomy graduate student once asked me whether it was possible to hold a genuine discussion in an undergraduate science course "when there *is* a right answer," he observed, "and you [the teacher] know it.") As a consequence, any attempt to integrate writing and speaking with learning in a science course is likely to be innovative—*unusual*—even though many of these innovations are based upon established forms of professional communication. Elaborate peer review exercises, critical analyses of research articles, collaborative writing, field notebooks, research proposals, review articles, and poster sessions replicate standard forms of language use in scientific communities, which one biochemist described to me as "beehives of communication." Within the undergraduate curriculum at a large research university, however, these are extraordinary ways of teaching and learning.

Most of these practices in the sciences are also alien to the humanities and would not have emerged if we had tried to export ways of writing and teaching typically found in literary studies, composition, history, or philosophy. The problems science teachers identify, their motivations for change, and potential solutions reside almost entirely within their own disciplines. Even if they hold to the necessity of teaching "basic knowledge" in conventional courses, most scientists are aware of the stark contradictions between methods of undergraduate instruction and the actual demands of scientific careers, in and outside higher education. When they attempt to resolve these contradictions with their own imagination and expertise, science teachers invent new forms of writing, reading, teaching, and learning in undergraduate courses—forms transposed, more often than not, from their own professional experience. To figure out how to give students extensive feedback on research proposals in their population genetics course, for example, Charles Aquadro and Laura Katz did not need to learn about forms of discussion used in humanities courses. They relied upon methods used in their own research groups and professional conferences: short oral presentations followed by intense, "open-fire" question periods. When Melissa Hines decided to use peer review for the revision of student reports in an analytical chemistry lab, she did not need to read up on peer review methods in the WAC literature. She structured anonymous peer reviews based upon professional journal guidelines and procedures, including letters from authors to the editor, explaining how they would respond to suggestions and reconcile contradictions among reviews.

As potential teaching strategies, these practices flourish in disciplines in which many kinds of communication have instrumental functions connected with physical and social activities, such as field and laboratory studies. In an ecology course, for example, the process of inquiry can begin with observations recorded during a field trip to a marsh, and can proceed through group activities in which students formulate viable research questions toward the development of research proposals. The process of research and writing can then include literature searches, additional field studies, team presentations, and many other kinds of communication prior to that conventional moment of transaction in schooling: when students turn in their papers for grading.

Models for similar kinds of activities exist in the social sciences and can be extended to some humanities courses. Kathryn March's anthropology course, Sex and Gender in Cross-Cultural Perspective, includes collaborative ethnographic exercises carried through stages of observation and analysis, with close attention to the process of social research. Our projects in the interdisciplinary field of cognitive studies include extensive laboratory studies that students design and conduct, with many kinds of writing in the research process. In her courses on Buddhism, Asian studies professor Jane Marie Law transports her students to regional monasteries where they can observe and experience Buddhist practice, and their informal notes become the basis for further inquiries, discussions, and papers. Similar kinds of direct observation and analysis have enriched learning in fields such as political studies, history, interior design, and sociology.

The fact remains, however, that texts of one kind or another *are* the primary objects of inquiry and repositories of knowledge in the humanities, and necessary restrictions on the use of human subjects limit opportunities for real research activity in social science courses as well. Comparative literature is, after all, the comparative study of literature. Philosophy is the study of philosophical texts. And in courses based on theories and cases, sociology is, as my students say, "the study of sociology," confined to the classroom and to the individually authored text. What does it mean, in such courses, to do something other than "business as usual"?

Through the lens of the sciences we began to see interesting patterns, correlations, and problems that ran through the entire undergraduate curriculum, and these patterns increasingly informed our conversations with teachers in all disciplines. This was not simply a matter of transporting practices from one part of the curriculum to another, though that movement did occur. More important was an awareness of similarities among the points at which undergraduates are admitted to a line of inquiry, and asked to learn about it. Whether the object of inquiry is an assigned text, a chemical reaction, or an organism, how do we ask students to learn about it and to tell us what they have learned?

There is something oddly inverted about the way the university answers this question in practice, and this inversion tends to disconnect undergraduate education from real scholarship. Most scholars enter and remain in their fields because so many interesting questions remain unanswered, or as yet unasked. Yet we typically introduce undergraduates to these fields through knowledge already assembled, debates already held, theories and methods already formulated, and questions already answered. When teachers ask at the end of a class "Are there any questions?" they convey the message that lingering confusion and curiosity are weaknesses, and that remaining questions need to be answered as quickly as possible. Students reasonably conclude that writing, reading, speaking, and learning are about knowing things already known, and doing what has already been done.

Due to the need for "basic knowledge," this kind of learning is to some extent necessary. We can't ask undergraduates to enter the field of physics at the frontiers of research, where new questions are posed. But the unrelieved experience of absorbing and reproducing ideas and information creates a kind of intellectual and linguistic impoverishment that Harry Shaw had in mind when he proposed to "enrich" upper-level courses. This way of entering a discipline deprives undergraduates of many of the skills they will need as they enter graduate programs and professions, and it also creates epistemological misconceptions that are difficult to correct later.

Undergraduate laboratory science courses, for example, typically use "cookbook" experiments and reports to introduce undergraduates to basic experimental concepts, procedures, records, and forms of presentation. Yet these kinds of laboratory exercises also teach students that an experiment is, as the chemist Melissa Hines complained, "the shortest route between a known problem and a known solution." According to this definition, which science majors will need to abandon if they conduct real research, unexpected, puzzling results mean error. Lab reports, like lab experiments, should be completed in a single try, by following instructions.

In their own ways, courses in the social sciences and humanities also routinely misconstrue the processes of inquiry and writing in their disciplines. While writing assignments are more common in these fields, they frequently serve as forms of examination. As David Bartholomae observed in "Inventing the University," we ask undergraduates to write as though they had completed processes of inquiry they have not experienced, and to assume kinds of authority they do not actually possess (Bartholomae 1996, 134–65). To write effectively for him, Bartholomae says, students must appear to "know what I know and how I know it," even though they do not (140). And within the typical schedule of an undergraduate course, in a week, perhaps even at one sitting, students must construct a sense of authority that real scholars assemble over weeks and months, through many drafts. In such courses, revision, whether voluntary or assigned, does not represent an investigative process. It means that the first try, like a poorly conducted lab experiment, was flawed.

We observed these correlations most clearly in the weaknesses teachers observe in student research papers, usually assigned for the purpose of engaging undergraduates in real inquiry. Mary Beth Norton's dissatisfaction with the research papers in her history course, The Age of the American Revolution, made sense in a new way after Geoffrey Chester had abandoned research papers in Solid State Physics. Chester observed that research paper assignments attempt to replicate scholarship but cannot really do so, because scholars identify meaningful questions within a frame of reference undergraduates do not have, especially at the beginning of a course. Doing research then becomes a process of building that frame of reference in which students might find reasons for pursuing the topics they initially chose, more or less arbitrarily. And unless student writers thoroughly reformulate the project around the questions they have discovered, the papers they submit will simply contain bunches of information clustered around a topic. In Chester's words, "They want to tell you what the territory looked like as they walked over it." This fundamental problem applied equally to research papers on "Auger Electron Spectroscopy" and, in Norton's history course, "Slavery in South Carolina." In response to both, our central question is "What about it?" or "Why are you writing?" But students can't answer these questions without entirely rewriting and rethinking the draft. When they believe (or at least hope) that they are finished with the paper they have reached the point at which scholarship usually begins.

With recognition of this problem we could more effectively stage the research and writing process in Norton's history course, postponing a full draft until writers had developed a meaningful approach to the topic. Inheriting Solid State Physics from Geoffrey Chester, Chris Henley addressed the problem by changing the form and purpose of the research assignment, rather than abandoning it. Henley gave student research sharper focus on a smaller scale by using the model of a topical review article on primary literature. He believed that there was educational value in what he called "the Frankenstein work of synthesis," even if it sometimes created little monsters. Other teachers in a variety of fields have addressed this problem by concentrating their attention and guidance on the initial stages of inquiry: the building of frames of reference in which students can identify and pursue interesting questions. If we want undergraduates to know why our fields of study are exciting, these early stages of investigation are probably more important than finished products.

In shorter assignments teachers have similarly emphasized critical thinking, inquiry, and real revision by delaying the point at which students choose topics or theses for their papers. Reflective journals on lectures and readings, for example, allow teachers to assign drafts based on features of a text or lecture that students find puzzling or contradictory. These assignments ask students to write about their own questions: about something not yet explained or resolved.

A number of other teachers have recognized that conventional assignments ask students to pretend that they are real scholars, as Bartholomae observes, but also to pretend that they are not pretending. The result is a kind of pretense and caution, lacking the more playful, exploratory sense of the term "experiment": to try something new and see what happens. These teachers ask students explicitly to pretend they are someone else, and they find that students enjoy the challenge of trying on new voices and ways of thinking when teachers acknowledge rather than conceal the mimetic, imaginative dimensions of learning. Ross Brann made these dimensions explicit in the following assignment from his Near Eastern Studies course, Muslims, Christians, and Jews in Islamic Spain:

> Imagine that you are an Andalusian *adib* [a literary courtier] living in tenth-century Cordoba. Write a letter to a like-minded friend in North Africa (or Barcelona) and describe your life so as to convince him to join you at the Umayyad court. Also tell him something about your favorite genre of poetry and what you have been hearing and writing lately.

Explicitly imaginative assignments can liberate students from the routine constraints of trying to sound like scholars in the fields they are studying. And while this assignment is a challenging exercise in the use of historical imagination, the persona of an Andalusian *adib* is hardly more difficult to adopt or less useful, in the trajectories of undergraduate's lives, than that of a professor of Near Eastern history. The former is perhaps more useful, and certainly more engaging, for the purpose of assembling detailed conceptions of historical contexts, as this passage from a student paper on the topic suggests:

> I was sorry to learn of your beloved's death. It is said in Cordoba, "Once you were the moon on the night of its fullness, but then night decreed that you were to set . . ." Indeed it is a tragedy and I shall grieve the loss with you.
> I too, dearest of friends, bring word of bad news—indeed worse

than your own because it involves the one that we serve. As of late, my master has taken ill. It is also known that his son, al-Hakem II, prepares to ascend to the throne. I have spoken with the court physician and although he be a Jew and therefore untrustworthy in my eyes, I fear he tells the truth about medicine. He has told me that the Caliph will pass in but a few days. Ah, what gloom will come over this court if such an event happens!

## The Future of Writing in the Majors

About three years into the development of Writing in the Majors, Geoffrey Chester, then dean of the College of Arts and Sciences, politely asked, "When do you predict that Writing in the Majors will move beyond this *experimental* phase?" I offered a reassuring projection of two or three years, but I was thinking *"Never!"* and I might have asked in turn, "When do you predict that physics," Chester's field, "will move beyond *its* experimental phase?"

But his question was in many ways valid, and I've spent a lot of time thinking about its implications. For a variety of reasons, Writing in the Majors is unlikely to become the kind of institutionalized program that establishes formal guidelines, requirements, procedures, pedagogy, and assessment across the curriculum. A program that set out to maximize the variety of forms and contexts in which writing occurs cannot easily, or even sensibly, reduce that variety to uniformities and generalities. Nor are such formal designations and guidelines likely to become necessary. Writing in the Majors will not be able to expand to the scale at which all students, even in the College of Arts and Sciences, could be required to take a designated Writing in the Majors course in their chosen fields. Even if we had the resources for such expansion, the goal of administering a required, measured dose of writing instruction would conflict with our central goal of putting writing into solution with learning in the disciplines. In this respect, Writing in the Majors cannot become a model for large, mandated WAC programs, and such programs are not viable models for Writing in the Majors.

Geoffrey Chester's question had other potential meanings, however, including ones that apply to his field. Experimental research of all kinds both depends upon and builds an underlying body of knowledge or lore, collectively constructed, reconstructed, and shared. Professional journals, conferences, workshops, Web sites, and other forms of communication give current knowledge collective forms without undermining experimental work. Experiments do yield shared results, not just further experiments.

These are the directions in which Writing in the Majors is heading, along with other programs and projects in the expanding Knight Institute, under the direction of Jonathan Monroe. In coming years, Writing in the Majors will probably expand modestly, possibly in league with related programs among the undergraduate colleges at Cornell. But the main shift beyond the experimental phase of the program will occur through broader dissemination of the results of our work, both within and beyond Cornell. Some of the patterns described in this chapter have been digested into "Findings," available under the Writing in the Majors section on the Knight Institute's Web site. As part of her work for an NSF Postdoctoral Fellowship, Ann Stork has compiled extensive course materials and teaching strategies from our program on a Web site called *Resources for Scientists Teaching Science*. In addition to workshops and courses for Cornell faculty and teaching assistants, the Knight Consortium for Writing in the Disciplines extends our work to collaborative exchange with teachers from many other colleges and universities, in the United States and abroad. This book and other publications provide additional means through which Writing in the Majors, like the Knight Institute at large, can establish and share bodies of working knowledge without losing the experimental, inductive design from which this knowledge emerged.

# Finding Places for Writing in a Research University

## *A Director's View*

### HARRY E. SHAW

Chair, English; Director, Knight Writing
Program 1986–1992

⌒ "What is the place of writing in the university?" Questions like this confuse me, bringing to mind answers along the lines of, "Well, I think it's in the next building over—why don't you try the phone book?" Or perhaps, "It happens all over the place, doesn't it?" In 1986, I nonetheless found myself urgently asking the question, "What is the place of writing at Cornell University?" There's nothing like an endowment to focus the mind, and a substantial endowment, indeed, from the Knight Foundation materialized for the John S. Knight Writing Program, in the very week in which I became its director. This essay will discuss how I responded to the opportunity of finding new places for writing at Cornell and strengthening old ones. One of my underlying concerns here will be the relationship of abstractions to concrete, institutionally situated (which is to say, historical) practices. The Knight endowment opened up possibilities sufficiently large that posing more immediate questions wouldn't entirely suffice. Abstraction, prospective and retrospective, was inescapable.

The prospect of reframing the place of writing in a great university was exhilarating. A wish to distance myself from grandiose questions about teaching and its administration nonetheless persisted in my mind. My experience as a student and a teacher in the late sixties and early seventies had left me a distrust of those who "know what teaching is all about." It wasn't just that they were willing to tell you what teaching is all about, at considerable length (as befits the subject), but also that abstract certainties can bring with them a certain coerciveness, even when (or perhaps especially when) they dictate that classes must be places where people should be creative and free. In the worst case of this scenario, a student who can't or won't be creative and free in the approved mode is assigned an unenviable role. The tune of the other drummer becomes the only tune in town, and you'd better express your freedom by marching to it if you don't want to be belittled and ostracized. (For an acid view of this and related phenomena, one can turn to Malcolm Bradbury's *The History Man*.) Such goings-on disturbed me, not least because they often occurred under the banner of a politics whose general, abstract beliefs and goals I more or less shared. The devil really is in the details.

In leading our writing program into new territory, it was my pleasure and responsibility to chart new courses. But I wanted to do so with a minimum of abstract certainty and "substance." My ideal was to let others do the talking, while I made a few carefully chosen institutional changes that would allow those with the desire, skill, and wit to get on with their business more easily and with fewer distractions. If they didn't have real business to do, you couldn't talk them into a possession if it. If they did, you would have helped to accomplish something. It would be particularly useful to create situations where they would be led to confront, with their own skills and in their own ways, real problems. Having done this, you'd simply fade away. The underlying contradictions here will be obvious enough. What, for instance, does it mean to face "real problems"? Who defines them? Who decides when they have been met? Perhaps it's time to turn to the concrete.

First, let me address the context I entered. I was exceptionally fortunate in my predecessor, Fredric Bogel. He had begun his stint at a time when a conjunction of changing circumstances in the university as a whole had weakened the program. He reversed this. Freshman writing at Cornell has long been conducted in a wide range of subjects, from anthropology to women's studies. Bogel reasserted the power of the program to set standards that would ensure that freshman writing courses centered on the teaching of writing. He instituted and gained acceptance for a substantial (and required) course to train the teaching students—from all fields—who offered courses in the program. He presided over the administrative separation of the program from the English Department, of which it had hitherto been a branch—a change that, in our particular context, had salutary results. And he spearheaded and coedited Cornell's own manual for writing instructors, *Teaching Prose*. I inherited from Rick Bogel a writing program that had gained prestige, an appropriate amount of power, and a well-defined and well-accepted mission. It wasn't necessary to invent the program from scratch, or to spend lots of energy mending or replacing broken parts. I could concentrate instead on new levels of excellence. I had the further good fortune of entering a climate of solid support from the highest levels of

Arts College and university administration, including deans, the provost, and the president himself.

In such a situation, my belief in administration as the self-effacing making of fruitful adjustments could readily be put to use. Some aspects of the program could speak for themselves—for instance our Writing Workshop, which employed a group of greatly gifted writing teachers whose primary function at the time was to help students with special problems. They knew what steps needed to be taken; I furthered those steps as best I could. It was also easy enough to see how to give further strength to the program for training teaching assistants that Rick Bogel had initiated. We added staff, including (as a yearly visitor) James Slevin, a nationally known figure from outside Cornell, and we gave additional support to the excellent staff already in place, who, to this day, keep the training program fresh by constant revision and innovation.

The Knight endowment also opened up new vistas. It allowed us to match our TA training program with a program for training faculty members. It would have been possible simply to offer symposia and workshops, and in fact these are activities we have pursued to a limited extent. But wishing to put people in contact with what I've called "real problems" pointed in another direction. It seemed that we needed to open up a conversation with writing teachers who were focally engaged in the act of teaching writing at that very moment. We accomplished this by offering a number of faculty members each year the chance to teach a writing course during the university's six-week summer school, and to take a course from us at the same time. Our course involved close individual contact with our staff to create, assess, and readjust the course they were teaching, normally with a view toward giving a version of it, modified and enriched in the light of the summer's experience, during the regular school year. Faculty members were paid for participating in both the course they taught (the funds came from the summer session) and the course they took (the funds came from us). Our outside writing expert was the keystone of the course we offered them. Among other things, this meant that Cornell colleagues didn't need to bare their teaching souls to their neighbors. I would claim a certain administrative elegance for this set of arrangements (for instance, our program doesn't wind up bearing its entire cost).

This venture occupies just the sort of place I wanted our program as a whole to occupy, one of putting special expertise gained from years of teaching and thinking about writing at the service of people interested in teaching a course in their own fields of academic expertise and, as part of this process, working with their students' writing. And it helped turn potential confrontations into collaborations. Debates about who should properly set the standards for "real" writing courses, for instance, tended simply not to arise in this setting.

Denials of the appropriateness of the program's set of guidelines for all Freshman Writing Seminars (six to ten papers per semester, serious revisions, and the like) were less likely to be voiced by those actually engaged in teaching students than by faculty members debating the point as a matter of departmental prerogative, with appeals to the wisdom of the ages.

Our training programs expanded upon an already firmly rooted endeavor. Most of my own energy increasingly went into another project, where the program had been less active. When I assumed the role of director of the John S. Knight Writing Program, it seemed clear to me that our offerings for freshmen were basically sound. It seemed equally clear that, as with other institutions of higher learning, there was a striking disproportion between the energy officially put into writing instruction during the freshman year on the one hand, and during the sophomore, junior, and senior years on the other. This disproportion was more striking because of the strength of our freshman offerings and their cross-curricular character. One could argue that attention to writing occurs naturally in upper-level courses, but given the realities of the demands placed on a university's instructional staff, the notion of letting nature take its course in this matter produced uneasiness. Underlying that uneasiness was, of course, the assumption that freshman writing courses—even *two* of them—cannot provide an inoculation against all future problems with writing. In time, I learned to put this positively: attention to writing can enrich learning in all the disciplines pursued at a major research university.

How, then, could the writing program expand the teaching of writing beyond the freshman year? Cornell is a large and administratively complex place. Indeed, as a hybrid of a land-grant university (four colleges and one school), private university (three colleges), and hotel school (not to mention a set of professional schools), its complexities are probably unique. Shortly before I became director, one of the university's smaller schools had instituted a requirement in upper-level writing, and I became involved in devising ways to ensure that enough courses existed in the university curriculum to allow students to fulfill the requirement. This exercise provided a testing ground for a number of plans for strengthening writing beyond the freshman year, none of them original. We tried the idea of attaching "satellite" writing courses to popular courses given in the Arts College. We tried designating special writing sections of courses normally given with sections anyway. We expanded the number of sections of our upper-division expository writing course. We supported a faculty member who wished to add a writing dimension to a course she regularly taught in the school, offering her a place in our faculty training program and helping in other ways.

All of these expedients—especially the last two—had their uses, and by refining the mix, we found ourselves able to accommodate the relatively small number of students involved. The difficulties we encountered even on this small scale, however, suggested the inadvisability of lobbying for a large-scale upper-division writing requirement mandated from above. In this regard, the sprawling complexities of Cornell's organization, and the fierce independence of its various constituencies, turned out to be an advantage. An administration far less capable than ours would think twice about mandating global requirements beyond the freshman year in such circumstances. We would have to work from the bottom up, not from the top down. But this meant—as it took me much longer to realize than it should have—a return to the principle of helping capable people deal with real problems in ways they made their own.

I've just suggested that I should have seen the connection between my views of administration and university realities sooner. Actually, the matter is a bit more complex than that. In the *Grundrisse*, Marx talks of "simple abstractions." These are, roughly, conceptions that gain a fully articulated content only when history has produced an entity to which they correspond—the idea of "the middle class," for instance. This sort of emergence occurred during the years I spent leading the writing program; it bears on my underlying concern in this essay with the relationship between abstractions and concrete practice. The style of administration I've claimed for my own actually began as a set of intuitions, or perhaps even prejudices. I was suspicious of general talk and doctrine about teaching, and especially of the process of deducing practices directly from general talk and then asking others to carry them out. At the same time, I was fascinated with (in certain instances, horrified by) what a few well-planned institutional arrangements and adjustments (as opposed to lots of philosophizing) could accomplish. The suspicion and the fascination crystallized into a clear concept (or, in Marx's terms, a simple abstraction) only when I saw an example of the concept at work for a particular purpose and in a particular setting. This crystallization began with the process of devising our summer training program for faculty members; it reached fulfillment as we developed the upper-division program we came to call Writing in the Majors.

Writing in the Majors took shape in response to the set of conditions and restraints I've outlined: it sought to turn them to our advantage. We worked under a succession of highly sympathetic deans (one of whom, as it happened, had participated in our summer training course), but we weren't laboring to fulfill a general mandate they had imposed. We had neither the means to create a new set of courses nor any interest in doing so (and our students couldn't have fit a new phalanx of courses into their schedules, anyway). We were forced to ask the question this way: how can we get instructors interested in making writing a focal point of courses they already teach? The answer turned out to be simple. We simply (!) needed to make it appear plausible that by concentrating on writing, they could fulfill *their own* instructional goals more successfully, instead of appealing to an altruistic belief in a general bettering of student writing. That is, we had to persuade them that coming to grips with the real problems of writing could help them teach the subjects of their expertise more successfully.

The most difficult administrative moments in creating Writing in the Majors came at the very beginning. The problem was gaining a hearing. Because we lacked an official mandate along the lines of "All students at Cornell must take two writing courses beyond the freshman year," getting the ear of busy departmental administrators and, through them, of busy faculty members was a challenge requiring patience and persistence. The dean of the College of Arts and Sciences at that time, Gregory Chester, added informal urging of his own, which helped but didn't suffice. A noted physicist himself, he created another problem, by persuading me (despite his rank, but in keeping with his character, the process was truly one of discussion and persuasion) that the best place to concentrate our efforts would be in the sciences—a harder conceptual nut to crack, we assumed, than the humanities. In the end, however, we did manage to make contact with faculty members from a wide spectrum of disciplines. Because we were working from the bottom up, the faculty members we met with were an ideal, voluntary, self-selected group. Typically, they were excellent teachers. As such, they had a lively awareness of how difficult excellent teaching is, and were interested in aid—from whatever country.

Our work with scientists proved particularly rewarding. It helped that not many of them considered themselves already knowledgeable about what making writing a focus of their courses might accomplish; then too, they seemed to enjoy solving problems in creative and unusual ways. A further advantage of working with scientists was that it helped us stay on track. Keith Hjortshoj, the member of the Writing Workshop who was the mainstay of our end of these discussions (he has since become director of Writing in the Majors) has a doctorate in anthropology, not English, but even he could hardly imagine himself to be an expert in the fields in which these upper-level courses were given (particle physics, for instance). A pattern was thus set in which we served, perforce, as facilitators, not dictators. In dealing with faculty members from diverse fields, we learned never to assume that we knew, on any level, more about the substance of their courses than they did. (We didn't suppose, for instance, that our work with language had given us a privileged insight into a fundamental deep structure of the discourse with whose epiphenomena they concerned themselves as professionals.) By the same token, we made it clear that we considered them experts in writing in their own fields, whether or not they realized it, and whether or not they found writing difficult themselves. They read and wrote papers and books; they knew the acceptable genres and forms of argument—indeed, they themselves were engaged in creating and transforming them.

Our modesty didn't mean that we were unable to hold up our end of the dialogue about their courses. We knew how to name and account for much of their concrete writing expertise when they explained its substance in terms we could fathom (which, in some subjects, was no mean accomplishment). We possessed a great deal of experience and lore about responding to sentences and essays. We had accumulated and were expanding a wide-ranging repertoire of examples of the remarkably varied ways in which writing can contribute to learning in courses across the curriculum. One aspect of the writing teacher's mindset proved particularly useful—a focus on audience, including the audience in the classroom. For many with whom we worked, writing had served primarily as a mode of testing students, not as a mode of thought. Imagining how writing could pass beyond serving as a means of evaluation meant imagining the situation of students taking a course, and trying to see things from their point of view. This cut against disciplinary norms in a variety of fields; it could lead to significant rethinking of what it means to teach. Finally we offered a further, non-negligible advantage: the ability to help professors from disciplines across the university to cope with the added work involved in making writing instruction part of their courses by training and paying for teaching assistants drawn from the field in which a course was offered.

Given the outlook I've claimed, I would be the last person to suggest that what's good for Cornell is necessarily good for the nation and the nation's colleges and universities. I will, however, comment briefly on what appear to me to be two implications of the versions of writing instruction the John S. Knight Institute for Writing in the Disciplines has developed, in the hopes that doing so may clarify the extent to which others might or might not profitably draw upon our experiences and models.

To begin with administrative practice, I trust that my generally negative view of top-down administrative decrees has become sufficiently evident. Such decrees seem likely to impede the real work that needs to be done with individuals; they can transform an opportunity into a burden, evoking resentment and a mechanical response. Top-down directives do have the advantage of moving toward quick results; our own bottom-up, course-by-course approach may well seem glacial by comparison. Which kind of movement has the greater reality? Glaciers can alter landscapes. When one adds the fact that top-down decrees are rarely accompanied by sufficient resources to support their realization, the case against them seems grave. Again, however, things may look different in other institutional settings. One could add that, in all conceivable settings, a writing program can hardly thrive if it lacks financial substance and administrative clout. A college or university administration needs to decide that it wants to have a real writing program, to the extent of imagining its situation and needs concretely and responding to them.

I move to matters more vexed. It's well known that historically, groups of practitioners in a variety of fields have gained professional status by claiming exclusive ownership of the expertise within them. When you've built a set of institutions that can make the name "quack" stick, you have a medical profession. The same goes for professors of physics, or English, or composition theory. Writing teachers, the majority of whom are grossly overworked and underpaid, may well wish to follow the same path to professionhood. This could solve the thorny problem of providing grounds for colleges and universities to grant tenure to writing instructors without rethinking the nature of tenure itself. (In the process, the nature of the jobs writing instructors do would itself change, in ways that would themselves raise a further set of intricate problems and possibilities.) For better or worse, our experience in Writing in the Majors calls into question hegemonic aspirations based on the idea that a profession of writing could own and police its field. If we had claimed exclusive expertise with respect to writing, we would have gotten nowhere. We made ourselves useful to teachers in traditional fields; we didn't try to claim (as some would have it) that a new kind of biology would arise from following our insights, in a move that would replace philosophy with rhetoric as the arbiter of all knowledge. The logic at work throughout the John S. Knight Institute for Writing in the Disciplines, from its broadly and genuinely cross-disciplinary Freshman Writing Seminars to Writing in the Majors, involves turning writing over to people in various academic fields, except in special cases such as bringing writers with basic difficulties up to speed. A small number of writing experts enable instructors across the university to make writing a lively part of the life of the mind.

As a practical matter, I believe that this historical moment is, in any event, highly unpropitious for a professionalization of writing instruction that would gain writing teachers the security, status, and pay they deserve. The present state of affairs is much too convenient economically and ideologically for it to be overturned on such grounds. Again, however, you can't unequivocally deduce general principles from specific practices, any more than you can simply deduce practice from theory; it might be possible to read the implications of our experience at Cornell in quite different ways. In any event, because we have large numbers of excellent graduate students and have developed the ability to train them effectively as writing instructors, Cornell itself hasn't developed a legion of part-time employees to fill the gap. Instead, we have a handful of writing experts, housed mainly in the Writing Workshop. As our mission has grown, these experts have found their tutorial work balanced by other commitments, from our teacher-training programs to Writing in the Majors. These different components seem likely to be mutually enriching. Intellectually and pedagogically, this situation seems to me admirable. Our experts command respect, especially with those in whose courses their palpable expertise has made a difference. In a faculty meeting at UCLA (which, nonetheless has an excellent writing program), a scientist summed up what by vote appeared to be the general sentiment of the faculty by suggesting that writing involves a process of recording thought, not of thinking itself. If such a discussion arose in a general meeting here (as I hope it will not), I believe it's a safe bet that strenuous voices would be raised in opposition to any such sentiment, even though Writing in the Majors is, as yet, far from having penetrated all quarters of the university.

I shall end on a personal note. What becomes of the director of a writing program conceived of in this way? In what place—or is it spot—does he find himself? The administrative style I've been advocating suggests that a director should be adept at disappearing acts. Does this mean that the directors should wither away altogether, like the state after the revolution? Well, to an extent that's just what happened during my own tenure as director. I entered a full-time position. I left a position that had, at my instigation, become half-time. It seemed better for the program and its director if the latter were able to maintain something of a normal life in an academic field. Moving in this direction was more attractive because of the gifts of Katherine Gottschalk, who had served as my assistant director. It was clear to me that she could run our Freshman Writing Seminars at least as well as I could, and I turned this part of my job over to her, having made the adjustments necessary to ensure that she would have the time to do it.

To be sure, the director of a major academic program ought not to fade away altogether. Given the realities of institutional rank and power at Cornell, it was essential that a tenured professor head its writing program. I've mentioned that one of the most difficult tasks in getting Writing in the Majors underway was to gain a hearing for it among those who hardly imagined themselves to be writing teachers. If I had not been a professor, it is most unlikely I would ever have got a foot in the door. There is also something to be said for vesting the overall direction of a large and varied program in someone not fully identified with any of its particular functions. Or to turn the coin over, it's better for the director of Writing in the Majors or the First-Year Writing Seminars not to feel obliged to balance the claims of their parts of the Knight Writing Program, now Institute, against those of the other parts, but to leave the balancing to someone else. (As, when chair of Cornell's English department, I asked the dean for a senior hire, I did not pause to consider the needs of other entities in the College. I advocated.)

The ideal mode of administration I gradually defined as I went about my business as director of the writing program nonetheless amounted in the end to something close to a pure formalism. My function as I conceived it was to create places where others could address substantive problems, not to "lead" them in any normal sense of the word. Such a role can be alienating, especially for someone who thinks of himself primarily as a teacher and scholar involved in a substantive discipline. You provide the equipment and the field; they get to play on it. And there's also the danger that working on a primarily formal level could mean losing a living sense of the very details one aims to rearrange for the benefit of others. I am told that Lionel Trilling once told a younger colleague that teachers shouldn't devote quite all of their energy to their students: it leaves you feeling "empty." It is the same with creating possibilities for others. Having experienced an administrative analogue to this emptiness has increased my tolerance for the penchant of administrators to visit what appear to be substantive initiatives from the top down upon large academic units. I still think it's a temptation to be avoided. The exhilaration of helping to make things work and happen ought to see one through.

Dealing with administrative forms and structures can also come to inform one's own scholarly work in unexpected ways. A provost under whom I served remarked to me that I was lucky to be running a program in my own field. I'd be able to "keep up"; I wouldn't have to retool after my stint as director ended. I longed to tell him that my activities as director had little (actually, nothing) to do with the presence of history in British fiction of the eighteenth and nineteenth centuries. Yet some infiltration seems to have occurred regardless. I currently find myself fascinated by the problem of how authors and narrators situate themselves with respect to the fictional worlds they create, and how they wish to situate us as readers. Do they place themselves (and us as readers) "in" or "above" these worlds, or somehow in both places at once? What does this imply about our situation with regard to the actual world in which we live? This is a structural quandary shared by novelists and . . . the directors of writing programs.

I close with a final misgiving I came to feel about an administrative style that seems to have been well suited for a period of exploration and expansion into new regions of the major research university of which it is a part. Jürgen Habermas is one of a line of distinguished social thinkers to focus on the problems involved with what is known as "instrumental reason." Instrumental reason leads you to do things simply because they are possible. The clearest examples come from technology: you build a bigger and better bomb, and so do your opponents, because it's possible; or you spend enormous amounts of money on computer technology because it's there. What's missing when one follows the logic of instrumental reason alone is an attempt to set reasoned goals, balancing priorities through a democratic process of rational choice. You develop bigger bombs or buy better computers because the context you're in makes you feel that you "have to." The modern world has proved excellent at following the logic of instrumental reason, poor at developing forms of institutional rationality that would allow us to make choices between instrumental possibilities. We keep at the cutting edge, but we don't know where it's cutting, or why.

Instrumental reason is a mixed blessing. But doesn't my own stress on making institutional adjustments embrace its logic? You see what can be done along certain lines in the structure of the university, and you do it, eschewing what you take to be windy discussions of The Nature of Writing in General. Well, that danger always exists. Happily, there's more to be said on this subject. For Habermas, instrumental reason is a mixed blessing, but under the right conditions it can *be* a blessing. He has no illusions about the possibility, or even the desirability, of doing away with instrumental reason altogether. What we require are mechanisms whereby the outcomes of instrumental reason can be regulated to serve goals arrived at in a reasoned and democratic fashion. I like to think that the discussions we had with individual instructors in Writing in the Majors exemplify this kind of goal-setting, and I hope that those who read Keith Hjortshoj's description of how some of those discussions proceeded will agree. To be sure, the goals were set on a case-by-case basis, but that, as a step in learning how to arrive at a more widely held consensus, might not be such a bad thing either.

# PART TWO

# Cultures and Acculturation

## Teaching, Writing, and Learning in Field-Specific Contexts

# Writing Animals

---

ELIZABETH OLTENACU

Animal Science

℘ The Department of Animal Science might seem to be a strange home for a First-Year Writing Seminar. Animal Scientists focus on the care and management of production and companion animal species. We are not, as many people believe, veterinarians, but are geneticists, nutritionists, physiologists and animal management specialists. Our concerns are the production of food from animal sources and the humane care of animals. When animal scientists write, their efforts most often take the form of a highly technical report on the results of a research project, or of a grant proposal written to convince some government body or philanthropic group to donate funds to support further research. Both kinds of writing must follow precisely circumscribed formats if they are to have any chance of success: the scientific journal will not publish any rambling, poorly focused submission; the granting agency will not even consider support for any hopefuls who fail to meet precise structural and page-limit guidelines. On occasion, the animal scientist might become involved in the writing of a textbook, again a technical piece of writing, although it does offer greater opportunity for reflection on, and integration of, a wider range of topics. All these forms of writing are technical texts written for technically competent readers. Some animal scientists are attuned to different audiences as their jobs include an extension component. Their writing extends the results of research to a "user" audience of farmers and pet owners, and must put technical information into layperson's terms. This is another tough audience: a dry, overly technical piece will fail in its ultimate objective and its information will remain unused.

What of the writing that we ask of our students? We expect them to learn

*75*

how to present technical information to a technically competent reader: often this is in the form of the traditional laboratory report. In addition, we want them to gain familiarity with the body of knowledge in particular subject areas and to develop the ability to find and integrate the work of others: thus, students conduct library research that culminates in the traditional term paper. Upper-level courses sometimes set the student an applied problem that might incorporate field trips and research as another source of information. The student then integrates information from these sources with classroom and library learning to develop a report that might reach more than one audience: the professor who will grade it and perhaps a farmer or agribusiness representative who will apply its conclusions to the solution of a "real-world" problem. The advanced student who has a more research-oriented interest will be concerned with developing an understanding of the scientific method and applying it to problems. This individual must become adept at the concise expression of a theory and its underlying assumptions, the careful design and articulation of an experiment to test the theory, and the technical discussion of its results. The unifying thread that runs through almost all our familiar forms of writing in animal science is the discipline imposed by the constraints of science.

But now let me turn to non–animal scientists' perceptions of our field, for, in reality, their opinions will have a major impact on the future of animal science. Their perceptions of the work we do and interpretations of our writings on it should be of great concern to us. If we are unable to express our goals and achievements in terms that are understandable to them, or if we fail to address their concerns, then we can anticipate difficulties ahead. And there is little doubt that the issues of importance to the layperson will force animal scientists to think and write differently about their field, as those issues demand that we, indeed that all scientists, reflect more on the ethical implications of our work. The layperson, in exchange, needs to develop a better understanding of the complexities of the relationship between humans and domestic animals if we are ever to hope for a constructive dialogue to take place. There are extreme views that cover the full gamut from animal scientist to animal rightist. Those at one end of the spectrum sometimes fail to recognize that there are legitimate calls to progress more cautiously; those at the other may fail to appreciate the evolutionary aspects that make our bonds with domestic species well-nigh impossible to break.

I had another concern, this one about student attitudes to learning, which led to this offering of an animal science First-Year Writing Seminar. It is a concern that relates to the very heart of the Knight Institute's concept. Many students "compartmentalize" their learning and fail to appreciate the need to integrate subject areas and skills that will face them in the working world. As an instructor who routinely uses writing as a method of assessing student learning in my junior-level course, I lost count of the times that my comments on students' writing were rewarded by "but this isn't a writing course" in my end-of-semester evaluations. Many students seem to believe that lucid, coherent writing is irrelevant in a science class; that the instructor should ignore rambling, careless text and react solely to the science facts. There is a failure on the part of some students to comprehend that even good, solid facts can be obscured by poor writing, and that even a writing assignment in a science course deserves the time and thoroughness of drafting and editing. In a more selfish vein, I saw this as an opportunity to do what instructors of science courses often cannot do: focus in depth, beyond the specifics of the accuracy of the scientific content of their writing, on helping students develop their ability to communicate ideas.

FWS: Animal Domestication and Behavior, ANSC 120, was a synthesis of two opportunities: one, the bringing together of animal science and non–animal science students to reflect on the evolution of domestication; the other the chance to explore how, why, and for whom animal scientists write. I chose animal domestication as my subject because I believe that a more informed dialogue on the sometimes contentious issues of animal welfare that are critical to the future of animal agriculture can be achieved only if all participants have a full understanding of the nature of the domestication relationship. Animal scientists need to pause in their daily interactions with domestic species to reflect on the roots and genesis of that relationship in order to tackle modern issues effectively. Laypersons need to develop the ability to evaluate the writings of those who protest the "enslavement of animals" within the reality that domestication is, in fact, a highly successful evolutionary strategy entered upon by humans and a few other species. It is beneficial to both animal scientists and non–animal scientists to stand aside from the details of modern science, take time to view the wider picture of how and why species entered into this covenant we call domestication, and explore the diversity of writings on this topic. The fact that each of us possesses, as a consequence of humanity's longstanding and intimate relationship with domestic species, a certain baseline knowledge of domestic animals, whether or not we are aware of it, allows a significant part of the course to be a sharing and discussion of experiences and a relating of "own" knowledge to the content of the texts we read. One of the writing exercises I set my students is the keeping of a weekly journal that has two specific goals: first, to reflect on our in-class discussions and put them into the context of their personal experiences with animals and, second, to set down any further thoughts they might have on our discussion topics, beyond what was expressed in the classroom. Each week, one of our class sessions begins with two or three students reading their previous week's journal entries as a review and as a starting point for the next topic. I ensure that different individuals read each week, thus maintaining active involvement in the course by all students. The students' end-of-semester course reviews invariably highlight their appreciation of this revisiting of topics after a few days' reflection as a satisfying learning experience. I confess their journal writing tends to be reviewed less rigorously than do their assigned essays, but the objective of the journal exercise is to encourage reflection on class topics and "loosen up" the flow of ideas from mind to paper.

As we progress through the course, we explore how people have written about animal domestication historically, with particular focus on authors' observations about the role animal behavior played in the ultimate determination of which species became fully domesticated. This encourages students to think and write about how our relationship with domestic species developed, and about how our attitudes have changed over time. For example, in reading the writings of Francis Galton, a cousin and contemporary of Charles Darwin, students soon perceive a great deal about the development of human attitudes to our own as well as other species. However, before we delve into the written word, we look at a pictorial "text" and try to interpret what it tells us of the history of domestication. The tomb paintings of ancient Egypt offer a wealth of illustrations of daily life at that point in history, including many depictions of how the Egyptians interacted with animals. A mural from Beni Hassan depicts a multitude of species and a wide range of human interactions with them. It forms an excellent basis for an essay that offers students a little more opportunity for creativity than is found in much animal science writing, as they put themselves into the role of discoverer of the mural and interpreter of its content. Observation is a key to the study of animal behavior, so this is a valuable early exercise for students in the course.

Animal science tends to focus on the "here and now" of modern agriculture. In thinking about how we arrived at this point, however, we need to look at a broader canvas. Domestic species in the United States did not, for the most part, originate in that part of the world, but were brought from elsewhere. We read a part of Jared Diamond's recent Pulitzer Prize–winning book, *Guns, Germs and Steel: The Fates of Human Societies*, which leads to a consideration of the role domestic animals played in the development of human societies and in influencing the outcomes of human interactions on a worldwide scale. For everyone in the class, this introduces new concepts of how profound the effects of the close relationship between humans and domestic species have been.

In the first half of ANSC 120, we focus primarily on reading texts written for a lay audience as students explore and write about the early development of domestication and the behavioral reasons why so few species were fully domesticated. The course text, *The Covenant of the Wild: Why Animals Chose Domes-*

*tication* by Stephen Budiansky, is read and discussed over the first few weeks of the course, alongside selections by Stephen Jay Gould from his books and writings for the periodical *Natural History*. This allows students to develop and write about a behavioral "profile" of domestic species from a nontechnical standpoint, and, incidentally, to think about how our own species fits into the same niche. The exercise is valuable for students who consider themselves to be animal science majors and have little time to reflect on the "why" and "how" of domestication as they begin their studies in the major, just as it is interesting for students who are not considering animal-oriented careers but who, in many cases, share their lives with companion animals, and fully intend to continue to do so in the future.

Once we have developed a shared understanding of the history of domestication and of the specific behavioral repertoire common to all our domestic species, we shift our focus to modern relationships with domestic animals. We explore the many forms taken by these relationships, and start to think about how the demands for high productivity may push animals close to their limits of adaptability, thus giving rise to concerns for their well-being. This then leads us into an exploration of the technical writing of current animal science studies on environmental enrichment for livestock, and of writings on animal cognition.

Students in ANSC 120 write six short essays over the course of the semester that parallel the class readings and allow them to interpret what they have read or to apply the information we have discussed in class. For example, after we have developed our outline of the behavioral attributes of a successfully domesticated animal species, I present the students with brief summaries of the behavior of two nondomestic species. I ask them to write about their evaluation of the potential and the shortcomings of each in regard to possible domestication, and then to present their conclusions on whether domestication is feasible for either and to hypothesize about how it might be attempted. In essence, the students are tackling the typical extension role of the animal scientist by applying the basic knowledge they have developed on animal behavior to solving a practical challenge.

Another essay, which students write fairly late in the course, sets them the task of analyzing the reasons why people often use the term "degenerate" in reference to domestic animal species. This assignment demands that students integrate what they have learned about the behavior of domestic animals with what they know about human perceptions of, and attitudes toward, wild species. In thinking about this topic, they must also incorporate the fact that individuals of most domestic species have returned to an independent, "wild" lifestyle and have founded successful feral populations. Thus, the neat compartmentalization of animals into "domestic" and "wild" species does not bear close scrutiny, and students must reflect further in this essay on a concept we first addressed early in the course when they read Galton's work and started to realize that wild animals may be tame and domestic animals may be wild.

In the second half of the course, we read several recent technical animal science journal articles that address modern issues related to domestication, with particular focus on production, rather than companion, species. This forms the basis for a discussion of the concerns related to intensive animal agriculture, an aspect of the domestication relationship that has arisen within the last half-century and is the root of much of the animal welfare/animal rights controversy. By this point in the course, all the students are able to think and write about current contentious issues of animal well-being in the context of a shared understanding of what brought species to this stage of domestication. I challenge them with reading a highly technical article, which reports a study designed to explore alleviation of some of the problems of an unstimulating intensive animal housing system through the use of environmental enrichment. We discuss this most technical piece of animal science writing in class, reviewing the structure of scientific journal articles, their purposes, and their intended audiences, as well as the factual content of this study. Then the students tackle a somewhat different kind of writing assignment: to distill the content of the journal article down to a six hundred-word report for their fellow students to read in the style of an article that might appear in the *Cornell Daily Sun*. At a point in the semester when they might be writing to satisfy what they believe the instructor "wants," students are forced to refocus on a very different audience and think about the needs and interests of a very different kind of reader.

I encourage students to explore a topic of personal interest to them (and relevant to the course topic!) through a more extensive writing project, which also serves to introduce them to the use of the Cornell library system. This project begins early in the semester, when I ask each student in the class to think of a few subjects that could be developed into a term paper. I explore their ideas with them in individual conferences. Each student then develops a brief outline that is shared with the class in a short discussion, which usually triggers further ideas that aid in development of the concept (or a change to a different topic!). Following discussion of all the project ideas, students pursue library research and develop a first draft of the term paper. About mid-semester, we devote one class session to peer review of these drafts. The papers then undergo a major revision, and their highlights are shared orally with the group during our last two class meetings, after I have read the papers. Again, class evaluation comments are positive about this exercise. For many of the students, this is the first Cornell experience of doing research for, and writing, a term paper, and it is achieved in the satisfying context of a topic in which they have a personal interest. The range of topics is greater that can be covered in my contribution to the course, so students also have the satisfaction of making an original contribution to the class. Some have even realized and appreciated that the stepwise development of the final product models the process that they (ideally) should use in writing projects in all their courses!

I have tried to incorporate the students' own observations and experiences into their thinking and writing in a variety of ways. Given the course's focus on animal behavior, I try to encourage some use of observational skills that all students should develop and learn to apply. Beyond what I have already described, I also use video several times in the course. In one instance, for example, it serves to introduce most students in the class to a relationship about which they know very little: that between humans, sheep, and the several breeds of dog which have been selected to perform very different functions related to the care and handling of sheep. The students are invited to choose one aspect of the video, with either a dog or a sheep focus, use the library to find one reference that expands on their chosen topic, and write an essay about it, interrelating what they observed in the video with what they learned from their research and, if appropriate, their own experience.

How would I evaluate the success of this first animal science venture into the teaching of a First-Year Writing Seminar? The course has evolved in each of the three years in which it has been taught to date, sometimes in response to student feedback, sometimes as a result of my own perceptions of the need to change. My goal of exploring a range of forms of writing by and about animal scientists leads us through a great variety of texts. When they are complex, I ensure that we have a class discussion about their content before students are expected to write an essay. Thus, students can guide each other to an understanding of the structure and function of the piece, while my input is to keep them on the right track and help them through the difficult sections. It is useful in this activity that the membership of the class is not limited to freshmen. The few more advanced students in the class have usually worked with scientific journal articles before, so can be of great help to the group. I discovered how valuable this class discussion could be, even with something as deceptively simple as the Egyptian mural essay assignment. A class discussion of it was introduced when I learned from the first-year students' essays how many different aspects there were to this illustration, beyond what I had perceived. The quality of student essays was markedly improved once I had initiated a group discussion during the class session in which they were first presented with the mural. Each individual perceived something different, comments sparked ideas on alternative interpretations, and the final essays often developed still more interpretations of the drawings.

Activities such as the interpretation of the Egyptian mural early in the course ensure that no one in the rather diverse group of students feels that the course content is beyond reach. The animal science majors have never had to deal with this kind of exercise: all students are on an equal footing. By the time we do reach the more technical texts, the students are comfortable with talking within our group and are not afraid to ask questions and express opinions. Their semester journal content reveals that all students, even those who were tentative about what the semester might hold at its start, reflect extensively on new topics and frequently relate them to their own experiences.

The blend of animal science content with the focus on writing in ANSC 120 confounds some students for a while, as mid-semester evaluations reveal. There are always a few students who protest the "slow" pace of the course, having failed to understand initially, despite my introduction to the course's objectives, that subject matter content is not the sole focus of the semester. Despite our many discussions of writing styles (of the texts we read as well as their own), despite our regular in-class exercises stressing common writing problems, there are still some students who feel we should be covering more subject matter. To my relief, however, there are more of the students who appreciate the time they have to reflect and to express their thoughts in essays, journals, and class discussions.

Most students who take ANSC 120 have ranked it fairly high in their First-Year Writing Seminar selection process. However, occasionally a student comes to the process late and has to take what is left in seminar openings. I close with comments from the last journal entry of a reluctant engineer in ANSC 120, as I believe his comments reflect a goal of the Knight Institute, indeed of a Cornell education: to expand students' horizons as well as demonstrating the importance of skills such as writing in all subject matter areas.

> Listening to everyone's presentations today was interesting. I am amazed at the amount of stuff I have learned in this class this semester. I am not trying to suck up here. Before the class began, I had no clue about anything having to do with animals. After all, the only exposure I had ever had with animals came with goldfish. Now, however, I feel that I am able to hold my own when discussing animals with other people and I find myself telling stories from class. Coming into this class I was not overly enthusiastic. However, I am thoroughly satisfied with what I have learned and I am glad that the balloting process was ineffective for me.

# Exoticizing the Familiar

## *Familiarizing the Exotic*

JANE FAJANS

Anthropology

With the publication of a volume called *Writing Culture* (Clifford and Marcus 1986), anthropology as a discipline became self-conscious about the role of writing in its intellectual project. Self-consciousness in this case is not simply an awareness of writing as a genre but a debate over the way writing about a culture, society, group, or event becomes a representation, interpretation, and reification of that object of description. The debate in anthropology has been around the question of "who has the right (authority) to speak for the 'other.'" Writing has become the victim and villain in the debate since writing has become the channel for "speaking" in this equation. The conflation of writing with "speaking for" has virtually eclipsed other approaches and analyses of writing.

The result of this focus on writing has been that a good deal of anthropological writing, especially the work considered most trendy at the present moment, focuses on writing. By emphasizing the rhetorical and subjective nature of writing, many recent anthropologists have stressed their perspective as a radical departure from the work of earlier colleagues (Clifford and Marcus 1986, Marcus and Fisher 1986, Clifford 1988, Dwyer 1982, and others). They see themselves as shifting from a "relatively" objective and seemingly standardized mode to a very subjective and somewhat more experimental one (Jacobson 1991, 4–7). The differences, however, are perhaps not as striking as they first appear. Numerous anthropologists over the last century have been self-conscious about the mode and manner of their presentation. Anthropological writings are not travelogues. Ethnographies do not merely describe another culture;

they are usually theoretically informed and oriented to interpreting particular events in terms of more abstract criteria. They are interpretations. Only the most naive student sees an ethnographic monograph as a documentary of another people, culture, or society. The author must select, arrange, and interpret the material she/he presents. Such construction has always been the case, but earlier authors did not belabor their readers with the fact that their accounts were only partial perspectives on the topic. What used to be descriptive and analytical ethnography has been subsumed by a diaristic and reflexive discourse on the interchange between an anthropologist and those with whom he/she did research. These have occasionally become soul-baring confessions or philosophical musings about learning to understand another culture.

In declaring a revolution in anthropological consciousness, many writers seem to have lost the forest for the trees. While I am not fully persuaded that focusing on these issues is a great way to be an anthropologist, examining the relations between writing and knowing about a topic is a great way of stimulating students. By considering these questions, students must learn to interpret texts and to take responsibility for their education. While I am convinced that anthropology is more than a personal account of an encounter with a people, culture, or society, I think that showing the diversity of experience that individual anthropologists have in producing these perspectives is an insightful way to challenge students' underlying assumptions about textuality. Although students are increasingly more sophisticated in their empirical knowledge of other cultures, many still do not grasp the significance of ideological phenomena. They are naive about how race, class, gender, ethnicity, age, and cultural values produce and reflect their own understandings and interpretations of the world.

I aspire to teach students to examine their mundane assumptions about themselves, what kinds of persons they are, and how their cultural and social milieu contributed to their personas. Sometimes the mundane is the most difficult to see beyond. Most of us never ask why we eat three meals a day, consider some people kin and others non-kin, or differentiate our group from other groups. Anthropology examines these and other basic assumptions and often undermines them, but it is not sufficient to give students counterexamples. Students learn best when they uncover these differences themselves. I use writing to elicit both conscious and unconscious assumptions and then use classroom interaction and group work to try to get students to compare their own views to others. The writing assignments start out by asking for personal experience. Through drafts and assignments, students are expected to move from the particular to the general and eventually back again. Writing connects the personal and the general, the particular and the abstract.

I teach two courses in the John S. Knight Institute for Writing in the Disciplines, a First-Year Writing Seminar and an upper-division Writing in the Majors anthropology course. In thinking about these two courses, I have become conscious of the similarities and differences in my pedagogical practices. My overall aim is to make students conscious of the ways in which they understand and interpret events in their own lives and how these give them insight into other lives and other cultures.

My First-Year Writing Seminar focuses on the role and meaning of food from an anthropological perspective. Food is a topic to which everyone can relate. Everyone has personal experience with it. It is taken for granted most of the time and it is basically nonthreatening. I build on the familiar in this course, focusing the early writing assignments on descriptive personal experiences. The first assignment is: "Describe a food event in which you have participated." I define a food event and give them some questions around which to formulate a response. After they have written papers, these writings are shared with the group. The collective set of papers is used to illustrate the vast array of experiences people have with food. The design of the course and the sequence of writings are oriented to exoticizing this familiar topic. Even things that seem straightforward and functional are shown to be laden with cultural values and imbued with symbols of class, ethnicity, gender, age, and many other features of meaning. My goal is to make students aware of the importance of these social and symbolic features, as well as to help them to appreciate the different ways in which people create meaning in their lives. By examining the roles food plays, students begin to see that almost everything people do reflects their cultural subjectivity. Students also learn that their own actions strengthen their social environments.

I strive to achieve the same end in a dialectically different way in my upper-division writing course, "Myth, Ritual, and Symbol." While everyone can dredge up an experience with food, most "American" undergraduates do not see themselves as having myths or practicing rituals; that is, they often discount their beliefs in activities they label as myth or ritual. It is a put-down to call something by these terms. In this course, I start by teaching students to understand and interpret myths, rituals, beliefs, and practices from other cultures. My emphasis is on analysis: what do these symbolic forms do in the cultures we are studying? How do certain kinds of activities from the mundane (food, gender, body) to the exotic (initiation, sorcery, magic) create meaning for participants in these communities? I discuss and present analyses of these other systems of belief, but in their writing, my students have to apply the analytical frameworks and techniques to their own experiences. They have to analyze gift exchanges, fashion, beloved stories, and religious practices, among other things, as imbued with symbolic meaning and cultural values. This is not an easy exercise, and many students seem mystified that I expect them to find analytical and symbolic meanings in their own customs. In this course, they are again supposed to "exoticize" the familiar in order to familiarize the exotic. The approaches of the two courses are inverted as initially introduced (food exoticizes the familiar while ritual familiarizes the exotic), but the final analysis is the same for each; students examine the roles mundane and extraordinary activities have in constructing meaning in their lives, relationships, and sense of identity.

I have found that students are tempted to take shortcuts in their thinking on many of these topics. Although I share the Knight Institute's conviction that writing is a good way to find out what you think, I have found out through these writing exercises that most of my students do not really begin to know how to think about these topics. Over the years I have observed that the first drafts I get, even in the upper-division courses, are usually very descriptive. Students have a hard time being analytical about their own experiences, even when they can see strong parallels between their own experiences and the examples we have discussed. Therefore, I require that students go through at least two drafts of each paper. They need the two-stage writing process to get feedback on their ideas. My comments on their first drafts are oriented toward going beyond descriptions to produce strong interpretations and analyses in the second drafts. I emphasize a coherent structure and attention to the particulars students have chosen to include. Second drafts are often considerably transformed and show very different appreciations of the events than were evident in the first drafts. These papers would almost always benefit from yet another draft, but I am not persuaded that it would be as substantial a learning experience to require one.

Because I am trying to achieve a great deal conceptually in these papers, I have frequently not been as conscientious about attending to the pragmatics of writing as I could have been. As a non-writing specialist, I was initially very diffident about my qualifications to teach writing and I avoided commenting on writing per se. I have found that my focus on writing has shifted as a result of working with the Knight Institute. In particular, the Institute stresses the correspondence between thinking and writing, and this resonated with my experience. In my experience, pushing students toward conceptual clarity usually helps their writing. When they get absorbed in communicating an idea, most of them can do it well; if the idea is not clear, neither is the writing. With this basic premise, I can engage students both conceptually and pragmatically.

In the First-Year Writing Seminar, I have learned to moderate my desire to instill as much anthropology as possible in order to focus on more basic conceptual and communicative skills. I am much more aware of the underlying problems students have with writing and, to my surprise, I feel much more confident in my ability to respond to their particular problems in order to help them improve. I try to introduce students to a variety of writing genres. Most of them are familiar with three basic kinds of writing: the personal essay, the document-based analysis, and the research paper. The kind of paper we work toward producing is really a synthesis of all three. Anthropology combines description, analysis, comparison, critique, and aspects of personal experience. I see these as ultimately related and as part of a complex genre of research and analysis. Although I expect to combine these different facets of writing in my own work, I initially try to disambiguate them in the writing course. I give students a series of exercises. The first is a description of an event or occasion in which they participated; the second is to interview a friend or acquaintance about a similar event. In this sequence, the interviewer in the second exercise must elicit all the relevant information to write a description similar to the one in the first piece. This new writing, however, requires a shift in positionality; it is an exercise in voice, since the author has to distinguish his/her own voice from that of the informant. In the first assignment, the writer is constructing a personal essay; in the second, he/she is already distancing him/herself from the event, but is also to some extent implicitly comparing the informant's experience with her/his own. I follow these two exercises with a more formal one on comparison and contrast. In this assignment, students have to compare the importance of food in two societies very different from their own. Food is used quite differently in each of these societies but there are points of commonality, as well. I ask students to examine the way food affects age, gender, kinship, death, etc., thus giving them some structural frames on which to hang their own comparisons. I encourage students to incorporate a comparative view between their own culture and the ways these other cultures use food to convey meaning. Explicitly or implicitly, I want students to ask if their understanding of the way food works in these two societies suggests new interpretations of the way we create meaning in our own.

In the course of these and the next several exercises, I try to work on developing a sustained argument including a thesis, an analysis, and a conclusion that hints at directions for further thinking. The final exercise I offer my students is the challenge of rewriting, at the very end of the semester, the first paper they wrote at the beginning. At this point, I expect them to reformulate the event they have described as an analysis of that event in a complex sociocultural setting. They are to interpret the contexts of the events, the roles of the participants, the meanings for the participants, and the relevance of particular aspects and activities.

This last paper becomes, I hope, the culmination of our endeavor. It should represent each student's ability to describe, compare, and analyze an aspect of his/her personal experience in terms of the cultural norms and values that motivated the experience and the reason that this event came to hold personal and symbolic meaning for the individual. By saving this rewrite until the end, I hope my students can see how much more they have to say about their own experiences than they did at the beginning.

In aiming to achieve this sense of understanding, I see my methodology as derived, at least in part, from the hermeneutical school of interpretation. This approach insists on a dialectical movement between a part of the text and the text as a whole, in which the meaning of the whole text is focused on a part in order to elucidate the significance of that part. Arriving at an understanding of a particular aspect of an event or piece of text reciprocally enhances one's understanding of the whole. The expanded interpretation of the whole dialectically infuses greater meaning to the parts, and so on. While I do not fix the lessons of the course on a single event or text, I try to continuously refer to past readings or future analyses in order to illustrate this synthetic process. The final rewrite is, in a sense, the closing of the hermeneutic circle in which the totality of the course should be brought to bear on the slice of individual experience that each student unwittingly chose at the beginning of the semester.

Hermeneutics and the notion of textuality have been important theoretical premises in anthropology for most of this century. They became even more important about thirty years ago. At this time, a number of interpretive anthropologists began to examine culture as "if it were a text" and to interpret this text as if it were a story, perhaps even a story the participants in a culture might tell about themselves. Such a text becomes subject to intense interpretation, and these interpretations become susceptible to extrapolation. Although I admire and utilize the hermeneutic perspective, I do not feel comfortable reifying culture as a text. I take this interpretive stance as much metaphorically as I do literally.

There is a second important trend in writing anthropology, which comes out of the above but shifts the locus of engagement considerably. This approach sees all or most ethnographic writing as a kind of fiction—a partial truth so permeated by the subjectivity of the author as to be virtually fiction. This development in reading and writing anthropology emerged as part of a debate around ethnographic authority. The issues in this exchange focused on the points I mentioned earlier: who can speak for whom, and how we know that what we are saying has validity. These queries have emerged from a variety of interlocutors both inside and outside the discipline. Feminists were quick to query the authority of androcentric descriptions, and postcolonial scholars from Said onward were suspicious of the intentions and insights of nonnative observers. At first, these critiques seem to undermine the possibility of the ethnographic enterprise, and anthropologists responded with apologetic confessions for insensitive domination. But these critiques have lead to very insightful repositionings of anthropological analyses. New modes of ethnographic writing emerged, and the ethnographer emerged as a central player in a contextual drama. The social and cultural interaction cannot be seen as a text because each encounter is unique and ephemeral. In these new writings, the authors stress the subjective aspects of the encounters and the fact that no one voice can capture the multiplicity of experiences and perspectives. These texts strive to incorporate a dialogic polysemy; monograph becomes dialogue; account becomes encounter.

These new writing approaches are especially conducive to classroom writing. Undergraduate students rarely feel sufficiently confident to produce an authoritative paper, but they can produce very insightful analyses from the dialectical position of insider/outsider, describing their own experiences with insights from an analytical tradition. In both of my courses, I find that students really flourish when they see that this kind of writing allows them to remain true to their own values and ideas but also to expand on these with techniques and insights that come from a very different perspective. They have to apply the insights of theoretical arguments to their own experiences, keeping in mind the comparative and generalizable qualities of their interpretations. It is because anthropology deals with both the familiar and the exotic that the dialectic between them is so successful.

# "You *Can* Make a Difference"

## *Human Rights as the Subject Matter for a First-Year Writing Seminar*

BILLIE JEAN ISBELL

Anthropology

When I first chose Anthropology 171, Questioning Humanity: Discourse and Actions on Human Rights in Latin America, as my First-Year Writing Seminar, I expected to write a few papers and read a few books. I did not expect to hear testimony from a survivor of a village massacre in Latin America. I did not expect to be confronted with some of the most terrifying and disturbing events ever to occur in South and Central America.

In this course I not only improved my writing skills, I also improved my listening abilities, my reading skills, and my critical thinking abilities. At the beginning of the semester my writing was reserved. I rarely took a solid position and supported it with evidence. By the end of the semester I had written and revised an opinion piece that clearly explained my stance while also incorporating substantial evidence. I tried several styles of writing including fiction, comparative essays, and research papers.

Elizabeth Antczak (Spring 1999)

### *Why Is Human Rights an Appropriate Subject for a Writing Seminar?*

After twenty-three years of teaching at Cornell, I have become concerned about the kind of citizens we are producing in an increasingly interconnected global environment. As N. Giroux (1997, 690) has asked: "What kind of society do we want to create in the context of the present shifting cultural and ethnic borders? How can we reconcile the notions of difference and equality with the imperatives of freedom and justice?" I believe that our educational system is at odds with the demands of the complex world in which students will find themselves. This First-Year Writing Seminar dealing with the discourses and actions on human rights in three Latin American countries (Guatemala, Chile, and Argentina) allows me a small window onto the reality of tomorrow's citizens. Human rights as a subject matter presents students with political realities as well as ethnical and moral dilemmas that they have not encountered before.

The students who take this course are self-selecting. Nevertheless, I have found that only those students whose ethnic and cultural backgrounds provided some personal experience with these issues had any opinions or knowledge about human rights in Latin America at all. In the spring of 1999, six students out of sixteen were of Latino or Latin American origin, and these six students all had some awareness of the political relationship between the United States and their own or their parents' country of origin. For example, a Chicano from Texas could describe the conditions on the border and another student who fled Nicaragua with her parents could recount family memories of the war years. However, not even these students were aware of the widespread human rights abuses or the role played by the United States in maintaining repressive regimes. Nor were they aware of the human rights movements that are spreading like wildfire across Latin America. Ironically, as electronic communications provides immediate accessibility to human rights reports and rapid response networks, the majority of students who enroll in this course express feeling politically impotent. The most common refrain at the beginning of the course in the spring of 1999 was: "Oh, how horrible! I never knew these things were going on, but what in the world could I possibly do about it? I'm just one person and I can't stop such powerful forces as the U.S. government or the Guatemalan military." Students also expressed anxiety about the complexity of world politics. Apathy was often the result. These factors, coupled with the demands of competing for the rewards of professionalization at Cornell, too often result in students becoming less informed and less empowered as they become engrossed in the day-to-day demands of coursework during their first year at Cornell. I found that students did not read newspapers or listen to world news until we began using relevant current events for writing assignments and class discussions. Do students remain isolated from world events across the disciplines as they complete their degrees?

## Universalism versus Relativism

The first goal of the seminar was to introduce students to the conflicted history of human rights in anthropology. Students were assigned two opposing views on human rights that embody the debate: Panikkar's (1982) "Is the Notion of Human Rights a Western Concept?" essay that argues that human rights must be contextualized within a particular culture using the example of his native India. Most students were convinced by his arguments and wrote essays supporting cultural relativism. Then they were introduced to Preis's (1996) article, "Human Rights as Cultural Practice: An Anthropological Critique," in which she provides three case histories from Africa of social actors overturning cultural practices they consider detrimental. The cases demonstrate the dynamic processes of change as members of society challenge cultural practices and traditions. The essay also demolishes the dichotomy of "the West versus the Traditional World" fundamental to the relativistic argument that the West has no right to meddle with the traditional world by passing a Universal Declaration of Human Rights. Preis's essay carefully outlines the history and current theories of human rights as evolving paradigms and cultural practices.

Students summarized the crux of each of the arguments as writing assignments and then wrote a five-page position paper and engaged in a class debate on universalism versus relativism. This set of writing exercises gave students an understanding of utilizing the concept of a crux of an argument and constructing their own arguments. The next set of assignments centered on the Universal Declaration of Human Rights, which was analyzed in detail. When this declaration was passed by the United Nations, the Executive Board of the American Anthropological Association published a statement in the *American Anthropologist* (1947, 539–42) rejecting its universality. In 1999, the American Anthropological Association passed a Declaration on Anthropology and Human Rights. In practical terms, the anthropological statement builds on the working definition of the Universal Declaration of Human Rights and other international laws, conventions, and practices. However, the preamble of the AAA's declaration states that the capacity for culture is tantamount to the capacity for humanity and further states that violence limits the humanity of individuals and collectivities. The anthropological declaration goes on to argue that the concept of human rights is not static; rather, our understanding is constantly evolving as we come to know more about the human condition. Furthermore, anthropologists are urged to be involved in the debate on enlarging the understanding of human rights on the basis of anthropological knowledge and research. Students read, analyzed, and discussed both of the declarations and wrote short essays on each. Class discussion focused on the politics of enforcing rights and the impossibility of guaranteeing all of the rights everywhere. I pointed out the United States has not ratified the Universal Declaration because we practice the death penalty. A heated debate ensued around the death penalty.

## Anthropology, Writing, and Human Rights

If students are to live in a democratic, global world where differences are to be respected, then they will have to learn that other cultures and languages construct truth, history, and memories in a variety of ways. Authority and writing are still contested grounds in the field of anthropology. One of the major goals of this seminar was to introduce students to the complexities of the anthropological craft of representing other people's lives through the lenses of our own observations and interpretations. Students became aware of their own observations and representations by engaging in encounters and interviews with: a survivor of a massacre in Guatemala; a Mapuche human rights lawyer from Chile; and one of the founding members of the Mothers of the Plaza de Mayo of Argentina. Students listened to these testimonies in Spanish and translated into English, took notes, and wrote short essays on what they heard and understood. Comparing the versions in class gave students concrete experiences to bring to the issues of writing and authority.

## Teaching with Testimonials

One student, Liz Antczak, became informed about human rights: she formulated opinions that she was able to express clearly in various genres. Her final research paper, "Guatemala and the United States, 1944–1999" was motivated by the "testimonio" of Jesús Tecú Osorio, a twenty-seven-year-old Mayan (Aché-speaking) human rights activist, who spoke to the class on 8 April 1999. CUSLAR, the Cornell Committee on United States and Latin American Relations, brought him to campus in conjunction with Guatemala Partners, an organization that supports speaking tours, exhumations and identification of victims, and witness protection programs for activists like Jesús Tecú. Tecú was instrumental in creating the Widows and Orphans of Rabinal, a human rights group of one thousand Mayan survivors of massacres. In 1993, with the cooperation of forensic anthropologists, the exhumation and identification of over 170 victims in Rabinal was completed. In 1994, a ceremony was held in Rabinal to rebury the dead. Tecú was awarded the Reebok Human Rights Award in 1996.

Tecú delivered his testimonio in quiet Spanish, in a matter-of-fact tone of voice devoid of emotion; nevertheless, he was visibly exhausted when he was finished. A CUSLAR volunteer simultaneously translated his speech into English, and each student rendered a version of the testimonio for class discussion. Lively debates ensued on the reliability of translations with many Spanish speakers questioning the translator's version of his story. The accuracy and detail of students' representations varied widely and many wondered why they could not capture much of his reality at all. A Spanish speaker noted that Tecú even contradicted himself a couple of times. All of these events provided the class with the bases to question "ethnographic authority" through their own collective experiences. Here is my version of his story.

On 31 March 1982 in Rabinal, seventy-one people, including his parents, were killed by the military. One month later, a civil patrol, made up of Mayan civilians from other villages that were required to kill or be killed, attacked Rabinal. The patrol rounded up the remaining women and children, tied them together, and marched them to the top of a hill. The killing began at 11:00 A.M. and they were still killing at 4:00 P.M.—seventy women and one hundred and seven children perished. But Jesús Tecú managed to flee into the woods, clutching his two-year-old baby brother in his arms; there he encountered an armed man raping a young woman. The man captured Jesús and snatched the baby from his arms and declared: "I'll let you live if you come with me to my village and work, but my wife doesn't want to take care of any babies." With that, he smashed the baby's head against a tree and led Jesus Tecú off to begin a year and eight months of servitude. The third attack took place in May of that year. The military searched for survivors, killed all of the men they could find, and carried the women and children off in helicopters.

In 1983, the dictator of Guatemala, Rios Montt, declared a general amnesty and survivors gathered at the military base where Jesús encountered his sister. She had been giving birth when the military first attacked Rabinal and miraculously, she, her baby, and the midwife were spared. They fled to the mountains. She denounced the man holding her brother captive to the regional military commander and Jesús was set free in November of 1983. Ten years later, the regional military commander marched again on the community, with two thousand members of the civil patrol, to stop the exhumation and identification of victims. The commander declared that the exhumation was the work of guerrillas. International attention in the form of human rights groups working in

Guatemala, facilitated by electronic communications, denounced the military action. Jesús Tecú and other survivors of the Rabinal massacres formed a human rights organization, called the Widows and Orphans of Rabinal, which was able to bring to trial three members of the civil patrol who had participated in the genocide of Rabinal. They were given death sentences in 1998 but the sentences were overturned by later appeals. The Widows and Orphans of Rabinal are seeking new trials.

## Exploring Voice and Style

Why bring such a moment of tragic history into the classroom? Prior to hearing Tecú's testimonio, the class had read two examples of the Latin American genre known as testimonial literature: Montejo's *Death of a Guatemalan Village* (1987)[1] and Burgos Debray's *I, Rigoberta Menchú: An Indian Woman in Guatemala* (1984).[2] They also read Asturias's prize-winning novel, *The President* (1997). Writing exercises included comparing these three volumes in terms of writing style and voice. Students quickly came to the conclusion that testimonios generally use straightforward first-person narrative devoid of metaphorical language. In contrast, Asturias's powerful metaphorical language captured their imaginations and allowed them to experiment with short pieces using these contrasting styles and voices. Several students pointed out that the testimonios had greater truth-value than the figurative language of Asturias, but that the latter had greater power to capture and hold the reader. Issues of audience and readership were discussed. Debates ensued over the most appropriate language to write an account of human rights abuses such as they had just heard and struggled to represent. We experimented with one-page assignments in both styles. Those inclined to do so were encouraged to write poetry or fiction, others wrote straightforward accounts in their own voice as the listener. Now students were prepared to confront another level of the controversy over ethnographic authority.

## The Rigoberta Menchú Controversy

The controversy over the veracity of Rigoberta Menchú's story first appeared in *Active Voices*, the on-line journal of *Cultural Survival*, in the summer of 1998 after anthropologist David Stoll published "The Construction of I, Rigoberta Menchú: Excerpts from a Work in Progress" (1997, 38) in *Brick*, a journal of literary criticism. Stoll claimed that in her testimonial, as told to Burgos Debray, Menchú had lied to advance the interests of the Guatemalan guerrillas, which in turn prolonged the war. Between January and April of 1999, contrasting articles appeared in the *Chronicle of Higher Education*, *Time Magazine*, the *New York Times*, the *New Republic*, and the *New York Review of Books*, to name only a few. I copied and distributed many of the articles to the class for discussion in mid-February. Students were dumbfounded. Was Stoll right? Menchú had convinced them of the truth of her story. Many asked: Why had I assigned a book that was full of lies? They felt betrayed.

The class focused on the complexities of the debate. Stoll contests three events in Menchú's testimonial story. He claims that she was not an eyewitness to her brother's murder by the military because other Mayans he interviewed recounted a different version of the story. He does not question that her brother was kidnapped, tortured, doused with gasoline, and burned to death. He states, however, that she did not see the event. Moreover, he argues that her father's battle over land was not with Ladinos, people of Spanish heritage, but rather with his own in-laws. Stoll says that according to informants (I never use this term) interviewed during his research for *Rigoberta Menchú and the Story of All Poor Guatemalans* (1999), Menchú lied about being a poor Indian with no education, and had actually attended a private Catholic school. Following the debate in *Active Voices* provided the class with an important controversy in contemporary anthropology and literary criticism.

Anthropologist Paul Gilles (*Active Voices*, June 1998) makes the point that Stoll confuses testimony (as in a court proceeding) and testimonial as a literary genre. Stoll ignores the research on testimonials as a form of collective autobiographical witnessing that are coauthored texts, as in the case of Burgos Debray's publication of Menchú's story. Burgos Debray's methodology of recording a "native Indian" for several hours illustrates the classical authorial practice of anthropology before George Marcus and others questioned "ethnographic authority" by asking: Who has the authority to create a narrative or a history? John Beverley (*Active Voices*, July 1998) puts it succinctly when he says that what seems to bother Stoll, above all, is that Menchú has an agenda. Beverley asks Stoll to clarify his own agenda. Stoll is uncomfortable with what he calls a "postmodernist anthropology" that frames the text and narrative. Ironically, Stoll is claiming authority for his own collected narratives over those told by Menchú to Burgos Debray. Menchú never saw the final text. Moreover, the French and Spanish editions differ considerably from the edition in English. Have Stoll's Guatemalan "informants" seen his texts? I directed students to several passages that Stoll considers offending in *I, Rigoberta*: the story of her brother's massacre (Burgos Debray 1984, 178–79); the recounting of her father's struggle over land (102–116); and Burgos Debray's passage that says Rigoberta declared: "I must say before I start that I never went to school, and so

I find speaking Spanish very difficult" (1). Stoll claims that Menchú attended a private Catholic school and completed the eighth grade. Her answer to these allegations in a press conference was that she had worked as a maid in the school in exchange for learning Spanish. In neither of the other passages in her narrative does Menchú claim to have been an eyewitness to the events described. Both texts have the tone of a shared family history. For example, she says: "This was the first time my father went to prison. My brother said: 'we don't know what to do for him because the lawyers say Papá will be in jail for eighteen years. We need money to get educated people to help us'" (102).

In the passages about her brother's massacre, she is clearly recounting a story told and retold by her family. I invited students to read closely and examine pronoun usage in the narrative. The use of the collective "we" is very common, with the notable exception of a passage that describes description of Rigoberta's tenth birthday (43–49). I asked the students to discuss examples from their own family stories that have become exaggerated or idealized. But still, several students held Menchú to a higher standard of veracity. After all, she was a Nobel Peace Prize winner. I countered by saying that yes, she was, but not for her testimonial told to Burgos Debray, but rather for her efforts to bring peace to Guatemala.

Yes, she painted an idealized picture of her father and recounted the family version of land battles with Ladinos rather than the version told to Stoll. Aren't all family stories filled with truths, half-truths, and exaggerations? I suggested that students try interviewing family members, especially different generations, about some significant event that is retold at gatherings. One student wrote a moving piece about his grandparents' arrival in the United States. Another contrasted a family origin story from the perspective of two generations.

In the essays on the Stoll-Menchú controversy, the majority of students came to realize that as Menchú states on the first page of *I, Rigoberta Menchú*: "This is my testimony. I didn't learn it from a book and I didn't learn it alone. I'd like to stress that it's not only my life; it's also the testimony of my people." Nevertheless, some students still held Menchú to a higher standard of veracity than they would their own family members. One student quoted Machiavelli: "Men are so simple and yield so readily to the desires of the moment that he who will trick will always find another who will suffer to be tricked." He concluded his essay with, "It makes me wonder if we are the ones who are willing to be deceived." However, another student ended her essay with: "If Stoll considers Menchú's rendition of the events that took place in Guatemala to be so flawed as to burn the flesh that holds her radiant bird of misery together, [a reference to Menchú's testimonial as the Quetzal Bird of Guatemala], perhaps it is our turn to question the wick that keeps his warning flare alight."

While most of the students were uncomfortable with the debate, their writing reflected thoughtfulness and even passion. They came to the realization that in Mayan languages, as in many New World languages of the Americas, a story cannot be told without a listener present who can contradict or confirm the narrator's version of the events. The speakers of these languages have formalized the true nature of narrative in which all discourse is a negotiation in meaning. If there had been another Mayan present who knew the realities of Rabinal, we would have heard a negotiated testimonio rather than a single voice. The students have learned that some cultures construct truth through such negotiations. The students in this seminar had been conditioned by their education to give greater truth-value and authority to the printed word. Now they had experienced a mini–anthropological experience of turning their own words to the printed page. Hopefully, our discussions and debates in class provided the springboard for illustrating how anthropology continues to deconstruct the authority and power of our colonial past and question our own participation in human rights abuses. And, in questioning ethnographic authority, students have gained the confidence and skills to construct their own arguments and participate as global citizens in a complex world.

# Writing from (Field) Experience

KATHRYN S. MARCH

Anthropology, Women's Studies,
Asian Studies

℘ Writing is pivotal to my upper-division classes at Cornell. Over the years of teaching anthropology, women's studies, and Asian studies courses, the way in which I teach writing in those classes has shifted away from the conventional term research paper to look increasingly at the many other ways in which writing links students to scholarship. The completed papers, articles, and books of experienced scholars are largely the windows through which we introduce students to intellectual life, but such works are the capstone[1] of a much longer process that often begins with precarious personal discoveries and only occasionally culminates in collective appreciation and acceptance for published work. Writing does not simply summarize this process; it is entangled in every stage of the enterprise, from observing to recording, testing to verifying, disseminating and critiquing, revising and finalizing. When we as teachers emphasize only the authoritatively (and often individually) written outcome, we obscure and reify the many tentative, exploratory, negotiated, experimental, and collective junctures through which the work has passed and been defined. My emphasis in teaching writing attempts to explore more of these interstitial moments, where writing is integral to the larger tasks of seeing, recording, understanding, and communicating the world around us.

The class on which these thoughts are based is jointly in anthropology and women's studies: it introduces students to the global diversity in the relations between women and men, and in the cultural constructions of those relations. As an upper-division course, it also expects students to be able to respond critically to advanced materials and, even, to explore both the disciplinary roots and the research potential of complex topics. Students come from many majors, some with prior experience in anthropology, some with experience in women's studies, but few with both. Typically, about one-third of the class has had some experience outside of the United States. As a group, the students in this class are energetic and engaged. This course—with its daunting title, Sex and Gender in Cross-Cultural Perspective, placed at the upper-undergraduate level in both anthropology and women's studies, and fulfilling no requirements in any of Cornell's colleges—attracts an extremely demanding, and rewarding, group of self-selected students.

My first objective in this course is to provide an overview of how cultures have shaped what it means to be a woman or a man. I focus upon non-Western examples and try to explore different regions of the world in some depth. The course is not, however, organized geographically. Instead, we look at a variety of facets to the cultural construction of gender. I begin by exploring biological sex differences, to show some of the ways in which our ideas, even about sexual dimorphism, menstruation, conception, pregnancy, and birth, are shaped by culture. Over the semester, as we look at how people become sexed through their socialization, family structures, divisions of labor, ritual and religion, popular culture, law and politics, I encourage the development both of greater sympathy for non-Western situations and of heightened critical sensitivity to the challenges of equitable change.

Although most of the course lectures, readings, and videos deal with the non-Western world, I am concerned that students also confront and understand the gendered world around them at Cornell. A parallel objective throughout this course, then, is to provide opportunities for students to learn and apply various anthropological field methods. I want students not only to be able to read analyses and ethnographies of gender, but also to appreciate the field situations and the field research apparatuses that produced them. To help students understand how the sources they read were produced, and to launch them into research experiences of their own, I have designed options for weekly mini–field research exercises I call "practicums." These practicums guide students through various anthropological methods, such as participant observation, use of field notes and note taking, interviewing, ethics in human subject research, ritual processual analysis, structuralist analysis, symbolic classifications, and visual content analysis. My goals in these practicums are, in part, to dismantle the common misapprehension that anthropological fieldwork is primarily intuitive or commonsensical. I want to substitute (and teach) a fuller appreciation for how systematic work must be done and, as well, allow students an opportunity to move beyond textual learning into the practical world.

In this, my course joins the recent anthropological call for a better understanding of disciplinary practice. Anthropology, and specifically ethnology, distinguished itself early as that offshoot from the ancestral tree of Western social theory that attended to the rest of the human world. Throughout the years of its establishment and rise in European and American universities, anthropology as a discipline lay claim to nothing less ambitious than everything human—biology, family, society, economy, religion, culture, language—in short, to all human history and activity, whether of mind, body, or community, throughout all time and everywhere humans had wandered on the globe. The magnificent embrace of the discipline's hubris no doubt exacerbates the present anthropological anguish: in precisely as much as grace lay in the promise of a full and final understanding of human nature, experience, and potential, the fall has plunged to the deepest foundations of that understanding itself. As we teach anthropology today, then, we must not only open student eyes to human possibilities they had not yet envisioned, but we must also help them develop a critical eye to—if I am not stretching my metaphor too far—understand the many historical and cultural lenses through which the rest of the world has previously been viewed.

The cornerstone of this enhanced critical awareness is writing, or, more exactly, is transforming the primary experience of fieldwork, observations, and research into its secondary materials, our articles and books. Many theorists have explored these problematics by investigating the ways in which anthropology has had as its primary focus knowledge of "other" people but has only partially come to terms with the underlying assumptions about selfhood and difference. Others focus upon the ways in which insiders and outsiders have differential access to knowledge, especially when "inside" and "outside" are produced in relations of exclusion and domination, especially colonial and postcolonial ones. Analogous critiques have been levied regarding the relative social positioning of women and men within gendered systems of knowledge and power.

As a teacher of sex and gender cross-culturally, I find it very helpful that so many of the students are sensitive to the postcolonial racist, ethnocentric, and sexist pitfalls plaguing anthropological work; it is less helpful that they have been more encouraged to be deconstructively critical than to attempt to move constructively beyond criticism. Many students—painfully aware of the historical forces shaping the disciplinary clay feet of anthropology, its multiple sources of bias, and the fundamental paradoxes of intersubjective and intercultural understanding—seem no longer able (or willing) to risk field research or ethnographic writing, taking refuge instead in wonderfully witty, even deeply insightful, critical self-introspections. They are so extremely skilled at critiquing all that is wrong (racist, sexist, colonialist, imperialist, romanticized . . .) with anthropology that they implicitly abandon the very enterprise of cross-cultural understanding as corrupt. The more adroit these students become at critiquing others' writings, it seems, the less able they are to produce any of their own. In my course on sex and gender, I am specifically concerned about unlocking the paralysis that this new critical awareness seems to produce in many students.

Because the course is also a women's studies course, students are especially ready not only to understand how profoundly the discipline might have been shaped by its historical biases, but also to work to change those biases. They may be more or less as disaffected as their peers with regard to academic writing, but they are far from inactive or mute in other regards. They always bring with them, to varying degrees and in various styles, some awareness of sex discrimination; although some suffer from the current allergy to the term "feminist," others equally enthusiastically embrace even its most radically lesbian separatist variants. All say they disapprove of sex discrimination, but few have examined how they decide whether they think any particular situation (such as women's primary commitment to child-caretaking, for example) is unacceptably sexist—that is, illegitimately traffics in sex difference—or whether they think it is legitimately structured by what they see as the inevitable realities of sex difference. I have been repeatedly struck, over the years I teach, by how varied students' assumptions about ("legitimate") sex differences are: what one student sees as clearly the result of human expectations, socialization, and culture, another sees as the result of biological, evolutionary and/or divine forces.

The course opens, then, with an exploration of their various assumptions, commitments, and biases. Discussed comparatively along with their awareness of the other sources of bias within the discipline of anthropology, this opens a door not just to damning the discipline but also to personalizing the very idea of perspectival knowledge. Students are quick to grasp the idea that anthropological accounts (like all human creations) are partial representations—and sometimes highly motivated or biased ones. It is a plausible intellectual trajectory, then, to this idea of perspectival knowledge, that knowledge is more than the representation of an objective reality. More than just an absolute question of what is there, knowledge is inherently adverbial; that is, all the adverbial questions asking who? when? where? how? and why? compose a particular form of knowledge that was produced to modify the very nature of the knowledge they produce.

Within anthropology, for example, we have argued for a very long time about whose Samoa was "right"—Mead's or Freeman's—only to discover several things: that both brought their own distinctive history to their portrait; that we can learn a great deal about Mead and Freeman as we describe the interplay between their histories and their accounts; that no one's representation of, say, Samoa can be without historical and personal engagement; but, still, that we also learn something more about Samoa with each additional version we encounter. That all our accounts are relative and partial does not mean that there isn't a Samoa out there; it means that there is neither a singular Samoa nor a perfect, objective, or totalizing account.

I try to translate these concerns into students' concrete writing practices with, for example, a practicum like the following:

*Example 1: First practicum assignment on ethnographic authority as described in the course syllabus*

IDEOLOGY, FEMINISM, ETHNOGRAPHIC WRITING, AND ETHNOGRAPHIC AUTHORITY

*Topic:* Anthropology has become increasingly self-critical about its biases, coming from a largely colonial, sometimes missionary, and often misogynist history, to ask: What is the basis for anthropological authority to study and write about other peoples? From the perspective of this course, how are the current critiques of anthropology informed by feminism and vice versa? All writing is done from some point of view. Most familiar, of course, are "first person" writing (which announces itself as coming from subjective personal experience) and "scientific" writing (which postulates a universal, objective viewpoint). Some of the most complex writing, however, must present, organize, and reflect upon information coming from several different sources simultaneously.

*Reading:* Hastrup, Kirsten. 1992. "Writing Ethnography: The State of the Art." In *Anthropology and Autobiography*, edited by J. Okely and H. Callaway. London: Routledge, 116–133.

*Assignment option:* If you choose to do this practicum option, you must:

1. Find a quotation, song, poem, or other short verbal piece on the subject of female power. It can represent a point of view that you either agree or disagree with. Choose a quote from any of the readings for this course, if you wish.

2. Interview one of the members of your small study group about their opinion of the citation you have chosen. Ask about:

(a) the nature of female power; (b) the possibilities for sexual equality; and (c) their opinions about what is at stake in sexual difference.

3. Write a one-page draft in which you try to represent the other person's point of view, then,

4. Show your draft to the other person and get them to write a one-page reply to yours, and finally,

5. Write another three-page paper in which you again present the other person's point of view, but this time, do so in such a way that your own point of view is also there.

(For this assignment, you will submit your quotation/source, your interview notes, your first draft, their reply, and your final paper.)

In preparation for this first practicum, readings, lectures, and discussions about the feminist critique of anthropology are linked to wider criticisms within the history of science about the misleading apparent objectivity of science. The challenge, however, lies not merely in accepting that much of orthodox anthropological knowledge was formulated from the self-serving and self-justifying vantage of elite, white, European males, but in appreciating the fundamental relativity of scientific truth(s), without losing all grasp of verification or justice: that many truths are possible, even necessary, does not mean that all things are true and it certainly does not mean that all are desirable in the creation of a more just world. The first practicum exercise, then, looks at feminism and the problematics of ethnographic authority. It asks students to investigate each other's points of view regarding sexual difference and to address the problem of point of view in their writing. In comments on and discussion of their writing, we look not only at the theoretical issues of situated knowledge and difference of opinion, but also at the historical moments through which female power, equality, and sexual difference have been constructed differently, and, finally, at some of the tangible practices in writing that reinforce or undermine various kinds of authority such as the use of passive versus active voices, quotation marks, and qualifying phrases like "I think" or "she believes" in contrast to ones like "I found" or "he showed."

The great strength of these activities is that, like other forms of "writing from experience," these exercises build upon the first-person power intrinsic in all of us. Writing from field experiences makes an anthropologist of every student. In every practicum, I have two primary objectives: first, to explore aspects of anthropological field method and experience and, second, to address issues in the writing and reading about those experiences. In the former, I want students not only to learn various anthropological field methods by trying them, but I want to encourage an understanding of other anthropologists' fieldwork that is both more critical and more sympathetic—more critical because students are better able to infer the precise field situations and approaches that produce it, and more sympathetic because they have tried fieldwork themselves.

I focus not only on critiques of the final product, but also upon understanding many other stages—formulating an opinion prior to undertaking any work, note-taking and making a record of others' work on the subject, note-taking and making a record of your own work, preliminary and further drafts, incorporation of other written sources, anticipation of readers' responses, and the incorporation of those responses— the whole cycle of scholarly reading, thinking, reworking, writing, and being read. In asking students to write about their field experiences, and to talk both about the fieldwork and about their writing, I hope to enhance their critical understanding of how anthropological material is produced and presented, and, at the same time, to develop their own capacities to construct interesting presentations based on original (if small) work themselves.

There are, however, serious challenges to writing from field experience as well, so a few practical notes about teaching based on practice are in order here. The first, of course, is that special precautions must be built into these exercises to make sure not only that the work proceeds ethically and without risk to its subjects, but also that the students are required to conform to disciplinary ethical standards, to understand those standards, and be able to apply them responsibly. To this end, each exercise must be carefully designed and the entire course must obtain approval from the appropriate university committee. In addition, each semester, one of the practicum exercises specifically asks students to think and write about the ethical issues of research involving human subjects itself.

*Example 2: Later practicum assignment dealing with the ethics of research involving human subjects*

ETHICS AND RESEARCH INVOLVING HUMAN SUBJECTS

*Topic:* Since you will be undertaking a wide variety of practicums observing, interviewing, and otherwise interacting with people, you must think about the ethics of research involving human subjects.

*Reading:* Handout on Human Subjects

*Assignment option:* If you choose this option, you must:

1. By yourself: Look at the remaining assignment options for this course. Pick any one that you plan to do. Write three short statements (one long paragraph each) to describe how you would deal ethically with the research principles of (a) informed consent, (b) privacy, and (c) no harm. Be specific (e.g., include examples of consent forms if you would use them).

2. Meet with your small group to read and discuss each other's ethics proposals. Also discuss: How well were these principles respected in the previous two section assignments? How well do these three principles address the ethics of doing social research? Can you imagine circumstances they would not cover well?

3. After your group meeting, make an annotated list discussing the limitations of this tripartite "protection of human subjects" framework (What is missing? Or what situations is it not adequate or appropriate for?) and write a brief essay (no more than two pages) assessing the strengths and limitations of the present human subjects framework.

(For this assignment, you will submit your three short statements, your notes on the group meeting, your annotated list, and your final essay.)

At this juncture, it is important to note a potential problem arising in the matter of time commitment: not only could any of these exercises expand to require an unacceptable amount of time, but the time required of instructors/ teaching assistants in responding to them is also dangerously elastic. Two solutions—beyond the obvious exhortation that no practicum should take students more than four to six hours total (one or two in fieldwork, and two to four in writing)—seem to have worked (and there are undoubtedly still others). The first has been to keep enrollment in the weekly discussion sessions at which these assignments are presented and discussed small. Limiting these groups to no more than eight students seems to work best; with more than eight, students need so much more oral and written feedback on their work that the instructors are forced both to hold an excessive number of tutorial office hours and to spend more time than is reasonable providing written commentary on the work. With a maximum of eight students, however, in-class discussions appear to be adequately satisfying to the students and teachers. Office hours can then be reserved for only those students needing additional special help, not serving the basic demands of the assignment. Furthermore, students are able to form good working relations with one another in these sections, especially because many of the assignments also ask them to work with two to four of the students from their section in small groups (these are the small groups to which the practicum assignments refer). I consider it one of the most tellingly positive responses to these sections (and their even smaller working subgroups) that students regularly write on evaluations: "I learned as much or more from the other students in this class as I did from readings, lectures, and videos."

The second vital change in the course design that made these practicums really workable was to introduce a substantial choice structure; that is, although there are usually a dozen topics and assignments outlined in the semester-long syllabus, students are only expected to complete about five (or at most eight, if there are no other evaluative requirements such as midterms). This means that it is likely that some (but not all) of the students in each section will have done the exercise each week; that it is possible to present and discuss each week's exercise (because of the first point); that it is possible to put adequate written comments on each week's work (ditto); and, last but not least, that it is possible to insist that all work be turned in on time. My stipulation that "airline rules" (serious doctor-certified illness, death in the immediate family, or commensurate catastrophe) apply to extensions has proven essential in keeping a timely flow of assignments and responses. Because students have control and choice in managing their own workload, this can accommodate almost all garden-variety problems.

Within these general principles then—that each practicum explores an anthropological field method, that each addresses specific related issues in disciplinary writing, and that each is done in a manageable and timely fashion—there has emerged over the years a sequence of assignment options, each of which pursues a topic presented in the lecture portion of class as important for understanding the anthropology of sex and gender. The earlier options tend to focus upon more observational methods and to deal with the related questions of note taking and record making. Thus, very early in the course, I usually do some sort of exercise (like the one below) asking students to decide how they make "diagnoses" of sex—that is, how they decide if someone is a woman or a man.

*Example 3: Observational practicum assignment from syllabus*

THE CLASSIFICATION OF SEX: MEN'S AND WOMEN'S
SEXED APPEARANCES

*Topic:* Because we often think of sex differences as "natural," "physical," and/or "biologically based," it is instructive to consider how we (and some other authors) actually use such evidence.

*Reading:* Buettner-Janusch, J. 1966. Brief selections on sexual
  selection from *Origins of Man.* N.Y.: John Wiley and Sons.
Errington, S. 1990. Brief selections on the body from "Recasting
  Sex, Gender, and Power: A Regional and Theoretical Over-
  view." In *Power and Difference: Gender in Island Southeast Asia,*
  edited by Atkinson and Errington. Stanford, Calif.: Stanford
  University Press, 1–58.
Mead, M. 1968 [1935]. Brief selections on sex and temperament from
  *Sex and Temperament in Three Primitive Societies.* N.Y.: Dell.

*Assignment option:*

  1. Observe ten to twenty people and guess/determine their sex.
  2. Be creative in how you record each of your observations.
Include what you think is pertinent information about the observed
person, the context of the observation, and the basis upon which
you made your sex diagnosis judgment. (Is it clothes? hair? gesture?
voice? body? what . . . ?)
  3. Try to be creative in how you select the situation for making
your observations. (The Quad is easy. But would the observations
and bases for judgment be different if you: saw only silhouettes?
Listened to voices on the phone? Looked at infants or elderly
people?)
  4. Consider the short Buettner-Janusch, Mead, and Errington
readings: what does each postulate is the basis for sexual differentiation in humans? Where do your own opinions fall in relation to
these authors?
  5. Write a short essay (no more than four pages) in which you use
the findings from your field practicum to support your own ideas
about human sexual differentiation in relation to these two citations
(and, of course, other class materials).
  (For this assignment, you will turn in your original record of the
observations as well as your final essay.)

As simple as this exercise sounds (and perhaps precisely because it is
simple), it inspires considerable originality in students, both in conceptualizing
a field situation and in relating it in writing to the two short excerpts provided
them. Students have, for example, sat on their front porches and tried to assess
the sex of drivers in cars passing by at forty-five miles per hour; or, they have
gone to one side of a semi-opaque glass-brick wall and looked at sex, as it were,
through a glass darkly. In trying to make a record of their observations, students

confront the first overwhelming crisis of field research: how to take notes as fast as the information presents itself.

In trying to evaluate their sex decision-making process, students must situate their own approach within the two counterpoised extracts provided: the Buettner-Janusch excerpt posits a decidedly sociobiological and evolutionary reproductive imperative to sex difference, the Mead excerpts (and what course on sex and gender cross-culturally could not incorporate at least some Mead?) embed the development of sex differences in different socialization practices, and the Errington one asserts that sex, as we know it, is a social and cultural construction. Rarely having ever asked themselves how they know someone's sex, and in conjunction with class lectures/discussions about the classification of sex difference, intersexuality, and *berdache* (the anthropological term usually applied to the wide variety of supernumerary sex/gender identities/roles found in many cultures), this practicum option, in my experience, is a good example of a way to link reading and the introduction of novel anthropological material in the classroom without exoticizing it.

Another practicum I often use looks at folklore or popular culture. The folklore option (below) surprises many students because they can't imagine (before they begin) that they will ever find anyone who knows any sayings, proverbs, rhymes, or other folkloric snippets on menstruation or ejaculation. After they try it, they learn (following the assigned article) not only the importance of coding in the communication of folklore, but also the related importance of making a record about the context within which information is collected, not as supplementary details about the information but as intrinsic to the very production of the information itself.

*Example 4: Practicum assignment option on folklore*

FOLKLORE AND THE ANALYSIS OF MYTHS OF MENSTRUA-
TION AND EJACULATION

*Topic:* Culture is not found only in dramatic rituals or life-threatening moments, but also in little bits and pieces of everyday practice: sayings, phrases, jump-rope rhymes, jingles . . .

*Reading:* Radner, J. N., and S. S. Lanser. 1993. "Strategies of Coding in Women's Cultures." In *Feminist Messages: Coding in Women's Folk Cultures,* edited by Joan Radner. Urbana, Ill.: University of Illinois Press.

*Assignment option:* Each person planning to do this practicum should collect a small set of folkloric material (proverbs, jump-rope or

other rhymes, euphemistic expressions, myths . . .) pertaining either
to menstruation (and menses) or to ejaculation (and semen),
remembering to:

1. Undertake the collection ethically (with project description
and consent form),

2. Record all pertinent contextual information (decide and be
prepared to explain what you think is pertinent),

3. Record your examples appropriately (decide and be prepared
to explain why you chose to record them in the way you did),

4. Record your own understanding of the "meaning" of the
example, and,

5. Record others' exegesis of their understandings of the
example (be sure to ask—at least—the original source of your
example and his/her listeners).

6. Meet in your small group to discuss and begin to interpret
your respective examples.

7. Write a short paper (no more than four pages) describing and
analyzing both the examples you collected and those that others in
your small group collected. What do you think is the underlying
logic of these examples? How well do you find that Radner and
Lanser's framework applies: for example, do you find that they are
examples of "explicit," "complicit," or "implicit" coding? How
does the issue of shared or non-shared identity play in these
examples and their coding? Are you able to use the examples you
collected and those you got from other group members in the same
way in your writing?

(For this assignment, you will submit your own notes, notes on
the group discussion, and your final paper.)

Among the most useful exercises, according to students, are ones dealing
with interviews. Most students are aware that interviewing—or, at least, talking
with people—is a central tool in human research. Some have heard or read
about the various kinds of interviewing possible, from structured to unstruc-
tured, individual, group or focus, singular or sequential. Few have ever done
any actual interviewing themselves. Most imagine that the best (in the sense of
scientific) interviews should be fully structured in advance and fully transcribed
afterwards. For this course, students begin by interviewing only other students
in the class, but after they have done the practicum on ethics they may interview
outsiders. They use interviews of various sorts in several of the practicum options during the middle portions of the course: to interview individuals about

how many gendered types of people they know; to interview both participants and practitioners in a *rite de passage* like a bar/bat mitzvah, a first communion, a fraternity or sorority initiation, or a military induction; and to interview people about sexual insults found in popular songs.

*Example 5: Practicum assignment option using interviews about* rites de passage

RITUAL AND PROCESSUAL ANALYSIS OF RITES OF PASSAGE

*Topic:* Rites of passage (including, especially, initiation rituals) follow a well-documented structure; VanGennep identified these as: (a) separation—in which the initiand is taken away from (or stripped of) his/her previous identity/role/world, (b) liminality— in which the initiand is kept apart and (typically) taught new skills appropriate to the identity/role/world into which she/he is moving, and (c) reintegration—in which the initiand is brought out (often with considerable fanfare) into his/her new identity/role/world.

*Assignment option:* for this assignment, you should:

1. Working in a small group with others from your section, identify an initiation ritual, life cycle ritual, or other rite of passage. Sorority/fraternity initiation, girl/boy scout initiation, confirmation, bar or bat mitzvah are all good examples but there are many others. It does not matter whether you have or have not yourself experienced the ritual.

2. Identify two people: one who has taken part in the ritual and one ritual specialist (someone who sponsors, performs, or is otherwise especially knowledgeable about it). Either or both of these people may already be members of your small group.

3. Divide up your small group so that some of you interview the participant and some interview the specialist. Ask each what happens in the rite of passage in question. Make a record of the sequence of events, the reported significance of the events, and their desired effect. (If possible, observe and record the ritual.)

4. With your small group, prepare to present a description of your fieldwork on the ritual. Be as creative as possible in deciding how to present this material: in addition to interview notes, you may want to use timelines, charts, or other visuals to enhance your description.

5. Individually, write a short paper (one to two pages) describing the identity transformations that this ritual is supposed to effect (i.e., from what identity to what identity—be specific) and the processes through which it attempts to effect them; remember to take into account your own position/identities in relation to the ritual(s) in question: how do your own position/identities affect the ways you might write about the experience of transforming identities?

Make sure that your conduct, your interviewees' understanding and participation, your record making, and your final presentation all embody the highest ethical standards, using project description and consent forms where appropriate.

(For this assignment, you will turn in your original notes, the materials you design as a group for the presentation, and your final paper.)

One of the greatest pleasures in working with students on these practicum exercises comes from the originality, talent, and insight of the students themselves; I learn a great deal from them every year. In this particular practicum, I sometimes think I have learned more than any faculty member should ever be required to maintain in confidence about college fraternity initiations. In many of these options, students also discover and share some astounding Web sites: on intersexuality, e.g., *Hermaphrodites with an Attitude* <http://www.isna.org/ HWA/Winter95–96/Winter95–96.html> and *Standards of Care for Gender Identity Disorders* <http://www.symposion.com/ijt/ijtco405.htm> or the *Intersex Support Group International* <http://www.isgi.org/>; and on menstruation, the *Museum of Menstruation and Women's Health* <http://www. mum.org/>.

The final exercises move into ever more sophisticated questions and methods, looking at aspects of symbolic and political analysis of, for example, popular songs, gossip, or commercial advertisements. In each case, the points in the projects are, simultaneously: to explore a topic derived from the substantive issues raised by the discipline in regard to women, men, and gender; to enter into another aspect of field research method; and, finally, to relate topic and field experience through writing and writing about specific aspects of writing. Exemplary of the kind of work expected in the final practicum exercises in this course is the one described below, which asks students to identify sexual insults in popular songs, to use a number of the approaches to symbolic analysis developed in other exercises and in class lectures, and to conduct a small focus group to discuss the insults and their interpretation(s). The practicum options that involve popular culture, such as advertising and, especially, songs, are extremely successful with students.

*Example 6: An option taken from (at or near) the end of the course*

SEXUAL INSULT TERMS IN POPULAR CULTURE

*Topic:* As we have seen (and you undoubtedly already realized), music and songs are powerful forms of cultural expression—and not just in "primitive" societies. Whether in the lives of the composers/performers or those of the listeners/audience, or in the institutional arrangements through which music/songs are produced, or in the symbolism of the lyrics, or in the music itself, music and songs have dramatic capacities to move and motivate us, including in/as our gendered selves/society. How do popular songs deploy images that degrade women, men, and sexual relationships?

*Reading:* Robertson, C. E. 1989 [1987]. "Power and Gender in the Musical Experiences of Women." In *Women and Music in Cross-Cultural Perspective.* Chicago: University of Illinois Press.

*Assignment option:* If you choose to do this practicum, you must:

1. Identify a song that includes lyrics you find insulting to women (some or all), men (some or all), or to sexual relationships (heterosexual or other).

2. Make a tape recording of this selection and print a copy of the lyrics.

3. Make a list of all the images you think are insulting. Consider what make them insulting: for something to be insultingly "wrong," it must assault the sense of what is properly "right." For example, it is an insult to call someone a "bitch" because (root contrast or inversion) humans are not dogs, and (contrastive details) because dogs eat their own shit, because bitches go into heat and then are sexually aggressive, because bitches have litters of puppies (not singleton births), because dogs are so loyal they put up with abuse from their significant people . . . For each of the images you list, explore what is the root contrast from which it arises and at least some of the details that contrast evokes. If pertinent, consider how the music (and video?) support or highlight these contrasts.

4. In some songs and contexts, people may attempt to claim an insult term for themselves, that is, to take it away from those who

would use it as an insult and redefine it as a self-referent of pride. Thus, for example, many people of African descent in the 1960s began to call themselves "black," asserting that "Black is Beautiful," although previously, that had been an insult term. Are there any similar recuperative efforts in your songs? Remembering especially the place of sexual insult in the West African uprisings, what do you think makes some such moves effective and others not?

5. In your small group, share your songs and preliminary findings. Discuss the contrasts or inversions your insults reveal. What are the similarities or differences in your findings?

6. Based upon your song, your small group discussion, class lectures, readings and videos, write a brief essay (three pages) discussing sexual insult, sexual power, and the relations between the sexes.

(For this assignment, you will submit the tape, the printed lyrics, your list of the insulting images, your notes on what makes them insulting, the list of instances in your song where the negative imagery seems to be reinterpreted positively, your notes on your small group meeting, and your final essay.)

In many ways, all of the options for practicums that call upon popular culture, especially songs, tap into concerns of exceptional salience for college students. The amount of time that they spend listening to, learning, thinking, and talking about current songs provides a vast reservoir of energy and interest that is easily tapped in exercises like this. Not only have they already done considerable interpretive work on these songs, but they are eager to add any other analytical approaches to their understanding of them and they readily get together to work on such assignments. They report these exercises as the most enjoyable of the entire semester. It is an annual challenge for me to engage in yet another round of new artists, new songs, and new insults, but the effort is amply rewarded in the creativity and responsiveness of the students.

It goes beyond the scope of this paper to describe in detail all the mechanics of this course. Other practicum options focus on topics like kinship (families and family support networks), sexual divisions of labor (in families and other living groups), childbirth (the social and ritual aspects of), ritual (the processual analysis of rites of passage), gossip (power and authority in speech and writing), popular culture (images of violence against women in advertising), mapping (gendered products and spaces in stores), socialization (children's rhymes), or identities (tomboys and sissies). Each builds upon the non-Western materials presented in lecture, films, and readings to focus upon a particular theoretical issue in the anthropology of gender along with the methodological and critical questions they raise.

Each of these practicum options also has a specific focus on writing. These vary but many include some component related to the overall course concern about attending to the position of the researcher and to the interactive context in which the information is collected as integral to the final production of description and analysis: in the example above about *rites de passage*, for instance, students are asked to compare the knowledge/experience of lay participants in a ritual with that of the specialist performing or organizing it. They must also explore how their access to, understanding of, and presentation of this information depends, in part, upon their own relationship to those they are interviewing or their own status as one who has or has not gone through the similar initiation. They work with well-established anthropological theory about *rites de passage*, focus upon gendered experiences of these ritual processes, and, through their own efforts to practice and write about the kind of research that produced those theories, can comment upon them more critically and constructively.

I ask a great deal of my students; they reward me with more than I ask. Although I have thought long and hard, over many years, about my objectives and alternatives in this course on Sex and Gender in Cross-Cultural Perspective, preparing this essay has been an interesting challenge to me. To convey all my commitments and struggles in this essay, it has been difficult to find the right balance among the theoretical, the pedagogical, and the practical lessons this teaching experience has taught me. My thoughts have been spinning with recollections from debates with teaching assistants about how best to direct, respond to, and evaluate student work, with remembered student statements about what they found new (and old) in this course, with excerpts from papers, or images from student presentations, with arguments about the significance of proper citational form—all in a twenty-year mélange of memory and intention. It has been worth the effort primarily because of my abiding commitment to the idea that all three—theory, pedagogy, and practice—are intimately and profitably braided into single coil, uniting concerns within the contemporary discipline of anthropology, feminist criticism, and the teaching of writing.

# The Invisible City of Color, or
# "I Thought This Was a Course on Writing!"

WILLIAM W. GOLDSMITH

City and Regional Planning

*⌒* "I thought this was a course on writing," fumed a restive high school senior in my writing seminar at Cornell one summer. "You haven't corrected
punctuation, spelling, or anything else on our papers. We're here to learn to
write. Teach us writing!" We were a full week into the summer course when he
erupted—that would be the third week of a regular term. The closest we'd gotten to "writing" was in-class work on revisions of essays about racial disparities
in the students' hometowns. I had told the students that their essays were not
good. The big problem was with their ideas, with what they were thinking, or
perhaps, what they were not thinking. It was this focus on the thinking that the
young man found so annoying. He knew what he thought. His high school
teachers had taught him rules of writing; he used them well. Now he wanted
more rules, more work on the business of writing!

This complaint arose in my writing seminar, Chocolate Cities and Vanilla
Suburbs, my first formal enterprise in the teaching of "writing." I had taught
much writing in less formal ways—as parts of freshman courses, senior seminars, and graduate courses on urban studies and city planning, responding to
term papers and theses, and editing journal articles. I had studied writing twice,
once forty years earlier when I was an engineering student at Berkeley, in English 1A with Frederick Crews, and the second time in a summer creative writing course at San Francisco State with George Logan Price. But teaching the
writing seminar at Cornell was new for me—a group of seventeen students expecting instruction not in a subject, but in "writing." This was a very different

matter. These summer students had not selected my course. They had been assigned randomly. They were not expecting the subject matter: racial discrimination, neighborhood segregation, and the whole mess of ethnic and class conflict that constitutes so much of the field of urban studies.

As in subsequent semesters, when the students *had* selected the subject, I aimed to work with them in three ways. First, we read fiction, essays, and journalism on race, inequality, "invisibility," and the city. My purpose is exposure to ideas, to controversies, to a few of the essential questions of the field: Who lives where, how do we see neighborhoods, why are cities and suburbs so imbalanced, what are some sources of racial and ethnic conflict, how can privileged people learn to see those who live invisibly and hear those whose weak voices don't travel? Second, I wanted to move the students beyond their hesitance to write and talk about race and social class. My purpose is to drag these young people temporarily out of their narrow communities and push them toward establishing a scientific personal distance, so they can understand the social conflicts that govern so much of city life. Third, I insisted that each student write for the public, expecting the whole group to read and listen.

The writing program, I had supposed, would push my attention away from my favorite subjects and toward a focus on "writing," on mechanics, syntax, and style. Much to the contrary, the program pushed me even harder in the opposite direction, to teach about the city. It was exactly where I wanted to go, into my subject matter, away from "teaching writing," away from mechanics, syntax, and style. Still, I find the program's organized restraint against the technical teaching of writing to be a test of nerves—the students' nerves and my nerves, too. None of us in the class is confident when I say early in the semester: "You are here to learn to write better. Stick with me. Keep working on your ideas; just think and write and rewrite and rethink, and then do it again—with criticism and help, to be sure—but work mainly to write what you mean. Although your papers are not satisfactory now, I guarantee that by the end of the semester you will write stronger, more convincing papers."

The students don't believe me. This method makes *me* terribly nervous. But it works! Of the thirty-four students in my first two terms, only one stagnated and only two or three made inadequate improvement. All the others, thirty or thirty-one in all, improved their writing considerably. Whether they would have improved as much in a course that focused on the technique of writing, I don't know, but I do know that they learned to write better. Based on my four or five semesters now of experience teaching "writing," I now believe students learn to write as their interests engage with their private experiences. Their writing becomes charged, alive, and competent.

In this writing course on race, class, and the modern city I have the students read writers who have found ways to convey the lives of people who might otherwise be invisible. Each of these writers reveals a community pushed to the outskirts of our world. Ironically, the most prominent outskirt, to which we direct much of our attention, is the inner city. The first times I taught the course, it ran like this:

The students first read Orwell's *Down and Out in Paris and London*. You will remember that Orwell writes from the bottom looking up, as an educated Englishman, a returning colonial policeman, a traveler who falls beneath respected society. He uses the accident of finding himself outcast and destitute to write about hunger and homelessness in ways well fed and comfortably housed students can understand. Next I have the students read Baldwin's *If Beale Street Could Talk*. His glimpses of life in Harlem in the 1960s and 1970s show students the pain and damage of racial discrimination. Baldwin has much to tell my students, much to make visible, as Fonny and Tish try to survive the city's hostility and indifference. Those two are more real than any characters I can invent from compendious statistics or news stories contrasting city with suburb, or African American with white.

Kathleen Norris comes next, as a city person who inherits a house in the prairie of western South Dakota and writes about small towns that "claim to be communities," places in decline, places in danger of losing hope. Reading her *Dakota: A Spiritual Geography*, the students resisted but finally managed to imagine invisibility from a new viewpoint. Newspaper reporter Alex Kotlowitz wrote *The Other Side of the River* as a documentary about adjoining cities, one black, one white, two places he has come to know after many visits to investigate the unexplained death of a teenage boy. Here I have the students solve the real-world mystery as they play the roles of murder suspects, friends and relatives, and investigators.

None of these five writers explores directly the American illness of multi-colored city and white suburb. Only Baldwin and Kotlowitz examine the American society to find the cancer of racism. Yet still the students learn, as each writer shows how one might examine and write about any places we and others live. I ask the students to imagine how each writer sees and thinks and writes. Then by seeing and thinking and writing themselves, and by rewriting and rethinking and reseeing, and by rewriting again, each of them can begin to use words to understand places and the ways people live. I encourage them to read *Pig Earth*, where John Berger uses prose, poetry, and sketches to show why the writer, in this case living with impoverished peasants in the French Alps, becomes useful to the people in a community only if he or she can write their stories and make their place real to others.

As I teach the seminar, we intersperse small readings now and then, using magazine or newspaper articles. We read a few short essays, perhaps see a video. Among my favorite items are Peggy McIntosh's essay "White Privilege: Unpacking the Invisible Knapsack," which helps white students examine the privileges they enjoy by virtue of their whiteness; a video by Lee Mun Wah called *The Color of Fear*, which documents an intense weekend of race-exploring conversations among nine men in northern California; and a deceptively simple article by Michelle Ling called "The Asian Invasion," about the campus at University of California, Berkeley, then and now.

## Writing in Urban Studies

The field of urban studies is loosely defined and extensively eclectic; it is defined by a problem, not by a method. The field does not have one body of literature, but many bodies, often mutually unintelligible. Scholarly papers in urban economics journals employ methods in mathematics and statistics that are mystifying to sociologists, anthropologists, public officials, and college freshmen. Papers in anthropology or political science employ methods and build on theories that are opaque to economists and laypersons both. The problem is like a spreading disease. Many in urban studies, as in the social sciences more generally, produce bad writing. They infect their work with words of public policy, an arena in which writers and speakers seek indirection and euphemism so as to obscure their meanings and avoid responsibility. They poison their work with "academese," a language used by professors and their graduate students to write to each other for promotion and tenure rather than for discovery and understanding. Writers in the social sciences tend to suffer severely from Thomas Kuhn's "paradigm" problem, biased by their hopes for influence and rewards in the worlds of money and politics. I thus frequently turn away from the scholars, turning instead to those who would call themselves "writers," who would resist "scientific" interpretations of their work.

Orwell, Baldwin, Norris, Kotlowitz, and Berger—each offers a very personal view, not scientific at all in the usual meaning of the term. They write about places where they live, about people they know as individuals, about the idiosyncrasies of community. In my own work in the field of urban studies, I have found that good questions about cities are often very complex and that viewpoint matters enormously. The most interesting questions often make students angry and contentious, because students can see that if they find answers and make them public, they will probably justify aid to some, penalties for others. Patterns of tax collection and public spending may help well-off white people in the suburbs, for example, while hurting poorer people of color in the cities. The key to getting rid of smog in the U.S. metropolises may lie in drastic reduction of automobile traffic, requiring the building of denser cities and in particular the reoccupancy of central cities. This, in turn, may require in turn huge improvements in city public schools along with unprecedented reductions in inequality of family income. What then? These are contentious, complex issues.

So why begin with stories, essays, novels, and journalism, if what we really want are good questions and solid answers—a manageable social science about the American city? If we really want students to figure out what it is that flavors our cities chocolate and our suburbs vanilla, or what harms city people so much and limits the imagination of suburbanites, should we not have them collect and analyze statistics, examine state and municipal laws, measure housing discrimination, study failing schools, and find out why so many people don't have decent homes? Of course we should, and we do. But I believe our students begin best by considering themselves and their own beliefs, prejudgments, and experiences. They should examine these very, very personal things against the focused, detailed, nuanced, and sensitive interpretations provided by great writers.

One major current in the flow of twentieth-century urban studies traces the influence and effect of what we call race. Although some scholars had hoped for an attenuation of urban racial injuries by century's end, unfortunately, with the start of the twenty-first century, they must muffle that optimism. Racial differences persist and strife has grown. Asian Americans and recent immigrants from many countries often find their housing choices restricted. Native Americans and dark-skinned Latinos suffer heavy discrimination. African Americans find that bank loan officers, real estate brokers, apartment renters, homeowners' insurance providers, and especially white residents continue to discriminate against them, forcing them to live in ghettos. In black neighborhoods especially, but also in many Latino neighborhoods, not everyone suffers hardship, but, overall, housing is inferior and more expensive, municipal services are deficient, and access to good shopping is complicated. Public safety is lacking, and public schools are appalling. As the metropolitan economy has restructured and jobs have suburbanized, access to work sites has become problematic. Since some 80 percent of the American people live in one part or another of highly segregated metropolitan areas, it is small exaggeration to refer to this state of affairs as apartheid. Indeed, *American Apartheid* is the appropriate title of the best known and most widely respected scholarly study on the subject (Massey and Denton 1993).

As students in the course learn, the suburb/city distinction starts as an imprecise symbol of the American racial divide and becomes an accurate reality. White suburbs fortify with zoning and building codes, they benefit from biased federal taxes and expenditures, they make sure their police challenge dark-skinned visitors and even residents, and they enact other exclusionary policies to maintain their privileges. Children growing up in black and Latino neighborhoods learn to cope with a hostile environment and with a periphery of exclusion. Children growing up in suburbs learn to expect their privileges, to avoid the city, and to fear difference. I begin the study of the city through an examination of these realities of racial segregation. Sadly, I see no reason to do otherwise.

In their examinations of city neighborhoods and suburbs, the students in my seminar write about their own neighborhoods and adjacent ones, about their high schools, their adventures into foreign turf and hostile zones, and their experiences with people not like themselves. I have discovered that white American students in my classes have had very few actual experiences with "others," with people who are not white. Only two of the white students in my first two classes had ever been inside the home of a non-white student. (One white male student had a Korean American girlfriend; one Eastern European immigrant female had a Latina best friend.) In my larger introductory courses, among those white Cornell students from a central city, many live in highly protected enclaves and attended private schools, thus escaping the potential mixing effects of the city. The majority of the white students are from the suburbs, and they have few non-white neighbors, although they sometimes mix gingerly with students of color in large high schools. In contrast, the Asian, African American, Latino, and immigrant students in my classes bring a rich set of cross-cultural experiences. In their wider urban encounters they face the world as "minorities," and they have all dealt extensively with whites.

### A Writing Sequence

After reading Orwell and Baldwin, the students all notice race and ethnicity, and many of them begin to talk about social class. As they begin to write, engage in peer review, and rewrite, something unexpected happens. In their concern to produce good writing, to get their ideas straight, and to think logically and use evidence honestly, the students forget to be careful; they forget to avoid race, and they begin to say what is really on their minds. This is an odd twist. In a sense, because the course is *not* officially or formally about urban studies, but instead about writing, the students are obligated to make their papers better. As they struggle to write, they become freer to think. I like that!

I aim in this course to sneak up on the students, lull them into dropping their defenses, coax them to think fresh thoughts about race and class. It isn't easy. I bait them and then switch the play. They are suspicious, they don't want the bait, they weave and bob. Because they have learned avoidance through tough, dangerous, sometimes damaging experiences, they know better than to talk honestly or openly about race and class. Because they don't talk straight, they cannot think straight. But crooked thinking doesn't mean no thinking. They are wary. Were I to come on to them directly, they would put up their guards, and that would guarantee my failure. So, as I've done in my other courses for years, I try to approach these raw and tender issues sideways, bottom-up, gingerly, jokingly, sarcastically. I avoid any standard, didactic approaches. I do try to provoke the students. For example, near the end of one semester I asked an Asian student who dressed, acted, and dated "white." "Well, if you are so comfortable, what would your grandmother say if you were to marry a white girl?" He got no chance to answer. "That's not the *real* question," a black woman quickly asserted, "We know sometimes it's ok to cross *that* line. The real question is, What if you marry a *black* girl?" In most circumstances, college students do not talk personally about race and class. This course works by the end of the semester because the students *do* talk experientially about these essentials of American life.

It helps that we begin the readings with Orwell, because *Down and Out* is replete with outrageous stereotypes, heaping the whole pile of mindless, insular English prejudice on the reader's head. Paris is plagued with Jews, blacks, Bulgarians, women, others, too—all of them useless, weak, untrustworthy, and incompetent. Orwell comments thus on the hotel doorkeeper who cheats him: "He called himself a Greek, but in reality he was an Armenian. After knowing him I saw the force of the proverb: 'Trust a snake before a Jew and a Jew before a Greek, but don't trust an Armenian'." I ask the students to figure out why Orwell uses these stereotypes. What effect do they have? What prejudices do they betray in the characters, or in Orwell himself? These discussions are relatively unthreatening, because *Down and Out* is about distant places and a distant time, Paris and London nearly eighty years ago. We read the book early in the course, and the students only rarely make connection to here and now.

The first six writing assignments build one upon another as they require the students to think about neighborhoods, people, and housing from their own experiences. In a short first assignment of a few paragraphs, students are asked to describe a hometown neighborhood. These pieces turn out to focus either on the natural environment of landscape and ecology, on the constructed environment of buildings, streets, and spaces, or on the human environment of culture, lifestyles, and politics. Next, students write a page or two about some particular person they know "who has suffered severe housing problems (lack of money to pay rent, homelessness, discrimination)" or alternatively "someone with a landlord's troubles (with tenants, city hall, restrictions on development)." Third, after some discussion of housing politics and also thinking of the person in the second paper, students write a two-page essay defending either a liberal position of higher wages, social benefits, and direct housing subsidies or a conservative position of permissive housing regulations, reduced restrictions like rent control and taxes, and expanded markets to cause filtering down.

In the fourth assignment, students respond to criticism from peers and from me by rewriting just the title of the liberal/conservative paper and its first paragraph. They also write another title and another introductory paragraph, but this time on Orwell's 125 pages on Paris, as they are asked to explain why Orwell fails to understand the lives of the Parisian poor, or why he believes he is a traitor to his class, or what he means by claiming that poverty frees the poor "from ordinary standards of behavior, just as money frees people from work."

Next, each student writes a full, four-page paper examining Orwell's use of stereotypes. They begin with just a paragraph imitating Orwell's style, but later they write this into a full paper, which most of them rewrite, many of them more than once. Then, finally in this sequence, each student begins to write from his or her own experience in dealing with a stranger, a difficult supervisor or coworker, or a bad housing situation.

Each semester, without fail, every student's memory yields up at least one striking occasion of racial conflict. As I read these papers I see how the act of writing works to clarify their thinking. Here is an example: When Brandon Hong (not his real name) stopped with his family for gas in rural upstate New York one sunny day in April, they could see a John Deere tractor dealer, a diner, and a bank. It had been a long drive, and Brandon, a big kid, was eager to stretch his legs. But, he writes, as the van stopped at the pump his heart thumped fast and hard, his muscles tightened, and his temperature rose. With teenage bravado (he was a high school wrestler) he prepared to protect his family. The other customers gave his family icy, hostile stares, and Brendan "took a deep breath and waited . . ." In his paper, Brandon was finally able to talk about and to interpret his observations: the next car at the gas station, with two African American men dressed in army fatigues, drew all the hostility away. The family paid and drove off. Not a word was spoken, ever, about the whole affair.

## Writing on Place and Race

Many students appreciate *If Beale Street Could Talk* and *The Other Side of the River* because the books help them to work out ideas about their own neighborhood experiences. The connections are obvious, because both books deal directly with the geography of the city and with black/white conflicts. But *Dakota*—about the isolation of western Dakota farmers, all white—seems to the students to offer less. Still, perhaps the best paper of my first semester was the one in which Lynn Crane related the pathetic, rural hopelessness of the Dakotas to her own rejection by Harlem. Harlem sent Lynn abroad, to a white school, for a better education. Caught up in the contradictions forced on all of us by our lives in a racially segregated country, Lynn wrote, "part of the problem is that our community teaches us that the ghetto is a place we must escape. There is an innate shame in being a part of this community." Her escape was through education, but her community rejected her, responding to her achievements with "jealousy, unrealistic expectations and greed, [and with] contempt, frustration, and confusion."

Much of the very best, most open writing comes near the end of the semester. By then each student is working hard to write better papers, to rethink earlier drafts, and—it seems—finally to lighten the load, to take off some of the protective armor. Lynn's paper on the conflicts facing a Harlem kid getting to a prep school came earlier, and it helped move the discussion along. But a whole spate of highly personal, reflective papers comes in near the end; some are new papers; others are very thorough revisions, almost unrecognizable. Most of the writers manage to get enough distance to figure out how the metropolis works as it isolates people by race and class, then throws them into conflict. They do this best by reflecting their own most troubling experiences onto a mirror of the readings.

Many students write of fear and violence related to race and class. I teach this material year in, year out, but only in writing seminars do I encounter such a rush of writing, such urgent struggles to get things straight. The experience is exhilarating as I become involved in working on the papers; and it is astonishing in sad confirmation of my professional findings about racial divisions. The following vignettes pulled from student papers provide illustration. One white student, when she was a little girl, emerged from the Washington, D.C. Metro to confront an angry, shouting, homeless black man. Writing about this as a young adult, she was able to work out on paper some of the twists and turns of her conflicting emotions, as she wanted to protect her mother, but also to sympathize with the man. In writing, she was finally able to examine the racial divide. Another white student, when he was a little boy in a well-off family, went across the Hop River from Andover, Connecticut, one Friday night to the poor and mostly Puerto Rican town on the other side to go to the movies. There he encountered hostility, a tough gang, and a cop on his side. He escaped a fight, but learned his lesson about race and turf. Only years later, when writing about it for class, was he able to understand how the city/suburb racial divisions provoked his personal conflict. A black student, when he was a young teenager, one day observed schoolyard racial insults and then a fight in which the violence got out of hand and might easily have taken someone's life. He was able to write in our class with some detachment, about the magnet school within the school, which enrolls all the white kids and only a few of the black kids, the play of geography, race, and school, and the inevitable conflict. An Asian American student, when he was a small-city high school student, bore direct racial insults alone in the cafeteria and with his mother in the shopping center. Sadly, his bitterness and confusion continue to muddle his writing, as I imagine they trouble his life. Still another white student had observed bullying racism in his prep school. He was only now able to write, to see that the racism was covered over by teachers and the headmaster, left to simmer among the students, no lessons learned but the cheap value of silence and avoidance.

At the lighter end, several papers one semester were stimulated by a brief assignment called "Asian Invasion." There were four Chinese American students in the class, and they especially responded with insight and irony, each struggling with the meaning of being "Chinese" while also being "white" in the American city. One of them, Zachery Po, wrote that the paper got through to him not as we read it aloud in class, but only when he was in his dorm room, "*really* reading it. It made me smile and laugh a bit; it made me nod a lot. I haven't read a piece that I could relate to this much in a very long time. . . . I could write the same thing, just differently." Zachery noticed "that I usually refer to myself as an Asian American rather than a Chinese American. I'm not really sure why. . . . But it took about thirteen years for me to become or realize that I've become a 'white Asian'."

Finally, several of the longer papers treated issues of neighborhood and the city/suburban divide quite directly. Isaac Galway wrote of his parents' nostalgia for Queens, their Christmastime visits to buy Polish hams, Lithuanian bread, and German sauerkraut, and their suburb's lack of identity or community and its emerging racism. They had left the city to escape crime and bad schools, and now found not just boredom, but also racist rot in their suburban haven. Paul Clark's white, working-class family lives in Northbrook, "a typical suburb sheltered from the harsh and frightening realities of . . . Chicago, thirty minutes south. . . . It is made up of mostly upper-class professional people." Paul's dad drives a freight truck; his mother is a secretary. He spent his childhood hearing comments like: "What kind of college degree do you need to become a truck driver? Paul's dad probably just needed his driver's license!" With his hand-me-downs, Paul writes that he took last place at the daily school fashion show and was the brunt of the jokes. The guidance counselor offered disbelief when Paul said his parents had been unable to save for his college. But Paul was a good student, and he could really play basketball, so he rose above these injuries and insults of social class, and he learned to connect class and race. In the summer going into his sophomore year in high school, he was the only white player on an all black team from Chicago's toughest projects. Most of the players had never met a white person their own age. They were a very strong team, but in a metropolitan tournament they played badly and lost, as it turned out to a team of Paul's white friends. After the game, one of these white kids offered Paul an outrageous racist insult. Later, Paul writes: "When I got home from the tournament, I called my grandfather, a former college player himself, to tell him about the weekend. He was not the least bit surprised at my friend's comments and said, 'that's what you get for being the only ping pong ball in a dirty coal bin'."

Barry Sampson grew up in Eastview, an established, well-off part of Frederic, about an hour outside Washington, D.C. Barry's family is Jewish, but the neighborhood seems to be hard-rock Christian. Barry's family often participated with the neighborhood by displaying Christmas lights, but the year they didn't, the neighborhood newsletter complained about those who "ignore the community spirit," and then one summer Barry and his brother were excluded from a neighborhood summer camp. Perhaps city/suburb was part of the dinner-table conversation. Barry writes: "The reason my parents moved out of [Brooklyn and Baltimore] and into the suburbs was for my brother and me . . . they felt a more suburban environment . . . would be safer and easier. . . . So what happens? We move to a suburb and are completely alienated! What is happening here? We live in a world with unsafe, destroyed cities and destructive suburbs. There is nowhere to go!"

The students from this writing seminar may become dentists, lawyers, accountants, teachers—and I hope some will become city planners. Even though they may live in suburbs, they will be helped by their efforts to write about, hear, and see the people who live in the central cities. I hope these students will write better on many subjects, for every audience, because they had once to think accurately and write precisely about these pivotal but usually avoided issues. I hope those who major in urban studies or another social science will continue to look to fiction, essays, and journalism for good examples of writing *and* thinking, and I hope they will aspire to bring about safe, well-organized cities with vibrant, productive suburbs.

# Writing in Cognitive Science

## Exploring the Life of the Mind

MICHAEL J. SPIVEY

Cognitive Studies / Psychology

A Buddhist monk walks up to a hot dog vendor and says, "Make me one with everything."

SOURCE UNKNOWN

### Introduction to Cognitive Science

☞ There are several academic disciplines whose scholars spend some percentage of their time and energy studying how the mind/brain works. The five disciplines that contribute the most to cognitive science are psychology, neurobiology, computer science, philosophy, and linguistics. Although portions of these disciplines address many of the same questions about the mind/brain, their methods, their data, their theories, and even their very styles of communication could not be more diverse. Moreover, the interdisciplinary subfields between pairs of these disciplines that surround the core of cognitive science are numerous and complex (see figure 1). Grasping the scientific literatures from these different disciplines and subfields, and connecting the links between them, is a difficult skill to acquire. But if you think *reading* cognitive science is hard, you should try *writing* it.

In our course, Introduction to Cognitive Science (cross-listed as Cognitive Studies 101, Psychology 102, Computer Science 101, Philosophy 191, and Linguistics 170), approximately 15 percent of the 200-plus students enroll in a writing section where, instead of taking exams, they participate in weekly discussion sections with teaching assistants, write journal entries, address thought ques-

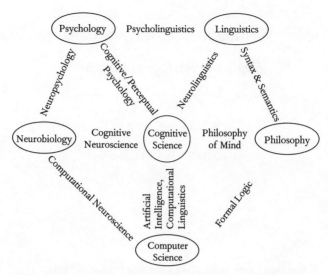

*Figure 1.* The five disciplines (circumscribed by ovals) that contribute most to cognitive science, and the interdisciplinary subfields that connect many of them together.

tions over e-mail, participate in formal debates, provide peer review for each other's drafts, and write and revise (and sometimes revise again) a major term paper. (Sadly, since we currently have only two teaching assistant slots available for the writing section, the remaining 170 students are doomed to engage in little more than the typical "memorize and regurgitate" test format that most large introductory courses involve.) The writing section of the course provides an opportunity for students to "get their hands dirty" with an in-depth exchange of ideas on lofty topics such as consciousness, free will, nature versus nurture, and artificial intelligence. It also gives them practice at dealing with some of the more practical topics in cognitive science, such as understanding how brain cells work, how psychological experiments are designed, how certain kinds of brain damage affect cognition, and how children learn language so quickly.

When initially designing this course, we envisioned two structures: (1) teach students about the five disciplines, or (2) teach students what the field of cognitive science knows about the major cognitive skills. Without the knowledge provided by (1), students might find (2) difficult to follow. Without (2), all that would be taught is independent methodologies and theoretical perspectives, without any integration of the disciplines. When we asked a colleague, Frank Keil, for advice on how to decide among these formats, he blithely said, "Do both!" and walked away.

In Introduction to Cognitive Science, the first five weeks are spent introducing the two hundred-plus students to the fundamental methodologies and perspectives of the five contributing disciplines. For example, philosophy and linguistics rely heavily on formal logical inference and introspection in order to reach conclusions about mental states and mental structure. In contrast, psychology and neurobiology tend to prefer meticulous experimentation. Computer science strongly emphasizes computational implementations of theories. All of these methodologies are important for guiding cognitive science in productive directions.

The remaining nine weeks of lecture are spent describing theories and research related to five major topics in cognitive science: language, learning and memory, vision, action, and artificial intelligence. Language is perhaps the best example of all five disciplines contributing almost equally to our growing understanding of how language is learned, comprehended, and produced. For example, there is a long tradition of philosophy and linguistics collaborating to develop formal theories of syntax (linguistic structure) and semantics (linguistic meaning). Also, in the 1960s, psychology and linguistics joined forces to create the now-thriving subfield of psycholinguistics, where researchers design experiments that test various theories about human language processing. Neuroscience has also participated in this effort. The subfield of neurolinguistics uses neuroimaging techniques and case studies of brain-damaged patients to show what brain regions are responsible for different aspects of language processing (e.g., Caramazza 1997; Damasio and Damasio 1992). Finally, the marriage of computer science and linguistics produced the subfield of computational linguistics, where computer simulations of natural language processing are developed.

### *Writing Curriculum*

One of the interesting weekly assignments that our Writing in the Majors students participate in is called "thought questions." The graduate student TA sends e-mail to the students discussing a particular aspect of the most recent lecture. Sometimes these assignments ask rather specific questions to test the students' memory and comprehension of the lecture (see example thought question 1). Other times, the thought questions are quite open-ended, encouraging students to take a side on some controversial issue and creatively formulate an argument supporting their position (see example thought question 2). The interesting thing about the medium of e-mail is that it is less formal than a paper that one prints out and hands to the instructor, yet, at the same time, it allows for more reflection and revision than a real-time conversation. As a medium of communication that is somewhere in between these formal and informal extremes, it engenders a balance of creativity and groundedness that often eludes the other media.

### EXAMPLE THOUGHT QUESTION I

The lecture on experimental design in psychology uses Lynn Cooper and Roger Shepard's (1984) mental rotation experiments as a model example. In these experiments, human participants examined rotated shapes (such as the letters in figure 2A), and attempted to identify them as shapes they'd previously seen upright (e.g., forward letters or backward letters). What Cooper and Shepard found was that the identification took longer when the stimulus was rotated farther away from upright. In fact, the reaction time increased linearly with increases in rotation (see figure 2B). It is as if the tilted image must be mentally rotated in real time before it can be fully recognized. This finding was among cognitive psychology's first and most elegant concrete measurements of the temporal dynamics of thought.

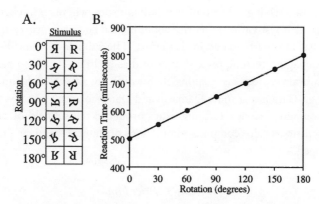

*Figure 2.* Example stimuli and schematic results from Cooper and Shepard (1984).

After the lecture, students were sent e-mail containing the following thought question:

Pick one specific experiment described in the Cooper and Shepard article. For this specific experiment, what is the:

    a. Hypothesis?
    b. Independent Variable(s)?
    c. Dependent Variable(s)?
    d. Procedure?
    e. Results?

Think of some possible flaws with the design/procedure of this specific experiment. Might these flaws threaten the conclusions that are drawn from the data?

Another one of the lectures, on computer science, introduces the concept of "search algorithms": computer programs that map out approximations of an exponentially large problem space, and search for the most advantageous series of steps to solve the problem. Each possible step in the problem space is called a "state." In figure 3, each diagram is a possible state that the chessboard can be in. There are typically about thirty possible moves at any one turn, and to compute the number of states in the problem space, the number of possible moves at one turn is multiplied by the number of possible moves at the next turn, and the next, and the next, etc. This results in an unimaginably large number of possible states for an entire game of chess—more than the number of particles in the universe. (In fact, in a search algorithm tree-structure such as that schematized in figure 3, even a ridiculously simple game like tic-tac-toe has many thousand possible

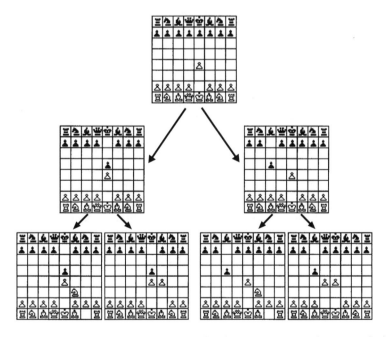

*Figure 3.* A tiny subset of the problem space for chess, as constructed by a search algorithm.

states in its problem space!) In chess, no contemporary computer could ever search the entire problem space in order to find a guaranteed pathway to checkmate. Therefore, computer scientists develop search algorithms that consider only small portions (in breadth and depth) of the problem space, in hopes to ignore only the hopeless pathways and explore only the fruitful ones.

After the lecture, students were sent e-mail containing the following thought question:

> In 1996, Garry Kasparov, one of the greatest-ever chess grand-masters, played Deep Blue, a computer that works by search algorithms similar to those described in lecture. Kasparov won convincingly, but said afterwards that he could feel "a new type of intelligence"—a thinking thing across the table from him.
>
> A couple of years later, they played again. Deep Blue had been modified somewhat. Kasparov lost badly. This time he angrily claimed that Deep Blue wasn't really playing chess, that it was nothing but a calculator with such raw, dumb power that a human being couldn't play against it.
>
> Is it only our prejudices that guide whether or not we view computers such as Deep Blue as thinking things? Or are there important cognitive qualities (perhaps creativity, consciousness, aesthetics, humor, morality) that a machine could never posses?

### TERM PAPER

The term paper is a chance for these students to tackle a big issue in the field of cognitive science, narrow it down to a tangible question, read and report on scientific approaches to that question, discuss the broader implications of these empirical results, and turn it all into an outstanding twenty-page paper. For many of these students, this is the longest paper they've ever written. Therefore, a fair amount of preparation is necessary. Early on in the course, they are encouraged to begin settling on a topic that interests them. The following is an example of the e-mail assignment instructing students to decide on a topic:

> The time has come for you to start thinking about your term paper, even though we have barely begun the course. An outline will be due soon, and a preliminary draft will be due early in the second half of the semester. Listed below are suggestions for the sorts of questions you might consider. You'll notice that they are deliberately quite open and vague. We'll narrow them down as the course progresses. Look through the syllabus, and perhaps glance ahead at

some of the readings, and see what sort of topic interests you most. Then phrase a question that reflects this broad interest, or pick one from below.

1. Is consciousness something science can study?

2. Can computers have minds?

3. Does our language determine the way we think, or does the way we think determine our language?

4. Can chaos theory and/or complexity theory inform our understanding of the mind?

5. Is language learned or innate?

6. How are memories stored in the mind/brain?

7. Is the mind/brain made up of separate modules or is it one vast network?

8. Are thoughts non-overlapping discrete symbols or overlapping fuzzy categories?

9. Does cognition constrain action, or does action constrain cognition?

10. Should we study the mind by starting with neurons and working our way "up" to cognition, or by studying cognition and working our way "down" to neurons?

Around the fifth week of the semester, students are expected to provide their TA with an outline of what the paper will look like. By the tenth week, a preliminary draft is due, on which they receive a considerable amount of comments and suggested revisions—from the TA as well as from their fellow students. A particularly bad habit that the writing section is designed to remove is the treating of one's own text as though it were sacred. Students are strongly encouraged to routinely erase and rewrite major sections of their papers. This kind of practice is crucial for good writing.

One student, in particular, wrote an excellent essay that addressed the topic, "Does our language determine the way we think, or does the way we think determine our language?" Benjamin Lee Whorf (1963) is often credited with first proposing that the semantic structure of one's native language molds one's mind into compartmentalizing the world into corresponding category structures. Thus, if two people speak very different native languages, they actually "think" and "view the world" differently. Elizabeth Tricomi's paper on this topic won her Cornell's 1998 John S. Knight Prize for Writing in the Majors.[1] The following excerpt demonstrates the clarity and precision with which she addressed this complex issue:

Facility with language requires a grasp of the somewhat extensive categorization of types of words and relations of words within language. So as children acquire language, they necessarily must, at least implicitly, come to understand the distinctions between word categories. Perhaps children's development of understanding categorization within language helps foster development of the cognitive skill of categorization in general.

Importantly, logical argumentation, and even compelling linguistic examples, is not enough to make a convincing case in cognitive science. Scientific experimental evidence is always the primary tool of persuasion in this field. Naturally, the appropriate source of experimental evidence in this case would come from research that compares children from two different languages, as described in this excerpt:

Gentner and Boroditsky (1997) discuss a 1993 study done by Imai and Gentner that examined infants' categorization of objects and substances. Linguistically, objects and substances are treated differently in the English language. Objects are described by count nouns, and can be counted directly (e.g., "two chairs") while substances are described by mass nouns, which can't be counted directly (e.g., one cannot say "two flours"). In English, count nouns require determiners, but mass nouns do not. For example, one would say, "This is *a* chair," but would say, "This is flour." There is no such distinction in the Japanese language. While infants show some prelinguistic distinction between objects and substances, there do seem to be very early effects of language on this categorization. Both American and Japanese two-year-olds could differentiate between substances and "complex" objects (discrete objects with complex shapes and functions). However, while American two-year-olds could differentiate between substances and simple objects (simple rigid entities), Japanese children responded at random when trying to do this task.

Overall, the Writing in the Majors section of this course is certainly more work than the standard version of the course (which has two prelims and a final exam). At the same time, it is also certainly more rewarding. Rather than simply memorizing the facts, these students get to *question* the facts. They get to amass studies from the scientific literature (source articles, not popular magazine articles or textbooks), develop an encompassing theoretical account of these findings, as well as point out gaps in the empirical data, or in the logical argumentation, and suggest novel experiments or data analyses that could improve our understanding. Most importantly, they develop writing skills early on in their undergraduate careers, which will allow them to excel in their higher-level courses.

## On Consciousness

In addition to cultivating writing skills and providing practical knowledge about how the mind/brain works and develops, this course tackles some very difficult philosophical issues about *what the mind is.* The topic of consciousness (biological as well as silicon-based) is by far the most popular topic that the writing students focus on for their term papers. For many of these students, this course is the first time they've sat down and really contemplated what it means for their personal and unique "sense of awareness" to be solely a product of the neural activity in their brains. The pattern of neural activation in your brain right now is not "under your control," it *is you.* And that pattern of activation is purely a result of the current and past input to your sensory systems combined with some genetically prespecified constraints on brain structure. Your consciousness is a deterministic product of two categories of external factors: environmental influences and genetic influences—neither of which are "under your control." There is no other scientifically viable category of factors that could contribute to your sense of self.

This is a difficult pill to swallow, and some students simply reject it. In our everyday lives, we tend to act and feel as though our minds are "our own," despite the fact that our brains are basically deterministic machines that are subject to the impartial physical laws of cause and effect. That is to say, a scientific study of the mind/brain leaves no room for nonphysical properties, such as the soul. There is, as of yet, no conclusive scientific evidence for such paranormal or supernatural phenomena. Therefore, although belief in a nonphysical self is perfectly legitimate and in fact encouraged in most cultures, it is not a matter of science—and that includes cognitive science.

This lack of control over the physical factors that determine the brain's "state" is consistent with what some students of the mind have called *the nonexistence of free will* (e.g., Hume 1739; Skinner 1971; Spinoza 1677). Even those people who are comfortable discounting the existence of a "soul" are often uncomfortable with letting go of their desire to bestow themselves with "free will." However, if there are no nonphysical causes of a person's behavior, and all physical causes can be traced to external forces (environmental and genetic influences), what is the force that is exerting "free will"? Think about this next time you're trying to decide what flavor of ice cream to choose.

The mind is not in an ivory tower. It is inseparable from the organism in which it is embodied, and, indeed, from the rest of the physical universe. Therefore, to the extent that the physical universe obeys the laws of cause and effect, so must the mind. There can be no physical "effect," such as deciding on chocolate ice cream, that does not have a physical "cause," such as the organism's recent depletion of sugar or a mild dependency on caffeine—each of which have their own previous causes. Thus, in some ways, the decision to choose chocolate ice cream over other desserts can be seen as "belonging" mostly to a convergence of local physical causes rather than solely to the organism itself. Indeed, even a so-called "willpower decision" to have no ice cream at all can still be seen as belonging to a culturally caused preference to avoid being overweight rather than belonging to the abstaining mind itself. Essentially, the scientific problem with attributing the responsibility for the mind's decisions to the mind's "free will" is that it posits an effect (a decision) that has no cause.[2]

### "Make Me One with Everything"

If you find it distressing to be told that you have no free will, and no soul, we believe there is a satisfying way to embrace this state of affairs. To begin, the solipsism that results from belief in a self that is independent from the rest of the universe can be quite frightening, if not crippling. By contrast, when one lets go of this feigned "ownership" of one's self, there is a profound sense of connectedness with the environment. (The joke at the beginning of this chapter was half serious!) Your mind and your sense of self are *part of* your central nervous system, which is *part of* your body, which is *part of* your environment, which is *part of* the universe. Take, for example, your state of mind when you hear your favorite song. Your eardrums vibrate at just the right series of frequencies to *cause* a brain-state consistent with happiness, which then *causes* muscles in your face to form a smile. But what *caused* your eardrums to vibrate? The air pressure waves comprising the song. In this chain of cause and effect, perhaps it is somewhat arbitrary to count one effect as "part of you" and the directly causally preceding event "not part of you." Especially when an environmental stimulus has as strong an effect on the mind as a favorite song, it seems perhaps reasonable to consider it as *part of* that mind. Consider what this must imply for when you hear the voice of your best friend.

Finally, this giving up of free will in no way makes you less "unique," or "just another cog in the clockwork of the universe." No other life form has ever had the exact combination of sensory input that your environment is providing your body with right now. That alone makes you undeniably unique in the entire history of the universe. Every state of mind you embody is a state of mind that no one else has ever embodied. Everything you do is something no one else has ever precisely done before. Given your unique combination of genetic and environmental influences, which have caused you to develop the way you have, your existence is irreplaceable and unrepeatable.

## *Artificial Intelligence*

Finally, there's one more major conclusion that this scientific/materialist view of the mind entails. If our compelling sense of self-awareness is an emergent property of complex deterministic neural interactions in our brains, then a silicon machine that approximated such complex deterministic neural interactions should be able to experience a similarly compelling sense of self-awareness. Of course, current computing technology is far from being able to approximate the billions of parallel processors (neurons) in the human brain. Moreover, the state-of-the-art in artificial neural network research is extremely primitive in comparison to most biological neural networks. Therefore, while it is possible, in principle, for a machine to have neural-like mental representations similar to our own, it is perhaps unlikely to happen in our lifetimes.[3]

However, system-internal processes may not be what are most important for detecting self-awareness. Instead, perhaps it is behavior that should be the measure of consciousness. If a machine's behavior is indistinguishable from a human's (regardless of the machine's internal programming format), shouldn't it be considered as self-aware and "capable of thought" as a human? After all, behavior is our only evidence that *each other* is conscious. This is precisely the logic that Alan Turing used in the 1950s when he described what became known as the Turing Test. In the Turing Test, a human judge communicates, via a computer terminal, with an artificial intelligence (AI) conversation program and with a human. If the human judge cannot tell which one is the human, then the AI has passed the Turing Test—and may as well be considered as intelligent, and capable of thought, as the human is. The following is an example transcript from an actual Turing Test. See if you can figure out whether the contestant is human or AI:

> *Contestant [13:41:17]:* Hi there, Judge 1!
>
> *Judge01 [13:41:45]:* Nice to know you. How are you?
>
> *Contestant [13:41:55]:* My name's Christine, by the way. I come from London.
>
> *Judge01 [13:42:39]:* My name is Paul, a Ph.D. student. How about you?

*Contestant [13:42:45]:* I'm over here on holiday.

*Judge01 [13:43:10]:* That is good. Have you been here before?

*Contestant [13:43:13]:* I haven't, no.

*Judge01 [13:43:45]:* Adelaide is a lovely city, isn't it?

*Contestant [13:43:55]:* I like the lake here . . . Flinders is a really nice campus.

*Judge01 [13:44:46]:* Do you know any persons in Flinders University?

*Contestant [13:44:53]:* Adelaide seems like a nice place to live.

*Judge01 [13:45:20]:* Are you a student?

*Contestant [13:45:29]:* Well, sometimes I am, but usually I'm not.

*Judge01 [13:45:53]:* Does it mean that you are a part-time student?

*Contestant [13:45:59]:* Don't mess me about!

*Judge01 [13:46:27]:* Sorry about that. Do you like Adelaide?

*Contestant [13:46:38]:* I'm going to go on a wine trip down the Barossa valley if I get a chance.

*Judge01 [13:47:12]:* That is great. Will you go yourself?

*Contestant [13:47:18]:* Give me a clue!

Obviously, by the end of this excerpt, it is clear that the contestant is a computer program. Mabel 1, programmed by David C. Hamill, provides a good example of the typical conversation between a human and current state-of-the-art AI: fine at preliminary small talk, but not so good at coherent discourse, conversational "give-and-take," or even grammar, in some cases. In a recent Turing Test Tournament, sponsored by the eccentric philanthropist Hugh Loebner, the best AI was rated by the judges as 11 percent Turing, or humanly intelligent. This may not seem a very impressive success rate, until one considers the success rate of the best human. The best human was rated only 61 percent humanly intelligent! Across all the human contestants, the average Turing rating (or human-like intelligence score) was 50 percent. Obviously, the Turing Test itself is a less than perfect measure of the capability of thought.[4]

Nonetheless, these advances in AI (traditional programs as well as neural networks), meager as they may seem, have developed over only a few decades. The remarkable acceleration with which computing technology, cognitive science, computational linguistics, and speech recognition are advancing suggests that some reasonably sophisticated and flexible spoken commands, and even genuine conversations, may be possible between humans and computers within the next ten years.

## *Writing in Cognitive Science*

With such broad implications for what it means to have a mind, ranging from "Am I conscious?" to "Can a machine be conscious?" this course is a real eye-opener for many of the students. More practically, Introduction to Cognitive Science is also an excellent way for students to get a taste of five different disciplines in just one course. Psychology, neuroscience, computer science, philosophy, and linguistics all have their own peculiar theoretical and methodological tools. When they join forces to study how the mind works, the result is an unparalleled interdisciplinary alliance that facilitates a cross-fostering of ideas guaranteed to continually stir the interest of students and experts alike.

This piqued interest is especially strong for the students who participate in the Writing-in-the-Majors section of this course. *Memorizing* the important facts from the readings and from lectures is not the goal for these students. It is merely a by-product of a larger goal: *thinking* about those important facts. The writing students get to try out their own ideas on these topics, engage in in-depth discussions and debates, produce regular writing samples, and craft and revise a sizable final paper that will make their parents proud of them. The writing section of this course is more than a learning experience; it is a growth experience.

# Freshman Rhetoric and Media Literacy

PAUL SAWYER

English

> [W]ho will deny that Oxford, by her ineffable charm, keeps
> ever calling us nearer to the true goal of all of us, to the ideal,
> to perfection—to beauty, in a word, which is only truth seen
> from another side?
>
> MATTHEW ARNOLD, *Essays in Criticism*, 1865

> Any new left in America must be, in large measure, a left with
> real intellectual skills, committed to deliberativeness, honesty,
> reflection as working tools. The university permits the political
> life to be an adjunct to the academic one, and action to be
> informed by reason.
>
> HAYDEN ET AL, *The Port Huron Statement*, 1962

℘ Freshmen writing courses used to be housed in English departments because of assumptions so widely accepted as to seem self-evident: that students need to write well, that the way to learn good writing is to read good writing, and that English departments are specially equipped to teach good writing—or more exactly, to define the "good" in good writing. With the advent of "writing across the curriculum," freshman writing no longer equals "freshman English," and the assumptions upon which freshman English was based no longer seem self-evident—in particular the idea of a special departmental expertise in the "goodness" of good writing. In giving the various disciplines responsibility for defining and teaching the kind of writing valued by those disciplines, the new model brackets the idea of "goodness" in general in favor of a plurality of discourses. "Good" writing ceases to consist primarily in an isolable but undefinable verbal quality that can theoretically be applied to any subject ("style," as it is still usually called); it becomes instead one of many possible modes inseparable from the particular interests and modes of inquiry that define the discipline in which it is taught.

The question this leaves unanswered is an old one, which might be put this way: Might not undergraduates need some skill or knowledge—a form of understanding, interpreting, or "reading" the world—that is not specific to a discipline and that might therefore fall through the cracks, not because it is a miscellaneous or unserious form of knowledge but, on the contrary, because it is so broad and urgent that it transcends disciplinary boundaries? Embracing, in a sense, the whole of the educational enterprise, such knowledge would involve not simply the knowable world "outside" but the observer as well—the student herself and her relations to all the other forms of knowledge. In putting the question this way, I am of course calling to life an old debate, one that more or less belongs to history—that is, in the terms in which it used to be discussed, if not in the felt needs that I believe survive. I mean the debate between specialization and liberal education. In older models of education, it was the humanities that provided the kind of overarching knowledge I have just invoked—that is, the broad questions of citizenship, value, and self-understanding—and at the heart of a humanities curriculum stood the English department, dedicated to a particular idea of the relationship between literature and moral teaching, and at the heart of English teaching (in the freshman year at any rate) stood the belletristic notion of style as central to the characteristic mode of expression not of a specialist but of a liberally educated person. Writing across the disciplines is one symptom of a more general shift from that older model of university education toward a newer one—towards the university as a place not of liberal but of professional education. Even though I am a professor of English, I hold no nostalgia for that older, humanities-centered model of liberal education, though, in fact, it survives with surprising passion and persistence among undergraduates. (I offer as evidence the single most popular text I have ever taught in a freshman seminar—the film *Dead Poets Society*.) What I want to do in this chapter is precisely not to return to the older humanistic model of teaching English but rather to raise in a different form the question of a freshman writing course as a place for exploring the nature of rhetorical engagement in general. To do so, I want to look briefly backwards for a moment to the older model of freshman English.

In the days before writing across the curriculum, when English instructors struggled to put together essays that were coherent and meaningful for the one course—virtually the only course in the curriculum—in which content existed not for its own sake but to serve the greater purpose of teaching some skill, it made good sense (it still does) to find essays with a broad, non-specialist appeal, capable of interesting all the students in the class while offending none, yet written with enough skill to serve as models of both style and rhetoric. Why, then (other than the fact that the authors were nearly all white men), do those old anthologies now feel so quaint, so oddly unlike anything else a student encountered, or a teacher taught, in the university curriculum? In even a good one of that older type—I have in mind the first edition of the *Norton Anthology*—canonical writers (Plato, Macchiavelli, Swift, Thoreau) found themselves grouped together with newer ones (Bronowski, Orwell, E. B. White) under general topics like "Democracy" or "Education" and surrounded by editorial prompts that rarely referred to historical context. By removing texts from their contexts, this kind of anthologizing encouraged students and teachers to see White on democracy or Macchiavelli on power as thinkers engaged in a timeless, genial debate on the "perennial" issues. What appeared as an advantage in the anthologies (breadth of appeal, universality) turns into their characteristic vice (blandness). Wayne Booth's "Is There Anything that a Man Must Know?", dropped from subsequent editions, is an extreme and therefore perhaps unfair example of this universalizing blandness (the answer to his question is, of course, the good, the true, and the beautiful); but even a work not inherently bland becomes so when anthologized. One remembers the ubiquity in freshman anthologies of Swift's "Modest Proposal"—the most violent public attack on colonialism in Western literature up to its time, evoking a social system so brutal that most college students can barely credit its existence—which was chosen and read over and over again as an example of irony. The freshman anthology, as Marshall MacLuhan would have put it, is a cool medium, no matter what the subject matter of the selections might be. We might even say that a literary work changes its genre as it enters an anthology, that the *Norton* "Modest Proposal" (that is, the freshman "Modest Proposal") bears even less resemblance to Swift's than Pierre Menard's Don Quixote does to that of Cervantes in Borges's famous story. I have already suggested the practical reasons for choosing debates with a low emotional temperature, but I would also suggest that the notoriously platitudinous "content" of freshman English reinforces an ideology of its own—a caricature of academic discourse that sees thinking as a kind of managed consensus and that separates the calm, the perennial, and the reasonable on the one hand from the urgent, the topical, and the emotional on the other. This attitude receives reinforcement from the most widely taught advice to writers in the entire canon of freshman rhetoric—Orwell's "Politics and the English Language"—which pits an approved, plain style (diction that is short, concrete, Anglo-Saxon, and clear as day) against the corruptions of political propaganda (diction that is polysyllabic, obscure, deceptive, and Latinate). Translated into the calm of the fresh-

man writing seminar, Orwell's impassioned plea for transparent writing reinforces the cultural prejudice that "ideology" (here "politics in our time," which
Orwell calls "a mass of lies and schizophrenia") is by its nature an impediment
to the free mind and the able writer. Anyone who, in the interest of accurate
reading, has tried to draw students' attention to what is distinctive, original, and
controversial in a prose argument, only to have the students translate "controversial" into "extreme" or "implausible," will know how deeply rooted and
even habitual is their conviction that—in the classroom at least—"truth" is
what is broadly acceptable. In many older courses, this conviction reigned in the
paper topics as well as readings. (Trying the opposite tack—introducing topics
that instantly divide a class into belligerent defenders, like abortion laws or gun
control, and then inviting the students to argue on paper in five angry paragraphs—only confirms by negative example the view that the classroom is the
place for bland thought.)

The second problem with the standard rhetoric course followed the first as
the night the day: blandness reigned in the writing assignments as well as the
reading. By presenting the essays as models of style and thought, one tended to
narrow the range of student engagement to a form of analytic appreciation—
usually clarifying the manifest content of the essays or tracing their structure. It
might be argued that these seemingly basic skills of reading—accurately com-
prehending a complex argument, "honing" a style that is clear and concise, developing a coherent argument over five or more paragraphs—are precisely the
verbal abilities incoming freshmen most need and most lack, and that is true.
And yet by removing context, audience, and occasion, one removes some of the
essential elements of rhetorical analysis. In short, the fundamental limitation of
the old freshman rhetoric course is that it was insufficiently rhetorical.

It is obvious that the "classic" freshman anthology no longer exists in the
pure form I have been describing. Very quickly, textbook publishers responded
to the imperatives of diversity, filling the newer editions with essays by women
and minorities and canceling out the most damaging tendency of the older selections—to present the realm of perennial, civilized discourse as inhabited by
males of European descent. As a result, the more recent *Norton* editions are, on
all counts, livelier and more pertinent than the old, and one can expect the same
of any course based on them. I wish now to describe the kind of course that
comes close to the spirit of the newer anthologies but departs from them in other
ways—chiefly in a concern with a textual variety far broader than the kind of
argumentative essay that still constitutes the backbone of an anthology-based
writing course in English. The course I am describing will ideally give students
an understanding of rhetoric so full and active that it will fulfill what the standard courses always purported to do, at least abstractly, which is to teach them

to comprehend not just "argument" or "writing" or "language" as such but rather to understand them as a variety of occasions, communities, genres, and interactions, and to comprehend this variety critically, with an awareness of how such occasions might concretely impinge on actual readers. (Terry Eagleton and others have similarly argued that the act of literary canonization as we know it abstracts the historical embeddedness and communal context of specific literary works and so gives us "masterpieces" at the expense of rhetorical awareness.) This awareness might best be called—after the title of a book by E. D. Hirsch— cultural literacy. Hirsch means by "literacy" something close to "what any educated person ought to have read," which for him is a conservative notion of "culture" as a canonical tradition. But in most uses, "culture" has a far wider range than what people used to call "high culture," a range that includes the sum total of whatever humans have attempted to think or express, whether in buildings or rituals or epic poems or laws or folk dances, in graffiti or learned treatises, or in the terse phrasing of the OED, "the intellectual side of civilization." The freshman writing course I describe here would be a course in "cultural literacy" in this expanded sense—not, indeed, a course about all of culture but about the legible products, the texts, likely to come their way as part of contemporary culture. This "literacy," I would argue, is not only useful as a skill and plausible as an aim but the most urgent skill freshmen today can learn—for the reason that in a media age, the ability to critically read newspapers and ads and video footage is a survival skill—a form of literacy almost as necessary to social survival as the ability to construe words and letters. This means I assume that universities can teach media literacy not simply as another specialization but (as I put it at the beginning of the essay) as a form of knowledge so broad and urgent that it transcends disciplinary boundaries and embraces the whole of the educational enterprise. In short, it belongs to the very idea of the university that I said above has been superseded, the idea of the university not as a place for specialized education but for liberal education. What do I now mean by liberal education?

The implied content of the old freshman anthology might be described as a very inadequate approximation to the idea of liberal education—the "space" within the practical pursuits of a college education where one can think, not just about those practical pursuits (chemical engineering or pre-law or clinical psychology) but about thinking in general, an activity that (as the old argument went) produced not a specialist but a whole or complete man. Matthew Arnold, the most influential theorist of liberal education in English, called this wholeness "culture," a form of internalized knowledge that, for Arnold, produced an internalized standard of judgment very similar to a moral instinct and that could be attained not in the heat of partisan debate but in a space of calm, where rational consideration was possible. This "space," which is also a frame of mind, Arnold called "disinterestedness." If you learn to think and judge as a cultured, or (a close synonym) a civilized person, this view holds; you will have a reference point from which to judge what is vulgar or banal or specious or transient or merely trendy or otherwise corruptive and vicious. This educational philosophy rests on an assumption that in order to transcend politics, it is possible and necessary to remove oneself from politics, and that the university can provide such a neutral space. This assumption is untenable as I have stated it, and so is the cultural (and class) politics underpinning it. In fact, it is precisely such an implied antagonism between "the best that has been thought and felt" (high culture) and the merely vulgar (low or popular culture) that the newer conception of culture as a totality of human expression undermines. But it would be hard indeed to think about the aims of education without some flexible version of disinterestedness—the possibility, as one might redefine it, of a relative autonomy from dominant commercial and ideological pressures, an autonomy that, by necessity, inhabits an institution very much bound up in the political and commercial pressures of society as a whole but which, at the very least, provides a chance to hear and to compare differing views and modes of speech. As the authors of the *Port Huron Statement* put it nearly forty years ago, outlining the possible emergence of a "new left": "In an unbelievably complicated world, [the university] is the central institution for organizing, evaluating, and transmitting knowledge . . . [it] is the only mainstream institution that is open to participation by individuals of nearly any viewpoint" (Hayden et al). In a media age, the university can act not as a place to pontificate against the evils of the popular but as a place of autonomy relative to the overwhelming ubiquity of "the media."

What is meant by "the media"? Used as a nebulous singular, the phrase connotes a whole set of experiences, assumptions, and mythologies that could form an interesting starting-point for a course; we might begin by noticing that it connotes a problem—a ubiquitous threat or assault (as in the phrase "we are bombarded by images from the media"), a scapegoat (as in the phrase "the media blew it all out of proportion"), a pervasive buzz of misinformation and error (as in "media hype"), an impermeable wall of representations, a mechanism for replacing realities with phantoms and sound bytes (as in "media events"), a general fluoridation of the knowledge supply upon which we nevertheless depend as the water we drink, and much else. Usually "the media" is short for "the news media," the contemporary economy of public information of unspecific (because corporate) source in which the medium of print does not dominate; but secondarily it seems to take in forms of corporate entertainment as well, especially as filmed or televised. As "the media" tends to denote the press, the response is hostile, but as it tends to denote popular culture, the response is friendlier. The purpose of a rhetoric course that centered on problems of reading in a media age would speak to both the paranoia and its attendant fascination by clarifying and making distinctions. I am not, however, describing either a "media studies" or a "popular studies" course, first of all, because its syllabus is open to texts that belong neither to the mass media nor to popular culture, and second, because it places less emphasis on describing forms and institutions (rap music, the broadcasting industry) than on the ways these forms mean and the ways they can be read. Described this way—that is, in terms of aim more than a subject or approach—the course fits into no established discipline; it does, however, come close to the methodology and purview of cultural studies.

Cultural studies, as the phrase makes clear, is a cross-disciplinary field, drawing together history, sociology, and anthropology as well as the humanities, but which in this country has nested mainly in literature departments, where it has transformed the traditional definition of literary studies and given its practitioners an expanded mandate as specialists in all forms of interpretation, not simply those developed in order to read the canonical texts of a literary tradition.[1] The chief pedagogical use of cultural studies in this country has been to contest the fiction of a universal subject—implicitly white, Western, and male—and to explore the multiple ways culture constructs the identities of the members of a society as female or Latino or straight or middle-class or European, always in relation to that implied dominant identity. In 2001–2002 at Cornell, the English department offered a number of first-year writing courses on these themes; a few titles are Gender and Cross-Dressing in the Renaissance; Sex, Cyborgs, and Miscegenation in Star Trek; The Politics of Representation: When the Postcolonial Writes Back; Blood, Blondes, and the Birds: The Films of Alfred Hitchcock; Images of American Indians: Myths and Realities; Race and Gender in American Sports; Boys Will Be Boys: Island Adventure Narratives; and Secretaries, Scandal, and the "American Way."

As even this brief list makes clear, cultural studies is not primarily a technique of reading the news media, yet its approaches and assumptions must profoundly influence any attempt at defining media literacy. This is because at its broadest, cultural studies is ultimately about all of us, as readers and as "subjects" in a world becoming increasingly globalized in the cultural sense—a world in which the older definitions of political identity (nations) and the older international order (domination by the West) are dissolving. "We" are no longer the world; the "world" is multicultural. This cultural globalization coincides with the main social mission of American universities since the 1960s, which has been to act as institutional advocates of cultural diversity. Teaching students to understand the complexity of social identity by understanding the rhetoric of identity formation—in ads, in "the media," in essays, in literary masterpieces—is crucially important work.

Conceived in this way, however, cultural studies contains a typically American omission. It is not always obvious how cultural studies reads or decodes or accounts for the workings of those broad structures of power without which no analysis of particular forms of "difference" can be complete. Even finding the word for these structures is hard. "Class" now seems inadequate on a number of counts; when used by literary theorists, it often gets associated with the various forms of discrimination (as in the series racism, sexism, classism, ageism, and so forth), as if poverty could be cured by political correctness. But the early works in cultural studies, particularly in the "culturalist" wing, were very clear that the idea of culture implies the idea of power among groups and cultures, of which one group with its culture is dominant in relation to the others. Now this technical description of a system that functions, not by dictating thought but by controlling the range of thought—the system called by cultural theorists "hegemony"—coincides exactly with a common criticism of the contemporary mass media. This brings me to a second main source for thinking about the rhetoric of contemporary cultural forms—the recent, influential group of progressive media critics, whose names include Noam Chomsky, George S. Herman, Michael Parenti, Robert McChesney, Jonathan Schell, and others. These writers point to the increasing concentration of power in the giant media conglomerates—a virtual monopoly of public access to events that sharply limits "the news" in ways that ultimately serve the interests of corporate elites and that have severely inhibited the functioning of a democratic polity. Taken together, critics like Chomsky and Herman and the increasingly broad body of work done in cultural studies provide both a general theory of cultural power and a set of reading techniques with which one can begin to think about a course in media literacy.

I will return at the end of this chapter to the question of a general theory; what I want to notice now is the problems and advantages for a course that attempts to engage the entire spectrum of "the media," from popular culture to advertisements to the press, as a field for interpretation. Advertisements are a good place to start because students already understand these texts as covert messages to be decoded, and students are already themselves competent decoders. With ads, as with all the other genres, the purpose of reading is to comprehend the surface and the depths at once—even in the most apparently straightforward genres (as in, figures of speech and apparent digressions of an essay), noticing how what is implicit colors and enriches or troubles what is explicit. One problem in defining interpretive techniques is that reading popular culture and reading the news media can be very different skills. The questions typically asked by media critics and by teachers of cultural studies would overlap in some cases (What language does this cigarette ad use to appeal to urban blacks?) but not in others. One group might ask, "How does this ad construct gender?" while the other might ask, "What news stories were displaced by the Monica Lewinsky scandal?" One might ask, "How does this film construct heterosexuality as normative?" while the other might ask, "Why does this article on an airline strike begin by describing the inconvenience of passengers?" The differences rest partly in different techniques of reading: in one case, "decoding" the covert implications embedded in an explicit statement or image; in the other, recognizing the ways of framing an event or debate (foregrounding, use of sources, function of layout, conventions of "objectivity"), which include, most importantly, the rules of exclusion. This heterogeneity suggests that no single course can do justice to all the forms of "media" texts and that in describing it, I am describing a series of courses rather than a single syllabus.

The first aim of such courses, then, is to interpret a variety of messages; the second is to understand messages as interpretations. That aim naturally implies some notion of truth or of truthfulness; and here the two methodologies on which I am drawing become not simply different but inconsistent. If the media critics, focusing on what has been distorted, buried, or excluded, speak implicitly of a cognizable reality, cultural studies experts, focusing on notions of identity, or the formation of subjects, tend to bracket "the real" in order to describe social constructedness. The reason I use the word "interpret" (as well as "construct") suggests one governing assumption of my courses, which is that truth is neither unitary nor purely factitious but a field of reference which, if never totally definable, makes it possible to talk about the relationship between interpretations and to make explicit the ways we judge and value those interpretations. In short, whatever "reality" is, texts are plural—a plurality that can best be studied as a set of relationships and best presented in a class as juxtaposition. Students will not all agree with or even comprehend the more abstract and radical accounts of hegemony and ideology provided by the pioneering theorists of cultural studies; that, I want to stress, is not the aim of the course. Rather, it will be enough if they begin to grasp the limits—to question the "givenness"—of the world as presented in the media, and to do so in concrete instances.

My first example of juxtaposition is not my own, but it clearly demonstrates the advantage of a contextualized freshman writing course over the older practice of presenting ahistorical snippets, prose arguments floating in a space of perennial thought. James Slevin, in his essay "Reading and Writing in the Classroom and the Profession," reports the results of looking up the actual issue of the *New Yorker* in which E. B. White's famous one-paragraph definition of "democracy" first appeared. Slevin finds that the essay (written in 1944, in the context of the global war fought for the very principles White was upholding) was surrounded by ads for luxury items, including one for Cadillac on the facing page, which uses a picture of a tank manufactured by Cadillac to advertise the car—a picture that links the war effort with privilege and ostentation as clearly as White links the war effort with the homely image of hot dogs and mustard. What are we to make of such a contradiction? Does it invalidate the ideas repeated in their pithiness and taken to heart by generations of rhetoric teachers and their students? Do we lose or gain by plucking the paragraph from the ads for fur coats or the "Talk of the Town" anecdote about a "lady" and her maid? Does the original issue form part of an overdetermined textual unity with the White piece—or are they a literary-historical accident, like the original appearance of "Ode on a Grecian Urn" in an architectural magazine? Whatever answers we come up with, and whatever further questions we ask, the point here is that, instead of centering our discussion on ideas in the abstract, we would be centering it on textual juxtapositions (in addition to the 1944 *New Yorker* and Slevin's essay, Fredric Bogel's stimulating reading of White to which Slevin responds; a current *New Yorker*; a magazine like *Details*, and so forth). Such a discussion would also, and perhaps ultimately, become a meditation on democracy.

I now describe one version of a course on media literacy, which I have been teaching under the title Fictions of the Real. The readings consist of print and televised accounts of events read next to book-length journalistic treatments of the same events. As I have described above, the course combines some of the concerns of media critics (what gets left out of the corporate press?) with some of the concerns of cultural studies experts (how does our culture construct us as gendered and racialized subjects?), juxtaposing texts strategically in order to come up with an adequate idea of "representation," one that—and this I have not discussed above—depends on understanding the relationship between the observer and the phenomenon observed. In my first version of the course, I chose the print and photographic materials from three crisis periods in American history: the Great Depression, the war in Vietnam, and contemporary urban poverty; texts included Agee's *Let Us Now Praise Famous Men*, Michael Herr's *Dispatches*, Jonathan Kozol's *Amazing Grace*, and Anna Deveare Smith's *Fires in the Mirror*, a one-person staging of the Crown Heights incident. I found that the topics were too disparate; an alternative version of the course would focus perhaps on a single historical period, creating a fuller discursive context for each reading. For example, a course on Representing the Depression, which included full works by Agee's predecessors Dorothea Lange and Margaret Bourke-White, writings by New Dealers, the Communist left, and others Agee found it necessary to attack, as well as issues of *Fortune* (for which Agee was writing), would illuminate Agee's perversities and mystifications as well as his unique achievement—all through a comparative rhetorical analysis that would have as its chief aim the problems of representing poverty in an affluent democratic state. In addition to illuminating issues I have mentioned above—the construction of an observer; the nature of an interpretation—these courses would also share a concern with uncovering or revealing, almost as a form of scandal, what is normally marginalized, avoided, or concealed.

In the remainder of this chapter, I want to draw on two of the texts I have taught, in order to give examples, first, of the kind of close reading possible to a cultural/media studies approach, and, second, of a writing assignment. The example of close reading comes from *Dispatches*:

> Because who but another correspondent could talk the kind of mythical war that you wanted to hear described? (Just hearing the way Flynn pronounced the word "Vietnam," the tenderness and respect that he put in it, taught you more about the beauty and horror of the place than anything the apologists or explainers could ever teach you.) Who could you discuss politics with, except a colleague? (We all had roughly the same position on the war: we were in it, and that was a position.) Where else could you go for a real sense of the war's past? There were all kinds of people who knew the background, the facts, the most minute details, but only a correspondent could give you the exact mood that attended each of the major epochs: the animal terror of the Ia Drang or the ghastly breakdown of the first major Marine operation, code-named Starlight, where the Marines were dying so incredibly fast, so far beyond the Command's allowance, that one of them got zipped into a body bag and tossed to the top of a pile of KIA's while he was still alive. . . . And if you saw some piece of helmet graffiti that seemed to say everything, you weren't going to pass it along to some colonel or tell it to a Psyops official. "Born to Kill" placed in all innocence next to the peace symbol, or "A sucking chest wound is Nature's way of telling you that you've been in a firefight" was just too good to share with anyone but a real collector, and, with very few exceptions, these were all correspondents. (225–26)

An excerpt like this demonstrates—if a demonstration were needed—that nonfiction prose can bear the same density of attention and response as fiction. Since so much of Herr's project consists of attacking the euphemized language and deliberate falsifications of "mission headquarters"—the "official" view that was promptly telegraphed to newspapers across the country—I begin discussing the book by asking what Herr's "truth" is. His Orwellian attack on jargon produces by contrast a style of absolute concreteness that registers with apparent transparency the experience of war in its overwhelming sensory immediacy. His descriptions are tactile, sensory, minute, rapid, and hallucinatory in their clarity, and at the heart of them is death—dreading it, living with it, staring at it, staring away from it, inhaling it—the erotically charged and all-but-unspeakable penumbra surrounding the experience that cannot actually be spoken or experienced. A rhetorical analysis of the ubiquitous comma-splicing and the episodic discontinuity helps identify the text's singular effect. But Herr's relationship to death and the men that inflict it and undergo it is problematic, since as a correspondent he is with the grunts but not of them; he tells their story but cannot quite live it. This and related ambiguities emerge in the context of a study question that asks, "What is the function of 'you' in passages like the text?" The word means—alternately and altogether—"I," "we," "one," "they," and the audience addressed; but in the passage above, it begins to take on a specialized context—the group of "alternative" correspondents with whom Herr identifies and whom he glorifies synecdochically in the figure of the astonishingly handsome son—Sean Flynn, ex-actor, war photographer (and later casualty), son of Erroll. Flynn, the ultimate connoisseur, merely by uttering a word, tells us more than all the "apologists and explainers" can about "the beauty and horror of the place"—two phrases that strikingly compromise Herr's apparently unproblematic notion of telling the truth, since "truth" has now become something unutterable, something that transcends political explanation, and "place" has become something like a projection of the connoisseur's sensibility, taking the place, literally, of Vietnam as a political region inhabited by people with a history and an economy separate from the American presence. The text therefore generates a tension between the "mythic war you wanted to hear described" and the unproblematic truth that "you" are also charged with telling, and once again, between the "mythic war"—which Herr half-reluctantly, half-defiantly describes as "merely wonderful," "not just terrible," and so forth—and political explanations, now relegated to the same position of inferior knowledge as that expressed in John Leonard's blurb ("it transcends politics"). This passage is pivotal in the book's move towards "myth," which, as we learn soon after, owes as much to the prose, imagery, and even racial sensibility of Conrad as it does to the immediately given sense-data of the Vietnamese conflict. "Vietnam" becomes in Herr a construction; what started out as a particularly compelling version of "truth" shifts to yet another representation, and an eminently literary one at that, arising partly from a rhetorical occasion (the need to tell the grunt's story in an unpopular conflict) that produces a political position after all—and an implied racial and gender politics. It is crucial for my class to recognize, however, that by using words like "construct" or "version" or "politics" or "representation" we are not thereby denying the reality of the Vietnam War (as in the popular caricature of deconstruction) but of recognizing how even a very compelling version of reality can contain its own "position" and its own blockages—even as it is possible to recognize in Herr's book a genuine, though complicated, moral achievement.

A common cliché ("war zone") links Vietnam and the South Bronx. Like Herr, Jonathan Kozol describes a subject that has been rendered unimaginable and all but unspeakable—not, however, because of official suppression but because of a collective unwillingness to know on the part of the very group for which Kozol writes the book. That resistance, which manifests itself contradictorily in ignorance and in the belief that we've "heard it all before" (to quote Christopher Lehmann-Haupt on an earlier book by Kozol), Kozol breaks down by a chilling quietness, even a modesty of demeanor, and a willingness to let his subjects speak for themselves. He manages simultaneously to familiarize and to defamiliarize—to defamiliarize the disasters that in fact face the very poor (bizarre fatal accidents to children, unprecedented rates of asthma and other illnesses, homicide rates) and to familiarize the victims of those disasters by letting them speak for themselves in casual dialogue. The children he meets, as he notes, do not speak the arcane jive of young thugs on television; nor do the poor in general match the twin stereotypes familiar from the media—criminal and victim; they suffer terribly, but in hope and in resistance, which is the principal meaning of the book's surprising title. Through the quietest of means, Kozol brings about the most savage of indictments.

In my paper assignment on the book, I asked students to explore Kozol's broadest implications through a discussion of rhetoric, specifically of Kozol's persona as journalist/inquirer. The following excerpt, from an essay that won a freshman writing prize in 1998, focuses on Kozol's ability to build an argument dialogically—by intertwining his observations with the words of his subjects:

> Jonathan Kozol . . . lets the reader know that he is angry, angry
> that we, the citizens of America, are ignoring the urban poor not
> because of our apathy towards their economic hardship, but because
> of our apathy towards their race. But he is prudent in these attacks
> against the American citizenry—instead of attacking the middle
> class directly, he masks his personal convictions in the commentar-
> ies of the poverty-stricken characters he interviews. We, the
> oblivious readers, are scarcely aware that Kozol is attacking us until
> it is too late; until we, along with Kozol, care about saving the poor
> from their misery. We are no longer indifferent. This indirect tactic

forces the reader to assess Kozol's writing on a more minute level. The reader is not allowed to accept the author's writing at face value. Even though Kozol often refrains from using personal commentary, it is present, hidden behind the voices of the poor. One must look not only at the content of the characters' commentaries, but also at the specific questions Kozol poses to provoke such (often heart-wrenching) accounts. The few times Kozol does comment directly, it is thus profoundly disturbing.

Other topics on this text asked students to do archival work, comparing and evaluating Kozol with the sources in the press on which he draws.

Paper topics of this sort, which link rhetorical readings to political meanings, do not belong to the expertise of any single discipline, a fact that underscores the deepest implications of writing across the curriculum. This approach, in other words, simply assumes not just that various disciplines can teach college writing but also that various disciplines (the social sciences, but also the natural sciences in the very important subject of interpreting science reporting) can teach writing in the context of a close rhetorical analysis. There no longer remains anything specifically "English" about freshman composition. But a political content does remain in the specific courses I have described, and this is the subject on which I wish to close.

The functioning of media conglomerates as Chomsky and Herman and others describe it correlates closely with one of the key analytical concepts of European cultural studies. For Chomsky and Herman, the corporate news media in America today manages to "manufacture consent" by selecting out ideologically disturbing elements according to a set of "filters"—criteria that limit and define what news is "fit to print." The aim is not, strictly speaking, to censor ideas so much as to limit and manage people's access to them. The corresponding concept in cultural studies is Gramsci's theory of cultural hegemony. For Gramsci, modern societies are hegemonic structures, which means that they are led (to a greater or lesser according to specific conditions) by a loosely defined elite rather than by a tiny, well-marked set of autocratic rulers, using the methods of persuasion rather than coercion—or more specifically, by using such institutions as the church, the school, the family, and the law. In the words of some British culturalists, "A hegemonic cultural order tries to frame all competing definitions of the world within its range. It provides the horizon of thought and action within which conflicts are fought through. . . . A hegemonic order prescribes, not the specific content of ideas, but the limits within which ideas and conflicts move and are resolved" (Clarke et al 1981, 59–60). This idea has an obvious pertinence to several of my texts—to the old *New Yorker*, which could bring even an impassioned defense of democracy under the sponsorship of Cadillac, and to Kozol's indictment of the marginalization of poverty in the mainstream press.

Would it be feasible to introduce a political concept this abstract and all-encompassing into a course that focuses on specific texts and specific writing skills? Would it even be fair, given that most Cornell students, if they achieve their objectives, will find the notion of a hegemonic social order a comfort rather than a threat? These questions return me to my original formulation of purpose, which was not to teach political ideas but to teach a skill—cultural literacy. More important than introducing freshmen to Gramsci (although this is perfectly legitimate) is to open up the kind of awareness in terms of which Gramsci makes sense. By using readings to question the conventional limitations of politics-as-usual as constructed by the mass media—texts that break through to the undisclosed, the marginalized, the neglected—I hope to bring some of my students—as a kind of by-product more important, ultimately, than the work on which they will be graded—to an awareness of the terms of their privilege. The nature of privilege, and not sex scandals or crimes or conspiracies, is the deepest repression in our society. For students to begin to see through this repression, and to form choices on the basis of a knowledge that is moral as well as political, is a survival skill of a particularly urgent kind, and one that only the relative autonomy of a university can still provide.

# Toward a Community of Inquiry

## *Teaching Cornell AP Students*

DANIEL R. SCHWARZ

English

## *Prologue*

℘ I have been teaching a course entitled English 270, The Reading of Fiction, for most of the past thirty-one years. It is one of three 200-level courses offered by the English department; the others are English 271, The Reading of Poetry, and English 272, An Introduction to Drama. Currently the 270 classes are reserved in the first term for those who have had a 4 or 5 on the Princeton AP test or who have scored 700 or better on the English Composition or English Achievement tests; in the second term, the 270 classes are open to those who have taken a first-year writing seminar, but the students understand from fellow students and advisors that these classes are more demanding and in the second term the principle of self-selectivity works well. Often the second term 270 classes include a few students who begin their freshman year in January.

The students in the 270 classes rarely need remedial writing help. Most come from the College of Arts and Sciences and many are thinking about majoring in literature or related fields. Even in the second term, most have had AP English in high school, and while a few in the second term have received a 3 or did not take the test, most have received at least a 4.

Under the current ethos, each 270 section has different reading materials. Originally the course had a common reading list, and that common list encouraged colleagues to discuss pedagogical issues including how to integrate the teaching of reading and writing. I would prefer to return to this, or at least have half of the reading be the same. Not only does the teaching staff learn from one another when they teach common syllabi, but, according to recent data, so do students taking common courses learn from discussing the material.

When I was part of the original group in 1968 developing English 270 with common syllabi, we used earlier editions of Robert Gorham Davis's *Ten Modern Masters* and Irving Howe's *Classics of Modern Fiction*, and while I have tried other collections, I still prefer these in their later, more inclusive editions. My section of English 270 reads sophisticated modern fiction: Conrad, Lawrence, Joyce, Woolf, Faulkner, Chekhov, Dostoevsky, Kafka, Mann. We characteristically begin with short stories by such figures as Hemingway, Joyce, and Chekhov, but begin to integrate short novels like Conrad's *The Secret Sharer*, Joyce's *The Dead*, Dostoevsky's *Notes from Underground*, and Kafka's *Metamorphosis*, and toward the end of the semester we read one full-length novel, recently Woolf's *To the Lighthouse*; over the years the full-length novel has been Dostoevsky's *Crime and Punishment*, Lawrence's *Sons and Lovers*, or Conrad's *Lord Jim*. I also include some more relatively recent stories by writers such as Welty and Malamud. I have the students buy Abrams's *Glossary of Literary Terms*, Strunk and White's *The Elements of Style*, and the *Harbrace College Handbook*. In the first two-thirds of the course I assign from Abrams five crucial terms per week.

## Teaching Goals

The challenge is to get students to think in sophisticated terms while they write on subjects generated by the reading assignments. Let me say at the outset that I believe in directed discussions focused on the material we read and the papers we write. I think of myself as an orchestra conductor trying to get the most out of each player and working with each individual to bring out his or her talent. We know that if a student finds a mentor or two in his or her college career, that student will usually have a better experience, and we faculty teaching first-year seminars need be accessible to fill that role. First, we must teach students to write lucidly and logically and to teach them to make an argument that uses the examples of close reading to support concepts *and* uses historical and cultural contexts. (My mantra is: "Always the text; always historicize"). Second, we must encourage students to think independently and challenge accepted truths when they think them wrong or in need of modification. Third, we should teach students how to compare, contrast, and synthesize—while I use 270 course materials as a paradigm, these skills are transferable to other courses and inquiries beyond our particular subject matter. We need to teach our students to synthesize, compare, and contrast the works they are reading, not only in the obligatory way that we require in "conclusions" to essays, but throughout their essays' arguments as well as in their thinking about the body of material that constitutes a course. This emphasis on comparison and synthesis has the added benefit of making the students think of the course as a coherent body of material rather than an arbitrary sequence of unrelated material generated by the teacher's preferences. Fourth, we should teach students to read closely and well, alert to nuances in language, and to see the *value of reading* in a visual age. Close reading—attention to verbal nuances from tone to phonics—teaches attentiveness to language in writing and in speech. Finally, we should teach students to articulate ideas orally. We as teachers need to develop student skills that are transferable not only to other disciplines but also to their future careers. At so-called elite universities, we need to place less emphasis on preprofessional skills for putative English professors and more on skills that will make students productive citizens who might participate in civic life, including service on library and museum boards.

## The Freshman Seminar as Intellectual Opportunity

I like to think of the subtitle of my 270 class as "Cornell Optics." I continue to think of my class as a process of opening doors and windows. I believe every freshman section of the writing program should, in part, be a course in opening eyes and helping the students see more. I call attention on a regular basis both on my e-mail list and in class to the vast variety of concerts, lectures, films, and writing opportunities for newspapers and magazines that are part of Cornell University.

I also utilize the resources on campus: the art museum as well as, more informally, the plays performed at the Cornell theater, films shown on campus, and the architecture and design of our campus. I hold at least one class session in the Johnson Art Museum and generate an assignment in which I ask the class to compare fiction with paintings or sculptures. Before that class, I ask each student to select a work that he or she will discuss. The class at the art museum emphasizes the distinction between the spatiality of the visual and the temporality of literary arts, while also showing students that, contrary to what many have thought, painting and sculpture may have a narrative element, and literature may have spatial organization.

## Teaching Writing

Our goals as writing teachers must be to teach precision of thought, clarity of expression, logic of argument, and individuality—and, yes, sometimes, controlled passion—of voice. My first class is necessarily mostly organizational

and introductory; I explain the logic of the syllabus and course policies and procedures. For freshman to understand that a writing course has a coherent perspective, the teacher must explain the *logic* of the syllabus: what he or she is doing on a regular basis and particularly *why* the class is reading the works it is
reading.

As a writing teacher I stress sentence variety. On each essay I stipulate
three or so sentence types that must be included and underlined; such sentences
might come from the following: "Not only . . . but also," "No sooner . . . than,"
" If . . . then," a rhetorical question, a subjunctive contrary to fact, a sentence
beginning with a gerund, a sentence beginning with a modifying present parti-
ciple, and a sentence beginning with a noun clause. I ask each student to mark
these sentences with a colored pen. I also stress the desirability of substituting
strong verbs for "there are," "there is," and "it is."

Because students are often on the frontier of their understanding when
dealing with complex texts such as *Notes from Underground* and *Death in Venice,* they tend to write convoluted sentences; by having them participate as a
community in carefully constructing paragraphs on the blackboard, I help them
learn how to discuss difficult and sophisticated texts in lucid sentences.

In this, our workshop aspect of the course, I stress strong conceptual topic
sentences, a taut evolving argument, and the ability to integrate a specific
story—or experience or piece of knowledge—with other stories and knowledge. Usually, in our workshop the focus is on one or two problems derived
from the prior set of essays such as the need for more use of the active voice or
ways of organizing evidence to make forceful arguments. Thus we might work
together to examine how to use evidence from the text, and how to structure a
paragraph that moves sequentially from concept, to a middle level of discourse
that negotiates between concept and specific, to specific evidence including perhaps a quotation, to precise comment in terms of the argument, to perhaps more
evidence and comment, and then back to middle level of discourse, and finally
back to concept.

I begin each term with short essays that increase in length as the term
progresses. I assign seven papers per term and, after the first one or two essays,
I offer a good deal of choice in my assignments. I also give students the option
of writing a short story so they can see how to handle point of view, characterization, development, and beginnings and endings. Most take this option.

I should make clear that I teach two seventy-five-minute classes a week,
and that the classes meet Tuesdays and Thursdays. Graded papers are always
handed back during the class after they are received. In the first few weeks, when
the students are not overwhelmed by other work, I assign shorter papers with
shorter intervals between assignment and due date. When we begin the longer

assignments, we have nine days between assignment and due date, and I correspond by e-mail with those seeking input on outlines and drafts.

Often, after collecting the papers on the due date, I immediately pass out student papers. Since I initiate this exercise after the first set or two of assigned papers, I am able to select for each student reader a paper that either exhibits writing problems present in the student reader's own work or a paper that provides an example of how to address successfully one or two of the student reader's major problems. I give the student readers about half an hour to make comments; sometimes I ask for a letter grade, too.

Of course, I regrade all the essays and provide substantive typed comments as well as handwritten marginal comments. As a way of learning more about the students, I observe how each student grader responds. My typed comments not only give an overview of the paper's strengths and problems but also refer to specific passages within the paper. Over the years, my emphasis has switched to the typed final comments—although I make comments within, too—in part because my English 270 students do not make a plethora of technical errors.

I do what I call "needs-based assignments"—that is, assignments based on the students' progress. Some students might continue to write shorter essays; some might revise more essays than others; some might propose topics that are a little outside the typical rubric of papers for an assignment. In addition to one stipulated revision assignment, each student may revise as often as she or he wishes. The original grade is not erased, but the second and subsequent grades are recorded.

Usually I have two office conferences with each student. However, if I think a student requires more conferences or if a student wants to discuss every paper, we might have several more. I also remain after class for informal discussions—sometimes continued in coffee rooms—which are often as valuable as formal conferences.

### Teaching Reading

My interest in narratology and in modern art informs my teaching as it does my writing. We should acknowledge the place of resistant reading perspectives—that is the perspective that *resists* the point of view that an author (or painter) thought he was expressing and built into his text. Often these resistant readings contribute rich feminist, gay, ecological, minority, and other multicultural perspectives that the author ignored. Certainly our student body has evolved into a much richer and more varied group where difference is respected. With these changes came changes in how we discuss reading assignments and the writing topics we assign. For example, discussion of the homoerotic implications of male bonding plays a larger role in my discussion of "The Secret Sharer" than it once did. Thus the canon changes even if the names of the texts are the same.

My teaching has always been closely related to my scholarship. If one believes, as I do, that the best readings are those that explain the phenomena within a text, one tests one's readings in a classroom. But, depending both on how we change and how our historical and cultural context change, the "best reading" is an evolving concept that varies from one reading to the next.

While I take cognizance of recent theory, in my teaching and writing I still find value in an Aristotelian perspective that stresses the *doesness* of a text and insists on the inextricable relationship between the aesthetic and ethical. Such a perspective asks how texts shape readers, what conscious and unconscious decisions an author makes to create a structure of effects, and what kind of form and genre the author chooses. I discuss the difference between Aristotelian approaches, which argue that the text generates effects, and reader response criticism, which stresses what the reader brings to the text. I suggest a transactional theory of reading that takes account of the differences between authorial and resistant readings.

Without using much of the jargon of contemporary criticism, I differentiate in one semi-lecture class between different traditional and more recent critical approaches and define deconstructive, Marxist, new historical, cultural studies, and, especially, feminist approaches. When we discuss texts I try to make the students aware of what approaches we are using. Thus when we do the full-length Woolf novel, *To the Lighthouse*, we particularly focus on issues of writing and reading as a woman and what that gender difference means.

## Building the Bridge between Reading and Writing

I believe that close reading of complex creative texts teaches that style enacts values, that the expectations of audiences change, and that *every choice* a writer makes affects how an audience reads his or her text. I discuss the first stories in terms of formal issues of point of view and show how they reveal the worlds in which the speakers live. Because these texts address problems of unreliable and imperceptive narrators, we discuss degrees of reliability and perceptivity. Later I move on to third-person omniscient narrators. I stress voice and persona as a way of getting students to be aware of how *their* structures and choices of language enact their voices and personas.

While acknowledging that scientific writing has different requirements than expository writing, I stress the need for the active voice. If students use the active voice to describe the author's creative decision and the narrator's self-dramatizing role, they become more aware of how creative and polemical authors make decisions that affect readers' responses, and they learn the difference between authorial and resistant readings. In discussion, to increase the emphasis on the creative act of writing, I insist that students use more accurate terminology to describe what is going on within a text than the clichéd "it says" or "they say."

As the syllabus progresses, the focus continues on ways of telling but includes such issues as doppelgangers ("The Secret Sharer," Lawrence's "The Prussian Officer," Joyce's "Counterparts," *Notes from Underground* and *Death in Venice*); the difference between character and characterization; how setting functions to reinforce theme and structure within an imagined ontology (Faulkner's "Dry September" and *The Dead*); the difference between story and discourse; the differences between, on the one hand, the realism of such writers as Hemingway, Joyce, Conrad, and stories that depend on fantasy and, on the other, parables such as Lawrence's "The Rocking Horse Winner," Kipling's "The Gardener," and Kafka's "The Hunter Gracchus" and *Metamorphosis*. In one informal unit, we discuss the implications of how stories and novels begin and end. Of course, the more complex texts need to be discussed in terms of most of the aforementioned issues.

After the first class, devoted to a discussion of how the point of view of the slightly older, retrospective teller functions in Joyce's "Araby," I might ask the class to discuss in the first assigned essay how the speaker is a self-dramatizing character in Hemingway's "Another Country." In my class on "Araby," we discuss how formal problems of point of view are inextricably related to historical issues such as Joyce's views of the effects of a stifling Catholic education and of the dominance of the British in Ireland upon the boy's perceptions. My stress in the early classes is that the narrator's words reveal as they conceal, conceal as they reveal. The first essay, perhaps a page and a half to two pages, assigned after the second class (but after the first discussion of the reading) also has, among other goals, the purpose of seeing if there are students who do not belong in the 200-level class, but instead in a course that provides more remedial writing help.

While discussing the literary works, I not only emphasize the issues I want discussed in the papers, but demonstrate how a paper on the assignment or—if I give a choice among topics, as I do after the first paper or two—assignments might be structured. Sometimes I assign papers asking students to write on works we have not yet talked about in terms of issues we have been discussing. Other times I ask students to build on issues within a text that we have been discussing—particularly when we are addressing complex texts, such as *Notes from Underground*, which they need to revisit to understand.

## Creating a Community of Inquiry

I wish my classes to be more than a site where I set assignments and the students do them to fulfill a course requirement. Needless to say, this is a goal to which we reach and often fall short. But I should like to suggest how we might develop a community of inquiry where all students understand learning as a process, take responsibility for being prepared each day, take assignments seriously, feel themselves part of a functioning group, and write their assignments with a sense of pride in their work and their evolving writing voices.

When we do a short reading assignment, I ask about half the class members to report orally on specific subjects; when I do a novella or the one longer novel, I might ask the entire class to prepare different subjects. Thus for "Araby," two students might address the retrospective telling, another the beginning, another the end, someone else the theme of Catholicism, another student the theme of empire, two others might be asked to think of the issue of guilt and how it shapes the retrospective teller, another would focus on the role of women, yet another the speaker's prepubescent psychosexuality. When two students are assigned the same subject, I encourage them to talk to one another and work together. The students are resources for the subjects when they arise; if, as occasionally occurs, they are not called on for a one- or two-minute presentation, they almost always raise their hands and participate.

Indeed, I teach writing in the spirit of, "This is true, isn't it?" and try to eschew the dogmatism about writing to which my generation and some of our students have been exposed. For does not the House of Good Writing have many rooms? My goal is to encourage each student to find his or her own voice rather than homogenize individual voices into one Proper Compositional Style. While I do not require it, I suggest keeping a loose-leaf journal, alternating days of writing about personal life with days writing about political and campus issues—or whatever is of interest to the student. I offer to read the latter pages during and / or after the course is over. Interestingly, a number of students have taken up this suggestion after the course—and after the demands on their freshman first or second term have lessened—and brought me their journals to read.

When reading in class a passage from a student paper or distributing papers for discussion, I have, over the years, alternated between anonymity and identifying the author. I discuss this issue early in the term and ask the class which they prefer. Within a class of seventeen—the maximum size for a Cornell freshman writing seminar—where the students come to know and respect one another, usually the student whose essay is being discussed identifies herself or himself. If one establishes a community of inquiry with a positive culture of learning, and begins by commending the achievements of the essay under discussion, one can, with some important exceptions, publicly identify students. However, when a paper is substandard, one should not identify the writer. And any student should be given the opportunity to approach the teacher and request anonymity when the issue is raised at the beginning of term.

My goal is to have every student take part in discussion in at least two classes out of three. Once students begin to participate they rarely stop. When they participate (rather than sit in the bleachers and watch), they feel better about themselves and the class. The class becomes the student's own experience, not something she or he observes as a bystander. More importantly, when students articulate ideas, they often clarify those ideas for themselves, and that clarification continues when listening to ensuing responses to their contributions.

E-mail has changed teaching, opening up new ways of bridging the gap between the dorm room and the classroom and creating an exciting nexus between the two sites. On the first day, I collect e-mail addresses and establish a course listserve; each student is expected to make a substantive contribution to the discussion of at least one text or recurring issue; most contribute more often. Indeed, as the term progresses and the students become better readers, the colloquies on e-mail are often stunning not only in their thoughtfulness and sophistication but also in the precision, lucidity, and energy of their writing. At the end of the term, along with their essays, the students submit their e-mail contribution in their folders. I might add that students are overwhelmingly enthusiastic about the listserve.

I encourage both e-mail comments addressed to the entire class and individual dialogues with me. Freshmen—and except for an occasional transfer or student who has postponed one writing seminar, my 270 students are freshmen—look to their teachers in small classes more than they do to their formal advisors. We teachers need to make clear that we are accessible to them in office hours and open to e-mail and phone inquiries. I answer e-mail several times a day from home, and I am also accessible by phone from 8 A.M. to 10 P.M. Of course, the students write each other "off list," and that is exactly what I want. I have no problem with a student showing a draft to a friend or roommate or other class member as long as the student writes his or her own paper. But e-mail has another important function in building a community of inquiry. Students are also encouraged to share with the class information about concerts, plays, or sporting events in which they participate; as a result, students attend one another's activities and build commitment to our community.

One way that a class becomes a community of inquiry is regular and prompt attendance, even for classes beginning at 8:40. We *need* to have rules for attendance and make a show of knowing who is present. Last term in English 270, I had, over the entire term, less than one absence per student, and more than half the students did not miss a class. I usually arrive early, and, as the class assembles, I ask what films they have seen and share my views of films I have seen; at other times we might discuss Cornell theater plays or campus issues, or adult choices with which freshmen are faced such as whether to join a fraternity or sorority and how to organize time among the demands of schoolwork, activities, and part-time jobs.

In these pre-class discussions, which, on occasion, overflow into the first few minutes of our seventy-five-minute class period, I might mention such freshman anxieties as what resources are available to students who are having trouble with any of their courses. Or I might discuss how to address difficulties with study habits or time management, particularly at hectic times before midterms and finals. At the end of each month, a few students and/or myself bring a little food for a brief class party, and, while nibbling for fifteen minutes, we discuss films, course issues, or Cornell and even national issues. At the end of term, I give students an informal reading list, suggesting further reading in authors we have read as well as authors we have not read, especially authors related to those we have read. I offer to read the students' work in the future. I remind them that when they read they should always be aware of the way a piece is written. For examples of good (but not always faultless) writing, I suggest that they should continue to read the editorial page and the op-ed page in the *New York Times* and perhaps the *New Yorker*. We have class reunions the next semester, and sometimes these reunions continue for four years. Since the listserves remain in place, class members and I continue to write one another after the class is over. Many of the 270 students take other classes from me, some become my major advisees, and quite often we keep in touch beyond their graduation, sometimes for decades.

What, finally, is a community of inquiry? It is a class in which students commit themselves not merely to the teacher, but to the material and each other in a spirit of learning. In a community of inquiry, the class does not stop when students and teachers separate and the course ends. The students speak to one another outside the classroom and on e-mail about their reading and writing, and carry their intellectual relationships beyond the life of the course.

We need to stress learning as an end itself and as a lifelong odyssey so that our students, as Constantine Cavafy put it, "Keep Ithaka always in mind. / Arriving there is what you're destined for. . . . / Ithaka gave you the marvelous journey / Without her you wouldn't have set out. . . . / Wise as you will have become, so full of experience, / you'll have understood by then what these Ithakas mean." The students need to understand that Cornell—and life— is composed of many Ithacas and that these Ithacas represent the wonder of learning.

# Teaching Writing about International Relations

MATTHEW EVANGELISTA

Government

℘ My fellow political scientists sometimes joke that our field is not a coherent or legitimate discipline. Political science (called "government" at Cornell and a few other tradition-bound institutions) is made up of people who act very much like economists or sociologists, statisticians or historians. They sometimes seem to hold more in common with members of those fields than with each other. The same is true of international relations, one of the subfields of political science. The approaches to the subject are myriad. The extensive range of writing styles reflects that diversity. Game theorists and statisticians often use words only to introduce and summarize the most important material: the mathematical model, the equations, or the data. For some postmodern scholars of international affairs, the word, or "discourse," is everything—but that doesn't make it easy to understand what they write.

In my teaching on international relations, we chart a middle course, but still manage to cover a wide range of writing styles. Students attempt to do one of the few things that do seem to unite many political scientists: to account for some political behavior (international, in our case) by developing competing explanations and evaluating the evidence supporting or undermining each one. We approach that task step by step, beginning with exercises that develop the students' abilities to make consistent arguments and relate them to evidence. Students try their hand at writing short opinion pieces on topical issues, or even letters to the editor. We emphasize writing and rewriting drafts. We try to un-learn what many of us learned in high school: that you can't write something until you have a complete outline, that you have to avoid the first person at all costs, including tortuous passive constructions. Ultimately, if we are successful, the students learn to present even the most difficult theoretical ideas (mainly associated these days with the "social constructivist" school of international relations) with clarity and style. The skill of writing clearly is one that students will use throughout their careers, long after they have forgotten the difference between "globalization" and "internationalization," or how the Cold War began or ended.

Much work in political science is historical in nature. We draw on sources including archives, memoirs, interviews, and contemporary newspaper and journal reports. There is often so much material that we cannot keep it all in our heads at once. We need to begin writing before we have gathered all the information we will need, lest we forget what we had earlier discovered. As we work on a particular argument, we refer back to our sources (and discover new ones), and revise the argument as we go along, in an iterative process. This sort of writing, characteristic of much of political science, does not lend itself easily to an outline-based strategy.

Much of my students' writing seems better suited to the write-and-revise strategy than to the outline-first strategy. In my course on comparative foreign policy, for example, I pose questions for student essays that require them to use multiple sources and to integrate evidence into their arguments that the original authors (of the required course readings) might have used for very different purposes. The task is similar to historical research. On a more mundane level, students who write take-home essay exams, and perhaps haven't done all of the required course reading ahead of time, can benefit from a strategy that emphasizes writing and revising as new information becomes available (or as they recognize that they lack adequate evidence and need to read more). Here is sample paper topic in comparative foreign policy.

> In order to sort out the most important factors and explanations for a particular phenomenon, political scientists often employ "counterfactual history." To take a simple example, one might argue that if Roosevelt had lived longer or Stalin had died sooner, the Cold War would never have happened. Try to find from among the readings an explicit or implicit counterfactual argument and analyze it. Consider, for example, the assumptions it makes about the most important level of analysis (in the case above, it would be the individual level—the "great person theory of history"), and about the most important explanations for the Cold War. The goal of the paper is to think critically about alternative courses that postwar

Soviet-American relations might have taken as a way to understand the main factors that influenced the Cold War.

My approach to teaching an alternative to the outline-first strategy is to propose in effect an outline-second strategy. The emphasis is on writing a draft and then analyzing the draft to perceive the structure of the essay and how it should be revised for clarity, consistency, and organization.

In sorting through evidence and deciding how it relates to her arguments, a student will typically confront evidence that does not support the case she wants to make. I encourage each student to consider this a potential opportunity rather than a defect of her argument. If a student can address possible problems with her argument head on, she can often make a more persuasive case for her position. A student usually does this by laying out an alternative argument that is consistent with the evidence that she finds anomalous for her own argument. The alternative explanation might account for the anomaly, but it might not do so well in explaining the rest of the evidence. If the student's original explanation accounts for more of what she seeks to explain, despite some anomalies, by conventional social-science criteria it is considered the stronger explanation. The task of formulating rival explanations for some political behavior, and testing them in this fashion against evidence, lies at the heart of political science. Most journal editors and reviewers will explicitly look for a section of a manuscript submission that addresses alternatives to the author's preferred explanation. Recognizing and weighing alternative explanations against evidence is undoubtedly a skill worth teaching, even to the majority of students who have no intention of becoming professional political scientists.

After reconciling redundancies and contradictions within the body of the paper draft, and dealing with problematic evidence and alternative explanations, a student still might face an important task to address in a final revision. I always remind each student that if he writes without an outline first, he might find that his conclusion does not always agree with his introduction. In an introduction, one makes a guess about where the argument is going, but it might end up going somewhere else. Students seem to find very helpful the apparently obvious admonishment: "Make sure your conclusion does not contradict your introduction." The solution, as I teach it, is a straightforward one. Replace your introductory paragraph with your concluding one, and rewrite your conclusion to paraphrase your new introduction.

Some readers, not social scientists I hope, might be shocked at the cookbook quality of these writing guidelines. Must the conclusion simply repeat the thesis of the introduction? For most purposes—for example, publication in mainstream professional journals—the answer is yes. A good expository essay on politics begins with an introduction that sets out clearly what the author intends to argue, including a summary of the main conclusion or "findings." Each paragraph follows in an order that the reader will have anticipated from the introduction. The conclusion typically sums up the overall argument and often proposes suggestions for further research.

This form of organization, which leaves so little to the imagination, is very different from how students seem to prefer to write. Many favor the mystery-story approach. The writer gradually leads the reader toward her conclusions, saving the punch line—to mix metaphors—until the very end. Most readers do not have the patience, however, to follow the argument to the end unless they know in advance where it is going. Professional journal editors and reviewers are quite explicit on that point. In addition, many journals require an abstract. To write an abstract one must be able to summarize the main points of an article concisely, without repeating all the steps that led to the conclusion. Happily, if an article is well organized, the abstract can consist mainly of part of the introductory paragraph and the first sentence ("topic sentence") of several of the paragraphs.

When I first began teaching writing, I got the impression that most of my students had learned yet another of the key lessons I had learned about writing in high school: except when writing explicit autobiography, always avoid the first person. Recently students' hesitations about using the first person have given way to the opposite tendency—an overly conversational or colloquial style of writing. We might attribute this tendency in part to the culture of the Internet, where communication often consists of battles of personal opinion on a range of topics, including politics. There is a place for opinion in the field of political science. Even if some scholars seem motivated more by "science" than politics, others are eager to express their political views and offer policy-relevant (as our jargon puts it) advice. Many professional political scientists publish their views in the opinion pages of newspapers or, in more extended form, in journals such as *The Nation* or *The Atlantic Monthly*. The writing style for op-ed pieces differs from conventional academic writing and not every scholar (or student) can do it well.

In several of my courses, students learn to write op-ed pieces. Beyond the basics of clear presentation and coherent argumentation, what makes for a good op-ed is partly a matter of taste. I suggest three criteria: First, although an opinion-page writer presents her own opinion, she should avoid making herself the most important political figure in the article. Unless you are Dave Barry or Russell Baker, your op-ed should not consist of a string of your personal political pet peeves.

Second, an op-ed should provide some new information as well as opinion.

The reader should learn something that she has not already read in the news section of the same newspaper. For a writer, starting with that new information is a good way to draw the reader into an op-ed. For professional writers, the new information is often garnered from interviews ("As Yasser Arafat told me last week . . ."), but it can also come from scholarly sources or government reports that are not otherwise widely known. I tell my students who want to write about the wars in former Yugoslavia, for example, that they can find a good "hook" without looking very far. They might start with the scholarly works I have assigned in the course syllabus. There they would find, for instance, that on the eve of the breakup of Yugoslavia, one-fifth of the country's working population was unemployed. In Serbia, about half of young men in their twenties were without jobs, providing ready recruits for the militias that ravaged first Croatia, then Bosnia, then Kosovo, then Macedonia. The connection between economic conditions and political and military outcomes could form the basis for an opinion-page article that would provide both underappreciated information as well as a point of view.

Finally, I encourage the students, as they do in their longer papers, to entertain alternative points of view or interpretations of the evidence. In an essay of seven hundred or eight hundred words, a thorough presentation and refutation of alternatives is impossible, but an acknowledgment of the other sides of an argument adds, rather than detracts, from the credibility of one's own position.

A key purpose of the Writing in the Majors program is to integrate the teaching of writing with the substantive study of an academic discipline. The study of international relations for students consists mainly of reading—primary sources, such as newspapers; secondary historical accounts; and theoretical discussions. Learning to read critically is an important way to improve one's writing skills.

In fields as varied as political science or international relations, what qualifies as good writing may be a matter of dispute. I always ask my students at the end of the semester to give their evaluations of the course readings, so that I can consider whether to reassign the same texts next time I teach the course. I often find that students assert that a particular author "writes well," when they really mean, "I liked what she had to say." They sometimes describe as "a terrible writer" someone whose ideas they found offensive, or perhaps just hard to understand.

Many students seem allergic to political scientists' pretensions to "theory," so that any author who makes abstract arguments is dismissed as a poor writer. Most teachers of international relations would respond that theories always drive real-world politics, but policy makers are not always aware of their theoretical assumptions. Or, as Keynes famously put it, "Mad men in authority, who hear voices in the air, are distilling their frenzy from some academic scribbler of a few years back." By developing the ability to identify the assumptions underlying politicians' rationales for their foreign policies, students enhance their analytic skills. By studying the work of "academic scribblers" and assessing the validity of their arguments and the quality of their writing, students ultimately improve their own writing skills as well.

The basic skills I seek to teach in my writing courses include clear organization and exposition, relating evidence to arguments, and evaluating competing explanations. Despite the diversity of approaches to the study of international relations, most scholars would agree that these skills constitute the necessary core of good writing practices in the discipline. They are also skills that every college student should learn. So even if my students' futures in international relations are limited to foreign travel and reading about current world events, I will have done my job if they leave my courses with improved abilities to write.

# Writing Political Science

*Asking a Question Then (Actually) Answering It*

MARY FAINSOD KATZENSTEIN

Government

☞ Some months ago, the administrator in my department caught me in the hall just at the end of the day and asked if I'd speak with a family waiting in the department lounge. The family, three generations worth, hoped to talk with a faculty member about undergraduate life at Cornell. I reached the doorway of the lounge, saw a fellow member of the department already there, and turned to make a furtive retreat, but not before hearing myself being graciously introduced by my departmental colleague. Perching on the arm of a chair near the door, I listened as this colleague continued his conversation with the prospective undergraduate, a young woman who was sitting very upright, all earnestness, her grandparents and parents looking on devotedly. "Why are you interested in political science?" my colleague asked. "I know it will sound naive," she began—I eyed the exit—"but I want to run for office, for the Senate, maybe even the presidency one day. Can a political science major help me do this?"

I was suddenly *very* interested! Unlikely as it sounds, not once in my twenty-five years of teaching political science had I ever heard anyone pose the question of whether a political science major was useful to someone who wanted to enter politics. Law, yes, or the foreign service, or nonprofit work or grassroots activism, or the inevitable query by prospective majors—"What is political science good for?" But I'd never known a student to ask about political science as a path to electoral office. Naive maybe, but original! As I was searching for an answer ("We have a course on campaigns and elections, another on the presidency"), my colleague remarked, "Political science is just where you should be because in this department we teach you how to write. We know that no one in Washington," he went on to explain, "has time to bother with academic-style exegesis. We want to teach you how to craft strong, parsimonious prose."

Everybody seemed happy. I made my retreat and returned home reflecting on what, in fact, we *are* preparing our students for when we teach writing to our majors. Descriptively, if not normatively, my answer is somewhat different from the one my colleague ventured. When we teach writing, I'd wager, we do not exactly envision successive progeny of lawyers, diplomats, or activists, never mind politicians. Unwittingly perhaps, we set about cultivating our students to be bonsai political science professors (diminutive replicas of ourselves). The justification for this conceit is the belief that much political science writing is broadly fungible—that it will serve our students well beyond the requirements of an undergraduate education.

Yet even as the profession can cheerfully agree that learning "to read and write in the discipline" has definitive use beyond the university, we can probably also quickly come to blows about the content and relevance of the instruction. Just what is too narrow so as to be too much political *science* and what is too broad so as to render the instruction an amorphous collection of ideas and literatures that has no disciplinary identity whatsoever? In my own First-Year Writing Seminars and upper-level Writing in the Majors courses, seen from the point of view of my colleagues, I no doubt err on the side of the "indisciplined." But as the anecdote at the essay's conclusion will betray, and as the title of this essay implies, when seen from the vantage of other disciplines, my view of political science writing instruction is indelibly marked by the identity of my vocation.

## Asking an Interesting Question

Empirical political science approaches writing much as the public understands marriage and monogamy, by which I do not mean the obvious point that the rules are observed largely in the breach. I am thinking, rather, of Ann Swidler's wonderful description of how the institution of marriage frames societal attitudes toward relationships. "The institution of marriage and 'courtship'," she observes, invites a very different set of questions from the one that might be applied to friendships. If there is a prospect of marriage, the questions asked of a relationship are likely to be: "Could this be 'it'?" "Is this the one?" "Will this be forever?" As Swidler points out, these are questions to which we subject only potential marriage partners, never our prospective friends. This is so despite pervasive popular recognition that marriages may be no more faithful or long-lasting than friendship. Political science writing, much like the institution of marriage, borrows from the idiom of monogamy. There is a corresponding irony in political science, moreover, that despite a broad acknowledgment of the transience of truth-claims, much political science writing repudiates plurality. Rarely are political scientists content to broach several interesting sets of ideas or offer a menu of different perspectives. The norm, rather, is (sequential) monogamy—to never lose focus on "the" question (and to provide "the" answer to the question posed). Before you start writing, you better have decided what "it" is, even as you are cognizant that many other "its" are possible and are likely soon to follow. "What's *the* (thesis) question; what's *the* argument this article makes?" These queries are the professional *lingua franca* of graduate education and they are basic to how many political scientists teach writing at the undergraduate level, as well.

If I sound skeptical, I do not, for the most part, mean to. Focusing on "the question" is how I begin my own writing courses. In my freshman writing seminar on India, we start the semester with an example of monogamous writing at work—a single, powerfully posed question that frames a compelling book on child labor written by Myron Weiner (1991). This reading invariably proves to be one of the semester's highlights, partly because of the clarity of its core question. Seven paragraphs into his 213-page monograph, Myron Weiner asks provocatively: "Why is the Indian state unable—or unwilling—to deal with the high and increasing illiteracy, low school enrollments, high dropout rates, and rampant child labor?" (5). When I ask what sentences students have underlined or highlighted from the first pages, it is a rare student who hasn't painted that question in yellow. No other questions compete for space. The assignment calls for students to circle all the questions in the chapter. Other than in this paragraph, there is not a single further question posed until the very last page of the eighteen-page chapter. Even these questions, on the final page of the chapter, are all derivative of the primary query: "Why were coalitions for reforms created elsewhere, but not in India?" (18). "If the impediment to change comes because of the attitudes of those who make, implement, and influence policy, and if these attitudes are based on deeply held beliefs that are not easily shaken, is reform likely?" (18).

I sometimes suspect that when "the" question in a particular political science reading is this assertively posed, students are cowed into believing that there *is* only one question to be asked—that every topic has "its" question. Is there only a single question to be asked about child labor in the Indian context? Clearly—no. As we discuss in class, Weiner might well have made his primary focus the question of how systems of property and production encourage the perpetuation of child labor, or how globalization impinges on child labor, or the question of whether gender inequality is its source, or all these concerns. He chooses, rather, to focus on the state—on personal agency and the failure of bureaucrats and other elites to require and enforce compulsory education. Arriving at "the" question, I try to emphasize, is a process of construction, not manifest destiny.

This is less obvious than it seems, particularly for freshman whose high school educations have typically been structured by preformulated paper and exam questions rather than by open-ended assignments. That "assisted" habit of thinking accounts partly for the anxiety that afflicts many students as they set about writing their first papers—at least as much as the novelty of college, a particular discipline, or subject matter. Until recently, my assignments in the early part of the semester prolonged this dependency, I think, offering in the syllabus one or several questions for students to address each week. Lately, I have become convinced that students are better served by (quite early in the semester) having to find their own way, floundering a bit while they try out alternative possibilities, and that it makes sense to build into the early assignments some opportunities to try out and share question-formulations for the essays that students intend to write.

But how to guide students not just toward "a question," but toward an interesting one? Indeed the risk of more open-ended assignments is seeing a student, even one with well-developed writing skills, pose a question whose importance is neither self-evident nor well established in his or her essay. In class, we talk a bit (not enough, I think) about what makes a question "important." I argue for a two-part process of identifying "authentically for oneself" what "really matters" and then, as a separate conceptual step, making the connection to the reader.

Trusting oneself to know what is interesting and to make critical judgments is the paramount challenge for many freshmen and sophomores in political science, indeed, across the disciplines. By freshman year of college, students are—no less in my day than now—skilled replicators of authorized interpretations. Then, at least as I experienced it, this meant scouring the card catalog in search of just the right secondary source that would unlock the secrets of the essay assignment due Monday, supplemented by the obscure encyclopedia article (where would I have been, at least so I thought, without the yellowed pages of a postwar edition of the *Encyclopedia of the Social Sciences?*); now it is the urgent combing of the Web with its addictive, ever-enticing sense that with just a little more time, one more set of searches, the crucial clue to an often unspecified problem will be unearthed; in both cases the search is driven by the uneasy quest for assurance that someone who "knows" can tell you what is worth saying.

The reading assignments in my freshman seminar are devised with the express intention of breaking through this protective cloak. I remember, with still-palpable pleasure, the first essay I ever wrote as an undergraduate that felt like it was truly my own. It was not, in fact, until junior year. The essay compared ideas of community and individualism based on the writing of two authors so obscure as to have warranted no attention from the literature. This is why I try in my courses now, where possible, to use recent books for which there are no reviews yet to be located or provocative articles that have left a long literary trail of already debated ideas. But obscurity is clearly not the answer. Students need to write on Mahatma Gandhi, on Partition—on people, events, and ideas that fill entire aisles of the library. For the majority of the semester, I try to generate classroom debates in which students, in the process of becoming involved, or better, impassioned, will develop a personal stake in (albeit much-rehearsed) issues and will gain confidence from joining their voice in a collective conversation.

To know as the author what is "important" for oneself, however, requires a different awareness from that which enables the writer to make an idea seem salient to others. What marks this process? This upcoming semester, I plan to introduce some short music listening—segments of a raga and sonata that will allow us to discuss why a particular rhythm, run, or chord is "interesting" to us, the listeners, and to open up a discussion of the way "interest" is contingent on familiarity/unfamiliarity and on the construction of existing paradigms of knowledge. In discussing how intellectual agendas are created and the need to connect to them, I talk in class about the subfield of comparative politics, into which category the study of India generally falls, and how this field represents "what is interesting" in terms of three formulations: (1) a question whose interest is established through comparison (an interesting contrast, a curious similarity); (2) a question whose interest is established through a claim of distinctiveness or uniqueness; (3) a question whose importance is argued in terms of a missing or unexplained gap or contradiction in a scholarly study or in the literature more broadly. I try to identify examples in the syllabus of each of these three "justificatory logics." Whether for undergraduate or graduate writing, I confess an impatience with the third of these three approaches when pursued devoid of its "real-world" relevance. Where I part ways with some of my colleagues is in finding the solipsism that "literature debates" can sometimes engender to be an acceptable price of "learning" the discipline.

With each of these approaches, we talk about how writers bring a "case" to the reader. Weiner's opening pages, I suggest, provide a wonderful model of the second "distinct case" approach and of the fascinating use of "specifics" to establish a problem's importance. We discuss how Weiner establishes the salience of his question within the first few paragraphs using a level of detail that belies what Daryl Bem has called the "hourglass" model of essay writing—start big, get small, and expand as you end. Only the first few sentences of the opening paragraphs of Weiner's book operates at the level of a general claim: "The governments of all developed countries and many developing countries have removed children from the labor force and required that they attend school" (3). But as soon as he reaches the second paragraph, Weiner establishes India's distinctiveness through a highly specific discussion of data. "This [the state's obligation to establish compulsory schooling] is not the view in India" (3). Right away, Weiner sets out some very detailed facts unfamiliar to the general reader:

> Primary education in India is not compulsory, nor is child labor
> illegal. The result is that less than half of India's children between
> the ages six and fourteen—82.2 million—are not at school. They
> stay at home to care for cattle, tend younger children, collect
> firewood, and work in the fields. They find employment in cottage
> industries, tea stalls, restaurants, or as household workers in middle-
> class homes. . . . Most children who start school drop out. Of those
> who enter first grade, only four out of ten complete four years of
> school. (3)

Even before the end of the first page, we have thus been handed quite specific "facts" and have gained the satisfaction of learning something both new and quite concrete. Armed with this newly acquired knowledge, we become quickly engaged by the "distinctive case" justification, "India is a significant exception to the global trend toward the removal of children from the labor force" (4). With the data that precedes it, the claim about India as a "significant exception" pierces our resistance to a broad generality. The contemporary reader has probably been desensitized by a surfeit of exhortations to pay attention to yet one more social problem in a world suffused by inequality and injustice; the way Weiner wins attention is to empower the reader right from the start with knowledge she or he is unlikely to have, thus enlisting the reader as an informed ally in the author's project.

Deciding on "the" question and convincing the reader of its importance presents different challenges for the freshman writing and upper-level Writing in the Majors classes. For upper-level students, it seems to be harder to come up with "the" question, but easier to make it interesting once they do. For freshmen, it is easier to define the question, but harder to get beyond the prosaic. In the beginning of the freshman writing seminar semester, there is often a trade-off between the pedantic but clear and the inventive but confused. These two opening paragraphs by freshman seminar students writing about the Weiner monograph are emblematic:

In the modern world, education has been made compulsory in all developed countries and many developing countries. In fact, most of these countries have come to regard education as a parental duty regardless of financial background and social status. Despite this, why has India, for one, not been able to implement compulsory universal education?

Is nothing simple? Is there no exact science in evaluating institutions embedded within the infrastructure of a society? Such would seem to be the case with child labor in India. It is superficial and ignorant to evaluate India's need for child labor and lack of compulsory education without understanding the motivation behind the people. Understanding motivation requires a cultural analysis which is based on what motivates certain behaviors. One way to study child labor is to evaluate the economic motivation of the people; however, economics and culture are interconnected.

With the first example, we talked about its exemplary clarity and then discussed ways of turning its somewhat wooden tone into a livelier, more interesting challenge. Could the writer locate a paradox, fix on an unusual or striking claim in the reading, or speak out of (in this case) his own experience? With the second example, we discussed its exciting implicit challenge to Weiner's argument; the class tried out ways to clarify terminology, sharpen and shorten the somewhat cumbersome prose, and pinpoint explicitly its between-the-lines critique.

In the upper-level Writing in the Majors course, which requires a long research paper in addition to several shorter ones, students find identifying an *area* for research and locating rich materials to be smooth sailing; honing in on "the question" is another matter. The task would be easier, I realize, if the course or paper assignment were organized around a set of competing theories. Carol Mueller, a political sociologist at Arizona State University (and colleague with whom I have collaborated), provides in her courses an exemplary, highly focused paper assignment that asks students to evaluate three competing theories of how the media treats political news as applied to an issue area of the student's choice.

My own course, by contrast—which takes up the broad question of how claims to gender equality are shaped by the political processes of a liberal democratic state—offers theoretical tools but no tidy set of opposing theories. The course focuses on how institutions restrict and enable. We look at how norms, rules, and structures confine and empower those who endeavor to challenge race, class, sexuality, and gender-based systems of inequality. We begin by looking at the "state" as an institution. We read Rogers Smith, who argues that "multiple traditions"—both liberal and exclusionary—are deeply embedded in American society, and that the history of inequality is therefore not one of the successes and failures of liberalism but of deeply embedded ideologies that compete *with* liberalism throughout American history. We read Catherine MacKinnon, who sees liberalism itself as androcentric, not merely outclassed by competing exclusionary ideologies, and we take up the case of reproductive rights to explore the characterizations of the state in Smith and MacKinnon. The course then turns to specific state and non-state institutions, to the military and the prison, to the church and the law firm, in order to explore how institutions create disciplining practices and at the same time harbor networks of activists who rely on the norms, rules, and institutional structures to mount challenges to the organization. On a more theoretical plane, we read Foucault and several contemporary sociological analyses of institutions.

This leaves, both for better and for worse, broad leeway for the paper-writer. I encourage students to choose a subject that is close to their interests. By the second week, when paper "topics" (subject areas—not "questions") are due, most students have easily fixed on an issue-area of particular interest to them: an art history major has chosen to work on "the guerilla girls" and discrimination in art shows; a Catholic student in the class elects to work on a dispute in a local parish; a student who worked as a summer assistant in an architecture firm decides to focus on architecture and the gendering of a profession. Another student who wants to think about volunteering in the local prison program works on incarceration, etc. The next step is to meet with students to discuss preliminary questions that their topics raise, and the process of research begins. From then on, numerous meetings take place involving the student, sometimes a teaching assistant, and myself, and we begin what I call a "perpetual dialogue." By this I do not mean that the student and I are in constant communication, although this aspect of the course does mutate into as many tutorials as there are students in the class; rather what I am referring to is the "call and response" between question and answer—between thinking about what research strategy is required given the putative question the student is asking and trying to define ever more sharply the question to which the material the student is beginning to collect is the answer.[1]

## Answering the Question

I devote far less space to this section of the chapter, thereby breaking the cardinal rule of spatially balanced subsections. But the reader will by now have caught my drift. If defining "the question" need not be a scientific process of identifying a query that can be confirmed or disconfirmed, then it goes without saying that I am unlikely to proselytize for rigorous case selection and hypothesis testing as a requisite of an acceptable "answer" to the question posed. But just as I have argued for the drafting of a question that is, above all, clear and important in the judgment of both author and prospective readership, so I will argue for the presentation of an answer to the question that is explicit in its method and engaging in its argumentation.

The questions and answers that students pursue in their writing projects are both descriptive and explanatory and in neither freshman nor upper-level courses do I seek to rank the value of one above the other. But what certain of the reading selections in both courses are intended to convey is that there *is* a difference, something that upper-level students may not apprehend necessarily more readily than freshman. In the freshman seminar, following the Weiner assignment, we read a long, rich, and recent analysis of caste in India, the purpose of which is to describe the changes that have occurred over the last decades. The book is predominately descriptive, although it presents explanations of societal changes, as well. And while it is the case that the description reciprocally serves the explanatory sections of the book, explanation is of secondary importance to the overall project. Although neither course seeks to favor one kind of writing over the other, I try to stress the importance of students knowing which they are doing and why so that their purposes can become clear in their texts.

Although upper-level students are more sophisticated in many ways than freshman, it is surprising, as with the distinction between description and explanation, that the more advanced students are not always much more self-aware about the ways that political perspectives enter into the presentation of an argument. In both courses we discuss at which points in the writing process an author's political views may enter—from the choice of a research question to the choice of methodology to the selection of an adjective. I do not urge upon students a "value-free" analysis, far from it. What I do counsel is making fully self-conscious choices and attending to the likely rhetorical consequences of those choices.

A number of years ago, standing by the Xerox machine at the Bunting Institute (an interdisciplinary research institute at Radcliffe that supports women's scholarship), a colleague in English literature asked if I knew a particular feminist scholar in political science whom she had heard deliver a paper at a conference in Santa Cruz. The presentation, my Bunting colleague remarked, was disappointing—a surprise to me, since this political science scholar was generally very well regarded among those I knew in her field. What was amiss, I wondered? My English literature colleague explained: "She asked a question and then simply proceeded to answer it." "Oh," I responded almost inaudibly, "but that is what many political scientists do."

Well, to be honest, that is not true of all dues-paying members of the political science association. Certainly there are many postmodern scholars and other social theorists who would decline to embrace the nomenclature of political "science" to begin with and who would find in the "question and answer" formulation that I have proposed already far too much that smacks of a positivism that is seen as perilously hegemonic.

For the methodologically inclined in political science, having a good question and providing an answer does not go far enough. To this phalanx of scholars, the simple formulation I have proposed might not sound as much wrong as anachronistic. A question should be not just any query but one that can be falsified. An answer is not merely a carefully argued position that is explicit in its premises and that weighs possible alternatives; it is what emerges from analysis that is based on a rigorous specification of competing hypotheses, variables, indicators, and case selection.

In my view, there are good reasons for the full spectrum of political analysis to be represented in the curriculum. But if it is instruction in writing that we are after, and if we envision political science students taking what they have learned about writing into the legal profession, the unions, into movement politics, the nonprofit association—even "into the Senate, maybe even the presidency one day"—asking an important question and providing an answer in clear, persuasive prose is what we should be teaching.

# The Politics of Writing

ROSE MCDERMOTT

Government

⌒ Integrating scholarship and teaching presents a challenge in any discipline. When attempting to combine the teaching of substantive knowledge and the teaching of writing techniques, the goal can appear even more daunting to achieve. The task of communicating effectively with undergraduates is often at odds with the goals of writing effective and influential arguments within a specific disciplinary culture. Yet a productive relationship can exist between research and writing, and between teaching substance and style. This chapter addresses this integration within political science in general, and international relations in particular.

Part of the synthesis I strive for when teaching First-Year Writing Seminars is achieved through understanding that pedagogical styles should be adapted to the particular level of the students. The way freshmen write differs from the way advanced undergraduates, graduate students, or professionals in the field might argue their interests, opinions, and ideas. Style is not the only aspect that differs across levels; the very topics that individuals find interesting and worthy of discussion vary as well. Recognizing that not all freshmen in my writing seminars in political science will go on to become professional members of my discipline grants certain latitude. I expect students to emerge from this course able to master a body of knowledge in international relations, as well as an effective means by which to communicate this information in writing. This goal creates a broad purpose that both allows interested students to continue their pursuit of political science, and less interested students to become more sophisticated consumers of political information in general. Structuring opportunities for effective political writing encourages this larger intention of creating more successful writers in general and more knowledgeable consumers of political writing in particular.

After some brief discussion of the relationship between scholarship and teaching writing in political science, I will note some specific aspects of the "disciplinary culture" of writing in political science and how these forces help shape the politics of teaching about writing in international relations. I will then draw on sections of my course syllabi, writing assignments, and student work to illustrate some possibilities for integrating scholarship and teaching writing in this area. I hope these samples demonstrate the quality and style of learning and writing that I strive to model and encourage in my students. These examples attempt to highlight the sometimes competing but often complimentary ambitions of teaching writing in a political context.

## Scholarship and Teaching Writing

We all probably wish at times that we only had to teach courses that were directly relevant to our current research interests at the time. However, as we all know, our particular research interests only rarely coincide with those of our colleagues, much less our graduate or undergraduate students. This is only natural, given different levels of personal development and intellectual background. But this tension in interest and background can offer a gift to teachers who wish to reconnect with what they originally found compelling and engaging in their own fields. Teachers can then aspire to communicate this enthusiasm to students in a way that is accessible and absorbing.

How is it possible to reconcile these disciplinary concerns with undergraduate interests? In international relations, students' interests are often sparked by current events in the world. In teaching political writing to undergraduates, the wedge into consciousness is not the door of abstract theory, but the window of these concrete events and circumstances from which the academic discipline also extracts facts, evidence, and arguments. Undergraduates are curious and motivated to explain why things occur as they do, and how they might get involved to change outcomes for the better. Indeed, few professional political scientists were originally drawn to the discipline out of an abstract interest in a particular theoretical perspective or method. Typically, they were originally compelled by a particular set of questions and problems in the world that they, too, wanted to understand and address.

Yet this interest in foreign policy decision making sparks little, if any, intellectual debate in the major journals in the field. Rather, major debates in the international relations literature takes a more theoretically bifurcated turn: much innovative work uses rational choice and game theory to provide quantitative or formal analysis of relatively abstract issues pertaining to the origins of conflict and the instigation of peace; other influential work has taken a more sociological turn to investigate the microfoundations of dynamic processes in international relations. Yet the steps from wondering whether the Cold War would blow us all up to a quantitative or psychological analysis of the dynamics of conflict escalation, bargaining, and negotiation are many and steep. Students must first stay engaged enough to learn the facts before the theories or methods can acquire meaning or significance.

Obviously the goal in teaching writing about politics to freshman is to both teach them something about politics and something about writing. Part of the benefit of teaching writing in a context of content lies in the wealth of topics and information that is available to students from their reading and experience. Part of the challenge is not to alienate students by disregarding concerns and interests that might seem too concrete in a higher-level graduate seminar. Remembering that the objective is not to create professional political scientists, but rather sophisticated consumers of political writing and information, can serve to help refocus exercises and discussions in more productive ways.

Teaching writing about international relations to freshmen can offer subtle contributions to individual scholarship for the teacher as well. Teachers are forced to enter the realm of immediacy, applicability, and pragmatism. Undergraduate students in general, but freshman in particular, are less concerned with what the theory of realism has to say about Slobodan Milosevic's policy of ethnic cleaning in Kosovo than in how and why this kind of killing can happen and what can be done to stop it. Theoretically, sophisticated larger arguments about the critical importance of open and stable access to cheap oil in the Middle East are much less convincing to freshmen than urgent questions about the deaths of Iraqi babies in the wake of a decade of sanctions imposed by the United Nations against Iraq. Being forced to clearly explain the connections between theory and practice in real-world situations encouraged me to examine more carefully my own thinking and writing on related topics.

Translating disciplinary knowledge in a way that encourages students to engage in persuasive writing to characterize and justify their opinions and arguments increases student respect for both the difficulty and the power of political writing and political propaganda. They come to realize that facts can be used selectively and manipulated in ways that are designed to garner sympathy for a particular political perspective. Teachers, for their part, discover ways to reformulate abstract theoretical constructs into more accessible, useful, and interesting arguments for students to integrate into their own intellectual development. In so doing, a teacher has the opportunity to both have an immediate impact on student understanding and to refine and extend the meaning and value of the more abstract work in his or her own writing.

## Disciplinary Culture and Writing Practices

There are several kinds of political writing. Much political writing falls under the rubric of journalism and consists of reporting and analyzing political facts and information for the informed and interested public. Professional political science writing in journals and books constitutes another main branch of political writing. The goals and the techniques of these types of writing often work in opposition to one another.

At its best, political journalism presents straightforward, accessible analysis with vivid imagery. Writers assume no prior knowledge on the part of the readers, and attempt to inform readers about the dynamics and individuals involved in particular events. Beginning students often find this work appealing and aspire to the directness of its style. Asking students to write succinct commentaries on current events, or to analyze newspaper articles for political propaganda involves them in active assimilation of political information. Developing a healthy skepticism toward the news advances students along the path toward becoming sophisticated and active members of a democratic civil society. Encouraging such involvement in the political process creates a habit and skill that will serve students well beyond their college writing course.

The professional political science writing that appears in journals and books is typically much more technical in nature and assumes a much greater degree of common knowledge and shared background information with the audience. Individuals who straddle the policy and academic worlds may call for greater policy relevance in theoretical work, but academic incentives work to reward the theoretical, not the political. Generating abstract theoretical arguments advances careers; choosing to write policy-relevant work closes down important professional options for the majority of political scientists.

So a tension emerges between teaching these styles in the classroom. Status accrues to the academic teacher who publishes in professional journals. A rare op-ed piece aside, journalistic writing or commentary is the subject of raised eyebrows, if not scorn. Yet these are precisely the works that generate greatest student interest and engagement at the undergraduate level. Few undergraduates will ever want or need to adopt the disciplinary argot of political science in their future writings. Fewer of them are prepared to invest the time and energy that would be required to learn the style, much less the content, of professional academic political writing.

The resolution in pedagogical terms lies in recognizing and understanding the different goals that are being advanced. Freshmen need to have experiences learning to write. Providing engaging content gives focus and purpose to those exercises. While political topics that freshman find compelling might not always overlap completely with those that the teacher finds most compelling, there can be an intersection between student interest and teacher pedagogy. Academics who strive to generate and maintain student involvement benefit in the lessons they learn about how to communicate their arguments more effectively to a wider audience. And making our own work more compelling and accessible, even within tighter disciplinary constraints, can ultimately only improve the influence of our ideas. Widening the scope of how we define our discipline and our work for undergraduates can facilitate this greater diffusion of ideas.

## Syllabi

I teach a First-Year Writing Seminar in political psychology in international relations, which is my primary research interest. My work applies theories and methods from social and cognitive psychology to understand decision making, especially in the realm of foreign policy.

My goal in teaching political psychology to freshman is to help them learn to write more clearly and coherently, and if possible, more easily, while learning something about political psychology. One of the ways that they can learn to do so is to read good writing. Truly great writing surpasses disciplinary boundaries; I have students read great writing in a variety of fields, including academic psychology, political science, and journalism. Having exemplary examples serves to both model and inspire excellence among students.

Reading is limited to seventy-five pages a week so as to allow ample time for writing. But this reading serves a very important function in terms of providing a common ground among students for class discussion and writing exercises. The writing assignments outlined below are examples of those I recently assigned to my first-year seminar.

One of the writing exercises that I found to be very helpful was to have students send e-mail essays once a week on the reading they have done. This worked particularly well for students who were shy or reluctant to talk in class. These e-mail essays not only gave students the opportunity to write about what they were reading and learning, but it also gave me feedback about questions that students might have had about the content of the readings, difficulties they might have had with a discussion or reading, and problems they might be having with their writing. Imposing length limits on the e-mail essays proved very fruitful both in helping students to become more concise in their comments and arguments and in reducing the time burden associated with grading.

The second way I encourage students to learn to become better writers is to give them numerous opportunities to practice their writing skills, in class as well as in homework assignments.

Depending on the week or the topic, I spent somewhere between one-third and one-half of the in-class time on writing exercises. Typically, these were focused on a particular technical aspect of writing, like topic sentences or essay organization. But after students had written a few papers, I asked them to bring in their past papers and find examples of some of the things we worked on in class in their own papers. Sometimes they found positive things in their writing, like the effective use of metaphors. Sometimes they were encouraged to find and rewrite sections of their paper that were not as carefully worded as they might have been. Students seemed to respond well to having the chance to directly incorporate the techniques they were learning into their own writing.

I found that one of the most effective exercises was having students read each other's papers. At first, I had students read and comment on each other's papers in class. Later in the semester, I had students take each other's papers home and write comments, including suggestions for constructive rewriting, which they gave to each other the during following class. Students then took their paper and their partner's comments home and rewrote their papers before turning them in for a grade. I found that students did much more extensive and effective revisions after these kinds of peer editing sessions than after receiving comments solely from me. They seemed to learn not only from the comments they received on their own work, but also by reading another student's work and noting what they thought was successful and what was not in the other's efforts.

## *Writing Assignments*

Over the course of the fifteen-week semester, students wrote six three- to five-page papers, two of which they were required to revise and resubmit. Only the revision receives a grade. I wanted the essay assignments to be relevant to the course material and to flow in some kind of sequence as well.

The first assignment started with something they should know pretty well: themselves. I asked them to write a political psychology of their own life. I wanted them to begin to think about how to analyze politics from a psychological perspective. My goal was to encourage students to start thinking about the kinds of questions that they might be interested in asking about a political leader that they hoped to understand, possibly someone they might consider voting for in the next election. I provided some guidelines in the assignment by telling them that they might want to mention their first political memory, or how they first became interested in politics. I encouraged them to describe their political beliefs, political issues they care about, or any political activities in which they have participated. In beginning to prompt students to make causal arguments, I asked them to consider whether they simply hold the political beliefs their parents espouse or whether their beliefs differ from their parents' beliefs and why that might be the case.

Students were eager to share these essays in class because they were interested in comparing their histories with those of other students. This essay served the purpose of providing substantive introduction among the members of the class without forcing anyone to disclose information they were uncomfortable sharing.

The second essay asked them to extend the first exercise to a contemporary political figure of their choice. By this time, students had read some psychobiographies of prominent political figures from the past and had some idea of the kind of topics that have been investigated. In this essay, students were not asked to do research on a political figure, but they are encouraged to think about the kinds of questions they would ask if they were to go about undertaking a psychological history of a political figure. The students were explicitly asked to discuss: the central question they were interested in asking about the person's life and political career; any hypotheses they might hold about the person's behavior; and the kind of evidence they would need to look for in order to answer their question.

The goal of this assignment was to get students to begin to see the biases they bring to their analyses and how these biases can influence the kind of questions they ask as well as the kind of conclusions they reach. I wanted them to begin to understand how others can use similar unspoken biases to persuade them in particular directions. In the process of discussing this assignment, I encouraged them to examine how the writers we read had been informed by particular theoretical positions, which then illuminate the kind of questions they ask and the kind of answers they seek. Once again, these readings serve as models for students to see how particular theoretical biases can either illuminate or restrict the insight gained into a specific person or event.

The third assignment asked students to compare two of the three psychobiographies that they read for class. They were asked to make a clear argument about which of the two they found more convincing and why. If they so desired, students could write their own interpretation of one of the people we read about and compare their own perspective to that offered by one of the authors.

The purpose of this exercise was to help students learn to separate fact from opinion in what they read and begin to think about how to use evidence persuasively. In this way, students also practiced comparing authors and arguments in writing.

The fourth assignment, along with the last, was one of the two most successful. I had students watch and discuss Leni Riefenstahl's 1934 pro-Nazi film, *Triumph of the Will*, in class. This movie was intended to portray a positive image of Adolph Hitler and the Nazi party. Riefenstahl devised innovative film techniques to invoke various verbal and nonverbal persuasion strategies to demonstrate Hitler's charisma and the compelling power of the Nazi party.

The purpose of this assignment was to encourage students to think about the psychological power of political propaganda. I wanted them to begin to explicitly recognize the way in which images and phrases are used by the media and other propaganda experts to influence their political, or other, beliefs and attitudes. Once students become more consciously aware of these techniques, how they are used, and what effect they have on a viewer or reader, they become more able to understand the appeal of seemingly incomprehensible positions. My hope was also that students would begin to develop some "screening" skills which, hopefully, will render them less susceptible to unwanted influence in their lives.

One of the students in my class won an honorable mention in the competition for best essays in freshman writing seminars in response to this assignment. His essay is a beautifully written example of the kind of thought and style I seek to encourage in my students. Setting out to answer the question he posed for himself, "How could an entire nation passively accept and willingly cooperate with an autocratic regime which genocidally slaughtered millions of innocent people?" Ari Zadok conducted a detailed analysis of how the subtle technical aspects of Riefenstahl's film, including the use of lighting, perspective, and movement, enhanced the early image of the Nazi party in Germany:

> Likewise, one of the most important lessons that Ms. Riefenstahl's film can teach us about propaganda is that the facts which you do not reveal are as important at the ones you do reveal. Manipulating public opinion is as much about hiding part of the truth as it is about showing people what you want them to see. Had *Triumph of the Will* shown Germans that the Nazi party was bent on global domination through military aggression, many citizens would have probably withheld their support. Had Hitler declared in all of his speeches that he was intent on exterminating millions of innocent people from the outset, it is a safe bet that he would have encoun-

tered far more opposition than he did. Instead, Hitler began drawing people's support through mainly positive propaganda such as *Triumph of the Will*'s message of German unity and strength. The tune of this "Pied Piper" seemed so sweet to the German public that they hailed him, literally, and soon were willing to follow him to the ends of the earth. By the time his enchanting tune had turned into a battle cry, they were so deeply under his charismatic spell that they were willing to contribute to the unthinkable.

I adapted the fifth assignment from one used by David Winter in his political psychology class at the University of Michigan. While some students originally balked at this assignment, it ended up being the most popular, and the one that students reported benefiting from the most. Students were asked to interview two people from among five different age cohorts. Students were encouraged to interview older relatives, particularly grandparents. They were instructed to ask their interviewees about their most important political memories and to ask for specific details about these memories. Students were told to ask their subjects about the events, how they understood and thought about them at the time, and what lessons they learned that they feel continue to apply today. Then the students were instructed to ask their subjects how they felt about any three of the following seven current political issues of their choosing: women's rights; race relations; gay rights; the appropriate international role of the United States; the Clinton presidency; and American economic issues. In their essays, students were directed to evaluate any connection they found between the generation of the person they interviewed, or the event that person remembered as significant, and the interviewee's subsequent political views.

The original goal of this assignment was to help students experience firsthand how historical experiences serve as analogies for current events in a personal psychological way. The biggest surprise was that while this objective was met, a much more important one was inadvertently achieved. Many students reported that this assignment afforded them with the first real opportunity they had had to talk to parents or grandparents about their lives as independent people. One student said that this was the first time his grandfather had talked to anyone about his experiences on D-Day. I was quite impressed with how this experience helped students better understand how people with intentions as honorable as their own could hold radically opposed political beliefs for good reasons that resulted from powerful personal experiences. In many cases, students achieved a much deeper understanding of their parents' or grandparents' positions on issues that had previously seemed incomprehensible to them. More than any other exercise I have witnessed, this assignment instilled a genuine sense of humility in some students who came to recognize, for the first time, that current political events in their lives might shape the formation of their attitudes and beliefs in ways that they might not fully appreciate, just as has happened to their ancestors. Although the particular content might differ from the views of their parents or grandparents, students found new respect for the similarity of the process of socialization.

The final assignment asked students to compare John F. Kennedy's 1961 Inaugural Address with William Jefferson Clinton's 1993 Inaugural Address. They were advised to discuss specific similarities or differences in content, style, images, values, attitudes, beliefs, perceptions, or issues. Students were encouraged to speculate about what they thought were the reasons for these contrasts.

This assignment was designed to provide a culmination for the class. I wanted students to be able to demonstrate that they knew how to: extract the implicit assumptions in someone else's argument; recognize propagandistic elements in the speeches; and think about why and how two leaders contrast in their approach to the same task. In short, I wanted students to write a persuasive, coherent argument demonstrating that they knew why they thought the way they did about the psychology of politics.

The goal of integrating writing and pedagogy within a specific disciplinary culture, in this case international relations, can be challenging at times. The primary academic goal of publishing in professional journals often requires a style that is antithetical to that which serves the interests and purposes of undergraduates. Yet the task of communicating effectively with undergraduates about the interest, importance, and relevance of a particular field is central to generating student engagement in both substance and style. Recognizing that students learn from the process, practice, and habit of writing as much as from the content of the course exercises and assignments helps teachers to interweave goals that might otherwise pull in opposite directions. Not all students will become professional academics. But all students will benefit from becoming better writers. And, in my discipline, they will hopefully benefit from learning to be more active and sophisticated consumers of political information as well.

Teaching writing in context provides a challenge and an opportunity. The challenge encourages teachers to keep the disciplinary learning and the writing related in an explicit, meaningful, and relevant way. The opportunity inspires teachers to model and nurture mutually reinforcing style and substance.

# Translation and Appropriation in Foreign Language and Writing Classrooms

JOHN WHITMAN

Linguistics

℘ This chapter grew out of the task of designing and teaching a First-Year Writing Seminar on translation at Cornell University in summer–fall 1998. I brought to the task no more direct experience than the memory of a delightful but ineffective expository writing class taken as a college freshman. The instructor, a novelist and short-story writer whose name I have not seen in print since, left one dark, vivid image from a piece of his own writing that he read in class. In the twenty-five years since, I have accumulated some experience teaching foreign languages. I was curious to find out how much these two kinds of teaching have to do with one another.

Translation in the general sense of language appropriation—giving or gaining control over texts in a previously inaccessible linguistic form—is the basic activity of all language workers—the community of interpreters, editors, translators, scholars, teachers, reporters, all manner of webcrafters—who deal everyday with two or more languages. It is also a shared part of the cultural experience of all persons trained in the humanities or social sciences, even in the home countries of the English hegemony. Outside those countries, of course, it is common to the background of all intellectuals. My project in this essay is to show how this broad sense of translation provides models for a type of language appropriation that I believe to be important for teaching academic writing.

First let me briefly develop the comparison between the teaching of foreign languages and teaching writing as these activities are normally constructed in the university. The contemporary versions of both kinds of teaching focus on procedural knowledge ("knowledge how") rather than declarative knowledge ("knowledge what"). It may seem that textbook-codified declarative knowledge (three thousand Chinese characters, the gender classes of German, "vocabulary") is at the core of foreign language learning. This is false. As Chomsky has remarked, the most important facts about the grammar of any human language are not contained in textbooks for foreign learners, because those facts are universal. The difference between lexical tools for foreign language learning (glossaries, dictionaries) and those used by students of writing in their native language is a difference of degree: the dictionaries are usually larger in the latter case. In fact the emphasis on procedural knowledge or "communicative competence" in contemporary foreign language teaching has led to a downgrading of the importance of textbooks, just as textbooks are rarely at the center of a writing course.

When textbooks are used in a writing course, the bulk of the declarative knowledge they set out to impart concerns matters of usage that are determined by sociocultural context. The same is true of foreign language textbooks. Besides listing and explaining vocabulary (something also done in certain kinds of texts for teaching writing), much of the factual information contained in foreign language texts has to do with how context conditions language use. Consider an example first from a language text, Jorden and Noda's modeling of the contexts for direct-style copula in Japanese (1984, 219):

|       |     |              |     |     |                  |
|-------|-----|--------------|-----|-----|------------------|
| 2'    | (J) | *Hontoo?*    |     | (N) | *Ho 'ntoo dà yo.* |
| 2"    | (J) | *Hontoo?*    |     | (N) | *Hontoo yo.*     |
| 2     | (J) | Is that true? |     | (N) | It's true.       |

In these four models, built around the word *hontoo,* "true," the direct-style copula *dà* occurs only in 2'(N). The absence of the copula in the (J) sentences is what we are accustomed to call a "grammatical rule." The absence of *dà* in 2"(N), on the other hand, establishes a sociocultural difference between this utterance and 2'(N). *Dà* is a marker of what Jorden and Noda call "blunt-style" (228): its presence marks a cluster of boundaries implicating gender, discourse type, class, and social role. It is not the job of a teacher to teach which of these patterns is "correct," for they all are. Her job is to make learners aware of the sociocultural dimensions of choice.

The factual information about language in writing textbooks is mostly like this. It also tends to focus on choices governed by sociocultural context. I selected for my course a book called *Style: Ten Lessons in Clarity and Grace*, by Joseph Williams (1996). I came to admire this book, although my students abhorred it. Williams's stance is that of shibboleth-debunker. Consider Williams's debunking of a classic shibboleth, the prohibition against beginning a sentence in written English with a conjunction. Williams puts this in the category of "folklore," a matter of choice: "not rules at all, but folklore that you can choose to ignore, unless you are writing for someone who can exact from you whatever kind of writing that person idiosyncratically prefers" (22). Williams ratifies his debunking with examples "from writers who are of substantial intellectual and scholarly stature or who, on matters of usage, are reliable archconservatives" (22). His source contra the conjunction shibboleth is a formidable one:

> *But*, it will be asked, is tact not an individual gift, therefore highly variable in its choices?
>
> *And* if that is so, what guidance can a manual offer, other than that of its author's prejudices—mere impressionism?
>
> Wilson Follett, Modern American Usage: A Guide, edited<br>and completed by Jacques Barzun et al (emphasis added).

Well, if Jacques Barzun did it, it must be OK . . . My students were happy to accept the dismissal of the conjunction proscription as folklore; they had already received the same message from high school and middle school teachers. But the following sample of their procedural knowledge in action shows that their instruction was less sensitive than what Jorden and Noda provide for Japanese:

> In capitalism, all the resources and the factors of production are owned by private individuals or firms. *And* they are free to use these resources to undertake production or to dispose of them. The system of price mechanism distributes scarce factors of production among entrepreneurs and allows the distribution of scarce goods and services among consumers. (Emphasis added.)

The point here is that the usage in question is neither good nor bad, from a normative standpoint: it is register-sensitive, to use a favorite term of sociolinguists, where high register includes written styles like academic writing. Sentence-initial conjunctions signal what might be called the "aggressive connectivity" of, for example, a hot-under-the collar editorial writer. They emphasize (and risk overemphasizing) the importance of the connection between the sentence they head and preceding discourse. They are characteristic of hortatory contexts, oratory and debate, more broadly spoken registers and their written imitations. The Follett/Barzun example involves an imputed question, and is thus perfectly appropriate. My student's example involves an attempt at nonhortatory academic writing, and thus comes dangerously close to unwarranted transgression of a register boundary.

So much for the common focus on procedural knowledge. The emphasis on knowledge "how" in the two enterprises is parallel and obvious. Let us turn to what I think is the most important difference in the characteristic attitudes toward language of these two professions.

On campuses that have a foreign language building, or even a floor, the difference between this space and the space consigned to writing teachers is obvious. Foreign languages occupy a decorated space: travel posters, Peace Corps recruitment brochures, exotic scripts, SCOLA schedules. These are the trappings of a serious enterprise: the culture of foreign language teaching is based on appropriation of something belonging to the Other, or appropriation of Others. The strong orientalist tradition in Asian language teaching exemplifies the first kind of adventure. The missionary-like commitment of certain countries to support instruction abroad of their national languages (the Alliance Française, the Goethe Institute, the Japan Foundation) as a virtual arm of foreign policy—almost as a type of surrogate colonial activity—exemplifies the second. Many students, especially the best students, are drawn to foreign language classes, particularly in the case of the exotics, the "LCTs" (less commonly taught languages), by the prospect of the first kind of appropriation. Both teacher and learner acknowledge that the learner owns nothing of the target language as beginner (*pace* Chomsky, because here we are talking about ratified ownership, not knowledge); the various stages of learning are recognized as a process of gaining possession ("After two summers at Middlebury, she has beautiful Arabic"). It is this frank, shared understanding of the process as a matter of giving and gaining ownership that confers on teachers the ready right to set standards and test mercilessly, and motivates learners to take special action if they desire real competence rather than mere certification (thus language houses, conversation partners, and summers in Seville).

The tradition in writing education is very different. A likely majority of freshman in writing classes, if asked, would maintain that they already know how to write. It is commonplace for a writing teacher to deny this ("None of them could write before they took my course"), but even so, the discourse of writing instruction tends to refer to remediation or honing of skills already partly possessed. More importantly than this, the kind of language that writing courses set out to teach (academic writing, for the purposes of this essay), is not regarded as an original possession of some Other. The cultural model for teaching and learning writing at the university level is not one of appropriation, but rather what we might call the Initiation Model. It is not unlike the model associated with activities such as learning to drive or gaining individual membership in the family country club. University-level writing skills are among the many perceived birthrights of middle-class children in the United States. Like pre-initiates in other societies, they are not expected to acquire this possession without training and the ordinary process of conferral, but it is theirs to acquire, if they follow the prescribed steps.

More than thirty years ago, the British sociologist Basil Bernstein caused a firestorm of controversy with a series of writings claiming that the spoken and written language produced by the working-class and middle-class children in the British schools he surveyed were qualitatively different. Bernstein character-ized the language of working-class children (and their parents) as "restricted codes": ritualistic, nonanalytic, and limited in rhetorical scope. He claimed that the educational success of middle-class children derived directly from their mastery of "elaborated codes": rhetorically flexible, adapted for analysis, de-bate, persuasion. Bernstein's dubious methodology and focus on qualitative difference was attacked by, among others, Chomsky and the American socio-linguist William Labov. Labov's article, "The Logic of Nonstandard English," remains a classic in the egalitarian tradition in American linguistics. But in a larger sense, both Bernstein and his critics missed the crucial point behind the differences in language-related education performance that Bernstein studied. This point has come up again in the more recent Ebonics debate. The language of school is the language of power, and that is the language of the middle class, conferred upon middle-class students by birthright or by initiation. It is only for outsiders—nonnative speakers, speakers of different class or ethnic varieties of language—that learning to speak and write in school is considered to be a mat-ter of appropriation.

To me, this distinction is a matter beyond pedagogy. It is a matter of poli-tics and morality. Assumptions about ownership of language are deeply embed-ded in all levels of our educational culture. There is no straightforward way to remove the birthright and even the stakes, except by changing the game. One change is to make the target not the language owned by some, but rather variet-ies of language that are up for grabs. From this comes the project of making everybody a translator.

Let me now turn to a few details about my class. In the event, my students all came to the class as capable writers. The many grades of nonnative speaker among them included two who were, in many ways, the strongest writers, from opposite ends of the Indian subcontinent. My class had the prosaic title Trans-lation and Writing Skill, but I made clear in the course description that I could not expect any particular level of foreign language ability, and certainly not competence in a single shared foreign language. As it turned out my students had a wonderful assortment of languages among them: Spanish, French, Chi-nese (one native Cantonese speaker, one seminative Mandarin speaker, one wonderfully sensitive learner from a California high school), Korean, Urdu, and

Bengali. So we were able to translate, in the conventional sense. The more challenging trick was to progress beyond that kind of activity to the core task of appropriating English.

The matter of appropriatory versus initiatory thinking about writing came up right away in the matter of composition analysis. The Williams text, which I used off and on during the first eight weeks of the course, is heavily analytic, in a manner attractive to a syntactician but repellent to recent victims of even half-heartedly Thistlebottomian high-school English teachers. Williams focuses on the uses and the dangers of particular syntactic and rhetorical devices: nominalization is useful for conciseness, but dangerous (as Orwell pointed out, politically dangerous) as a potential expedient for hiding agents and objects of actions.

This discussion is inherently boring. It is somewhat boring coming from Orwell, but "nominalization," "verb," etc., are terminal eye-glazers coming from a textbook. Our initial use of Williams was initiatory: we read the analysis (at least I did), we discussed it in class, we nodded our heads. Then we hit upon a somewhat more involved way of applying Williams's lessons. For example, in his discussion of Orwell's point about nominalization, Williams presented us with the two juxtaposed sentences below (1996, 47).

7a. Our lack of data prevented evaluation of state actions in targeting funds to areas in need of assistance.

7b. Because we lacked data, we could not evaluate whether the state had targeted funds to areas that needed assistance.

(7b) appears with a checkmark. My students sat, too polite to say what they were thinking ("Yeah, yeah, (7a) is turgid; sure, Prof., it's bad because it uses nouns instead of verbs, can we go now?") We divided up into teams, forgot about (7b), and attempted to write our translations of (7a) on the blackboards around the room. As the French and Spanish versions went up, I began to worry that colleagues from the Modern Languages Department might somehow stumble upon our classroom and blow my fraudulent cover. I cannot resist sharing the work of the French team: "(7a-F) Notre manque des donnés nous a empêché de faire une evaluation des procès d'état pour donner les fonds aux programmes qui en ont besoin." Meanwhile the Mandarin, Urdu, Bengali, and Korean teams had simply given up, writing: "(7a): most languages of the world, especially those relatively unscathed by the tradition of translation from aggressively nominalizing texts (e.g., Marx), simply balk at promiscuous use of inanimate agents; this is all the more so of the language of immigrant families or high school French and Spanish class." The expedient of intervening, so to speak, with actual translation activity in this case was successful for us because: it required doing something nonmechanical and difficult; it required analysis; and it legitimized analytic metalanguage. Thus, on the last point: "nominalization" and "verb" are pedantic labels within the high school English class experience, but in talk among translators, or for the Mandarin translator to explain her problem to the Spanish team, they are valued technical terms.

In retrospect, the class would have benefited from more conventional translation; I had not anticipated that my students would be so good. Translation is straightforwardly appropriatory. This fact accounts for its only quasi-respectable status as a Western cultural activity, needed but somewhat loathed, like leatherworking in Buddhist societies. (For a recent exposition of the translator's permanently marginal yet indispensable position, see Lawrence Venuti's 1998 book *The Scandals of Translation*.) My students produced some of their best writing in their translations. They produced these pieces with a sense of ownership (I've got Frida Kahlo—you've got Tagore) that shared writing assignments on our novel (*Lolita*) did not elicit in them.

The main challenge of our course was to transfer the activity of language appropriation to writing entirely within the world of English. To this end we did a number of rewriting activities, in addition to the normal editing and redrafting activities of a writing course and our perhaps less normal experiments in rewriting one another's texts. I will describe just one, built around three Orwell pieces, all chestnuts: the Burma essays "Shooting an Elephant" and "A Hanging," and "The English Language," alluded to above for its pronouncements on nominalization. This last essay was laid to rest in a parodic recasting in "verse." The teams assigned the Burma essays rewrote them as skits.

The skits were performed twice, both times to general hilarity, the second time for videotaping. I had not understood how foreign Orwell's stance and language would be to my students. They pulled off a bold, brilliant job of appropriation in rendering his essays as performance. The basic theme of the Burma essays is the idea of the European as a prisoner of his power: Eric Blair must shoot the elephant as a matter of face, despite the fact that it is the wrong thing to do. At an inexplicit level, the essays are about alienation in the service of power, but they also show Orwell's deep, stark, absolutely unbridgeable separation from the non-Europeans around him. My students noticed much more than I ever had about Orwell's language (that odd combination of Etonspeak, prissier to them than to me, mixed with occasional tough-guy modernist gambits such as second-person narration).

The "Shooting an Elephant" team cast a Pakistani woman as Orwell/Blair. Dressed in trenchcoat and hat, she had the best accent for the part and a flawless sense of irony. Both skits were narrated. Let us look briefly at the scene where the elephant is slain, contrasting Orwell's text with the work of the Orwell translator team. "Orwell(tr)" designates Orwell in the trenchcoat, the translated Orwell.

ORWELL: But at that moment I glanced round at the crowd that had followed me. It was an immense crowd, two thousand at the least and growing every minute. It blocked the road for a long distance on either side. I looked at the sea of yellow faces above the garish clothes—faces all happy and excited at this bit of fun, all certain that the elephant was going to be shot. . . . And it was at this moment, as I stood there with the rifle in my hands, that I first grasped the hollowness, the futility of the white man's dominion in the East. Here was I, the white man with his gun, seemingly the leading actor of the piece; but in reality I was only an absurd puppet pushed to and fro by the will of those yellow faces behind. I perceived in this moment that when the white man turns tyrant it is his own freedom that he destroys . . .

It was perfectly clear to me what I ought to do. I ought to walk up to within, say, twenty-five yards of the elephant and test his behaviour. If he charged I could shoot, if he took no notice of me it would be safe to leave him until the mahout came back. But I also knew that was going to do no such thing. I was a poor shot with a rifle and the ground was soft mud into which one would sink at every step. If the elephant charged and I missed him, I should have about as much chance as a toad under a steamroller.

ORWELL TRANSLATORS: *[Orwell(tr) transfers rifle over shoulder, uneasiness over his face. The group trudges across the soggy field.]*

*[Elephant enters, side facing Orwell(tr) and Burmans, tearing up bunches of grass and beating them against his knees to clean them and stuffing them into his mouth. Elephant does not seem to care about things around him.]*

*[Orwell(tr) halts on a road and sees the elephant; narrator joins him.]*

NARRATOR: As soon as I saw the elephant, I knew with perfect certainty that I ought not shoot him. It was a serious and costly matter to shoot an elephant. From that distance, he looked harmless as a cow, so I decided that I would watch him for a little while to make sure that he did not go savage again, and then go home.

*[Crowd gathers around Orwell(tr), chattering about the shooting.]*

ORWELL(TR): *[Looks around.]* These people came to see me shoot the elephant. I have to shoot the elephant—they expect it of me. I am a white man with my gun, standing in front of an unarmed native crowd, seemingly the lead actor in this play.

NARRATOR: But in reality I was only an absurd puppet pushed to and fro by the will of those yellow faces behind.

ORWELL(TR): When the white man turns tyrant it is his own freedom that he destroys. To rule, we must impress the natives, and so we must do what the natives expect of us. I have got to shoot the elephant. To walk away now—the crowd would laugh at me. My whole life, every white man's life in the East, is one long struggle not to be laughed at.

NARRATOR: But I did not want to shoot the elephant. It seemed to me that it would be murder to shoot him. Besides, there was the elephant's owner to consider . . .

ORWELL(TR): But I have got to act quickly. *[Burmans enter; Orwell(tr) turns to ask them.]* How has the elephant been behaving?

BURMAN #1: He takes no notice of you if you leave him alone.

BURMAN #2: He might charge you if you get too close. *[Burmans exit.]*

NARRATOR: It was clear that I ought to walk up to the elephant to test his behavior.

ORWELL(TR): I will do no such thing. I am a poor shot, and if I missed, I would have as much chance as a toad under a steamroller.

The line about the toad under a steamroller is not particularly remarkable in Orwell's text, but in the mouth of Orwell(tr) it was a showstopper, as she trained her umbrella on the tall blond elephant from engineering. Our translators perceived that Orwell uses two first-person narrators, the one in front of the movie camera and the one discussing matters "in reality." It was their brilliant accomplishment to establish a dialogue between these two, leaving past tense to the latter, and distributing the discussion of the White Man's Burden over both. They could not, or perhaps chose not to, replicate the loneliness of the original Orwell/Blair as self-portrayer or portrayed.

Translation as imitation, to use Robert Lowell's word, or remaking, is a favorite twentieth-century device, particularly in poetry and film. Rigid ideas about language boundary and ownership restrict this activity to foreign language originals in the former case; film exploits the ancient tradition of dramatic adaptation, and it was this that we used for our Orwell skits as well. It is helpful for me, in retrospect, to contrast the success of this activity with the general failure of everything associated with our reading of *Lolita*. *Lolita* was the worst possible choice for a text in a class with our objectives: Nabokov is a model of greedy appropriation, but the other half of his project is to make himself completely unappropriable. Having read the book, oohed and aahed, there was nothing more for us to do.

In a second running of this course, I would encourage my students to rewrite published material, to appropriate even more boldly. The foreign language classroom provides many more models of this sort. I recall a wonderful Chinese class where the students' task was to generate, taking turns, a continuous narrative based on the one-panel, uncaptioned *Family Circus* cartoons. It is a mistake to think that the difference in skill level makes this type of activity inapplicable to the writing classroom. The major lesson that foreign language learning has for the teaching of writing is the central understanding that any type of language learning involves establishing ownership, what I have called appropriation.

# Writing Religion at Cornell

## (Reflections of a Penitent Professor)

ROSS BRANN

Near Eastern Studies

&#8984; I have an admission to make: I have come to think of "writing" as an ersatz-religion at Cornell University.

Religionists will tell you they study belief-systems held by communities of adherents and that apart from their particular doctrines and hermeneutic procedures, such systems exhibit some kind of ritual praxis involving an array of obligations and prohibitions. By this standard, the unusual fellowship of individuals associated with the John S. Knight Institute for Writing in the Disciplines in the College of Arts and Sciences at Cornell University looks and sounds a lot like a religious community. Their religion is, quite simply, "writing," and its rites are elaborated in various prescriptions for and warnings against licit and illicit practices in the university classroom. As inscribed in the group's written dispensation and manual of the discipline, *Indispensable Reference for Teachers of First-Year Writing Seminars,* to follow the message to the letter holds out the promise of deliverance from the spiritual scourge of the academy that is poor pedagogy; to reject the creed or abandon the faith to one's colleagues consigns the instructor to an oblivion in which good teaching does not exist but bewildered students abound.

A few years ago I fell under the spell of this revelation and the sway of its devotees at Cornell. It wasn't that I had become a lost professorial soul searching for new meaning in the academy or because I was so completely jaded by the university's culture of incessant complaint that I desperately sought out some new, alternative source of illumination. Rather, it was my apparent destiny to be recruited for a mysterious venture called "The Summer Faculty Writing Seminar." "What exactly does it involve?" I asked somewhat sheepishly. The voice of authority on the telephone intoned: "You will assist the John S. Knight Institute in training and mentoring graduate students (who were to be sent to teach their own First-Year Writing Seminars the following fall semester), teach a section of Critical Reading and Writing, attend lectures and participate in discussions with colleagues on the role of writing in the university classroom, and meet for individual weekly sessions with a Master Writing Teacher." The latter, masquerading as a professor of English, turned out to be the functional equivalent of either a law-giving prophet or high priest. Since (the telephone voice of) the high-ranking priestess promised to share with me a portion of the Institute's sacerdotal emoluments in return for submitting to her fellows' indoctrination and for my subsequent service, I embraced the burden of these commandments, although not without the trepidation expected of a proselyte.

The Summer Faculty Writing Seminar's devotional regimen proved challenging and engaging as I discovered that talking religiously with colleagues about the roles of writing in the classroom, fine-tuning meaningful assignment sequences, sharpening the formulation of assignments themselves, and meditating on the critical function of student revisions effectively cut across the academic disciplines in a way few subjects or methods can. Although I piously encouraged students to regard writing as the single most important skill they could learn at Cornell, truth be told, I had never thought seriously about writing in the classroom before. In the course of that summer seminar, I came to appreciate that writing was not properly considered a skill at all but a significant, transformative vehicle for thinking and learning itself. And it turned out that the pleasure I take in challenging students' conventional wisdom on the subjects I teach and my avowed interest in the process as much as the substance of student learning made it rewarding to incorporate more and more varied student writing in my syllabus.

Now that I am no longer the neophyte and am deemed sufficiently worthy to traverse the edifying path that is Writing at Cornell, it appears I am obliged to share some narrative reflections on my quest to become a committed instructor of writing. However, I must confess concern lest too much of the esoteric lore passed on to me discreetly be conveyed in so public a forum as this book. In any case, I designed the first lesson for the section of Critical Reading and Writing assigned to me for the aforementioned summer session hoping to establish an Eriksonian sense of "basic trust" among the students, the teaching assistant, and the instructor. I also hoped to introduce the class to the religious cultures of the Middle East in a way that would draw them out as participants and draw their hidden assumptions out into the open. Accordingly, I asked the students, a diverse group of high school seniors with a sprinkling of Cornell freshmen and sophomores from around the globe, to volunteer the first thing to come to mind in connection with the term "Middle East." They responded with a list of ostensibly innocuous and wholly anticipated particulars and appellations such as "camels," "ancient ruins," "religion," "oil," and "Islam," as well as some predictable concepts and labels neither benign nor innocent, namely, "hostages," "terrorists," "religious fanatics," "gender discrimination," "hatred for Western civilization," all of which were, of course, related closely to the first items mentioned. Together, we rearranged the responses by category (historical, political, religious, economic, cultural). Just as I was poised to take the class in Socratic fashion through the *American* culturally and politically determined nature of the entire roster, one of the students who happened to be from abroad blurted out: "Body smell!" Astonished by this last-minute addition to the list and rendered mute along with the class, I somehow managed to collect myself and proceed with the discussion (of which I recall very little), as though nothing extraordinary or unsettling had happened. All the while my mind was fixed on what had been uttered. How should a teacher respond to such a provocation without reacting impulsively and humiliating the offending student? Doesn't singling out a student in this way, however justified it might seem, serve notice to the other students to be careful of what they think, say, and write, lest they too be taken to task in public? The Master Writing Teacher-cum-Priest or Prophet wasn't scheduled to receive me for my weekly consultation for another two days, so I was on my own. Overnight I reflected carefully how to turn this unforeseen crisis of the first day of class into an opportunity to broaden the course's horizons of writing and learning.

By the next morning, I had devised two exercises for engaging the class in an extended discussion of the common human complicity in cultural prejudice and judgmental misapprehension. We would return surreptitiously to the "smelly body" topos in the guise of the less inflammatory matter of cultural differences regarding food. The class wrote out typical menus from their respective cultures' cuisines. In the course of the ensuing discussion, it was apparent that what was delectable to some was downright loathsome to others. I posed the question whether it was possible for us to determine which cuisine could boast truly heavenly victuals and was deserving of reverence and which dietary habits and preferences were odious and demonic. In one voice the students asserted how *arbitrary* culinary differences seemed to be. And soon it dawned on them that cultural preferences regarding odor were in fact no different than foods in this respect.

They were then asked to narrate in writing a brief account of a misunderstanding based on culture, ethnicity, religion, gender, or age, if possible using a personal experience and relating the incident from the vantage of the other person. The students' alternately disturbing and stirring anecdotes and the articulate manner in which they related them to their classmates allowed a moment of unusual honesty to transform a group of strangers into a class with a shared experience and common agenda. The classroom incident had been a godsend. It made me aware that this group of students needed to approach the cultural and religious conflicts at the heart of the course by getting *inside* them, that is, by stepping into other personae and endeavoring to develop their distinctive voices. The course material and the peculiar resistance this band of students put up to it thus dictated the nature of the classroom activities and writing assignments. The experience of those first two days also taught me to treat any course syllabus I might ever prepare as a work-in-progress and not as an inviolate Text that could brook no emendation.

The class settled into a semester-long examination of conflicting cultural perceptions. The students eventually acquired a perspective on religious contention and cultural frictions from other times and places, and they developed an awareness of how the historical situation of culture informs the viewpoint of contemporary readers as much as the texts and their original and subsequent audiences. We moved into a discussion of the outcry over Salman Rushdie's *The Satanic Verses* for which students studied passages from the Qur'an and prepared (written) position papers for a series of formal debates staged in class. Next, we tackled paradigmatic tales involving gender and sexuality from the *1001 Nights* and struggled with the notions that every religious culture but one's own is insufficiently sensitive to gender issues. Posting a photographic portrait of a Muslim woman (in traditional dress) who seemed to peer at the class through the narrow eye-slits of her head covering was a particularly effective in-class writing exercise. The students' written extensions and embellishments on the introduction "I am Fatimah, a Muslim woman . . ." stimulated give and take and generated controversy lasting for several sessions but also seemed to take the class back a few steps to its previous sense of cultural privilege.

Fortuitously, I also uncovered in my files a slightly dated travel piece from the *New York Times* written by a sanctimonious American journalist touring Afghanistan. The students drafted blistering critiques of his smug representation of American society as completely free of gender inequality as opposed to Muslim society. I had an inkling, based on their previous behavior, that they would readily confront someone else's self-serving views before turning to their own. Based on our work with selected readings from *The Crusades through Arab Eyes* and the historical novel *Leo Africanus*, both by the Lebanese writer Amin Maalouf, the writing assignments shifted over the remaining weeks, by turns, from textual exposition, rhetorical exercises such as on-the-scene reportage for

the Crusades and the downfall of Muslim Granada in 1492, to analytical the-
matic essays. The material and assignments were building toward (somewhat)
more familiar contemporary depictions of Middle Eastern religion, culture, and
politics inscribed in *Lawrence of Arabia* and *The Battle of Algiers*. For that final
assignment sequence the class learned how to "read" and analyze films as arti-
facts of culture much as it had read texts. It was especially valuable for me to
experience just how energetically and creatively this generation of students responds to visual images as opposed to textual representations.

☞ Once the professor is initiated into contemplating the intimate relationship
between teaching, writing, and learning, there is simply no turning back to a life
of pedagogic transgression and the conduct of business as usual in the classroom. At summer's end, my thoughts, therefore, turned to the academic year
and how to tap into the possibilities writing offers for catalyzing learning in my
fall and spring semester courses. But is it possible to transfer the critical reading
and writing experience of a First-Year Writing Seminar into the format imposed
by a lecture hall? How often does the lecturer leave the classroom feeling up-
lifted by his own eloquence and command of material and, at the same time,
completely unaware of what the students were really thinking? The director of
the Writing in the Majors program, a singularly inspired and zealous advocate
of the religion of writing, generously encouraged me to reconceptualize and redesign the assignments for an upper-division "lecture" course on culture, religion, and society in Islamic Spain. The course's multiple cross-listings (Near
Eastern Studies, Comparative Literature, Religious Studies, Romance Studies,
and Jewish Studies) typically attract an extremely diverse group (between
twenty and fifty students) that mirrors, as it were, the ethnic, religious, cultural,
and social divisions of the subject studied. The different cultural and religious
"baggage" and expectations students bring with them makes it a challenge for
the instructor to harness the ensuing friction and serve as a mediator of the material as well as the students' contending religious, cultural, and political commitments as readers.

In reflecting on the previous incarnation of this course and the prescriptions and proscriptions set forth in the John S. Knight Institute's manual of discipline, it occurred to me that conventional undergraduate assignments (midterm, final examination, and term paper) do not always succeed in energizing
the kinds of thinking we look for from our students. And when their submitted
essays and papers fail to meet our high expectations, we reflexively regard it as
the disappointing result of the students' deficient effort, depleted energy, or divided attention. Often however, the problem really lies in the instructor's formulation of the assignment and the clarity and meaningfulness of the questions

posed. The timing of the assignments is also problematic. They commonly punctuate two or three intense moments in the semester but provide the students with no writing to undertake and the instructor nothing to evaluate in between.

I stumbled upon an unexpected solution to this problem. One afternoon, my elementary school–aged son happened to show me something called his "day book." It was a collection of mostly short entries he kept about the work of his "literature group" as well as his musings about his ongoing reading for pleasure. He would submit his journal weekly, and his teacher would respond with written notes of her own, typically in the form of encouraging comments or follow-up questions. This procedure links the acts of reading, thinking, and writing. It also affords the teacher periodic and intimate looks at the student's progress and provides the student regular and immediate feedback, extending the dialog between student and teacher beyond the confines of the classroom.

There is no reason to believe that we cannot incorporate similar methods of instruction at the university level, so long as we remain open-minded about how students actually learn and imaginative about how we teach. I therefore required the students in the Islamic Spain course to maintain a "reflective journal" in which they recorded their responses to the readings and other course materials (music, maps, slides, videos, and the spectacular course Web site designed by an enterprising and gifted teaching assistant) and their reactions to our combustible classroom discussions, including the instructor's contribution. The journal entries had no requisite page length or specified topics, although occasionally questions for thought on a session's reading were distributed or posted via the class e-mail list and course Web site. Teaching assistant support from the Writing in the Majors program enabled me to read and respond biweekly to these journals, and afforded me routine and continuous access to the inner learning experiences of the students as the course unfolded. Apart from the journals, review essays and mini–research papers replaced examinations and term papers.

A particularly electric moment transpired one day when Islamic Spain was opened to a group of visiting alumni. The syllabus had us reading and analyzing, among other things, a two-line Andalusi Arabic "love poem" (in translation). The transfixed poet narrates a scene in a mosque wherein he observes and ogles an unusually handsome young man bowing in prayer. Our guests were hooked on what they regarded as the lyric's beautiful spiritual dimension; the undergraduates were equally caught up by the poet's seemingly insolent preoccupation with the pleasures of the body at the wrong time and in the wrong place. It was one of those rare occasions when the instructor is content to step back and permit an animated discussion to run itself. Nearly every student in the class voiced exasperation in their journals for our visitors' blatant "misreading" of the verses. The interpretive impasse the session produced thus led us almost naturally into a study of the genre of Arabic "meditative poems," in which mature poets reflect upon the vanities of earthly existence and renounce the pleasures of their misspent youth (e.g., love and love poetry). The students ultimately expressed a renewed appreciation for poetry in light of the controversy our textual "exquisite trifle" had generated and the ambiguities of reading it revealed among different readers. Subsequently, I also found them trying their own hand at textual analysis of short poems in their reflective journals.

Classes vary from year to year as much as individual students differ, and it is not always splendor and light in Islamic Spain. In its most recent iteration, for instance, I found it necessary to take even the sharpest students through some "remedial" measures before engaging them in literary inquiry and cultural analysis. Many insisted they had been taught in high school honors English to frame their *explication du texte* with "the poem says . . ." They seemed to chafe when I resolutely corrected such phrases in their journals. As the offenses mounted in number we debated whether one could translate a poem into prose without rendering poetry meaningless. It was time to set the syllabus aside and apply the approach signaled by John Ciardi's *How a Poem Means* to the Arabic lyric, even if it meant temporarily neglecting much of its literary, historical, and social contexts.

With many more opportunities to write than are commonplace in upper-division humanities courses, the students took greater risks as writers. In the journals they seemed to worry far less about tailoring their discursive prose to the deliberate (i.e., ponderous) and dense (i.e., opaque and full of jargon) style they suppose their instructors prefer. Instead, they intuitively prospered as writers from the *semblance* of informality and freedom the genre bestowed on them. Occasionally, this resulted in sustained passages of lyric charm, brilliant insights of cultural analysis, or students taking conceptual leaps by making unexpected connections between texts or ideas. The journals seemed to represent a clear case of form conferring substance, and the entries reflected the students' alchemical transformation as writers. The adepts and illuminati of the Knight Institute at Cornell regard my experience with the reflective journals as evidence of Peter Elbow's "first-order thinking," in which "unplanned narrative and descriptive exploratory writing (or speaking) will almost invariably lead the person spontaneously to formulate *conceptual* insights that are remarkably shrewd . . . when someone manages to let the words, images and ideas choose more words, images and ideas . . ." (Elbow 1986, 56). The greater challenge was to foster writing assignments that would bridge the journals' flashes of intelligence and their lucid, seemingly effortless writing with more sustained systematic inquiry in analytic prose form.

In accordance with Elbow's notion of "second-order thinking" and its related methodical writing procedures, I encouraged students to revisit their most inspired journal entries and to revise and expand them into essays. One highly enterprising student was taken by the imaginative variations apparent in accounts of the Muslim conquest of Iberia in 711. He explored the literary and constructed nature of these materials in his journal and then in a paper went on to analyze in great detail similar literary and cultural transactions pertaining to Muslims he found in *Poema de mio Cid* and *Chanson de Roland*. To underscore his thesis regarding the evolving social meaning of orally transmitted materials, he drew upon an example from American popular culture in the textual history of Woody Guthrie's "This Land Is Your Land." Originally a song of social protest decrying relief lines and private property, it appeared in 1940 under the ironic title "God Blessed America." Later, with the politically charged lyrics expunged, the revised song became a folk anthem of American patriotism. The unusually bold turn the student's essay took had been inspired by reading a chapter of Maria Menocal's *Shards of Love* (1994) (required for the course), which explores the relationship between the classical Persian legend *Majnun Layla* and Eric Clapton's legendary rock song "Layla." With our avenue of inquiry thus attuned to correlating past and present, the students and I discovered that the power of religion, the power of the word, and the power of writing converge in Islamic Spain.

☞   If, God forbid, you should ever stray from the straight and narrow of this belief system at Cornell, you can be sure that one of the revered masters of the John S. Knight Institute will learn of it and you will have to answer for your transgressions. It sometimes seems as though they have an infinite number of vigilant eyes and ears trained everywhere you turn on campus. Once you have completed the novice's right of passage and gained admittance into the community of writing teachers, you are still never off the hook. The priests and their minions are always calling upon you to identify potential converts among the faculty, participate in soul-searching sessions, meetings, and fora about writing, serve on a faculty panel to award prize-winning student essays appearing in *Discoveries*, or, say, contribute to a book of essays about Writing at Cornell. I certainly don't mean to complain: I have come to accept that the training and insights I received from the John S. Knight Institute entail certain responsibilities. Although I have never been one to ascribe to any sort of orthodoxy or orthopraxy, truth to tell, these writing folks have made something of a believer and a better teacher out of me.

# Teaching Behavioral Ecology through Writing

PAUL W. SHERMAN

Neurobiology and Behavior

℘ Behavioral ecology is a relatively new and rapidly developing branch of evolutionary biology. Behavioral ecologists investigate how the behavior of animals, including humans, is influenced by natural selection in relation to the physical and social environment. At Cornell, teaching and learning behavioral ecology is facilitated by writing-intensive courses. Frequent writing assignments enable instructors to evaluate students' progress accurately and in time to adjust the level and content of lectures to students' needs, and begin early to engage and challenge students who are particularly enthusiastic and identify those requiring extra assistance. Students appreciate multiple, unhurried opportunities to synthesize and demonstrate their knowledge, and readily accept the challenge to rework essays in light of reviews by instructors and peers (especially because doing so enables them to improve their grades). Students flock to writing-intensive courses in behavioral ecology and faculty are committed to the nontraditional format. This chapter analyzes why.[1]

## Introduction to Behavioral Ecology

Behavioral ecology is a relatively new (less than years old) and rapidly expanding subdiscipline of evolutionary biology (Gross 1994). Practitioners study how behavior is influenced by natural selection in relation to ecological conditions. Behavioral ecologists share two theoretical perspectives, namely that (1) natural selection is the evolutionary process leading to adaptation, and (2) the principal focus of selection is the individual and its genetic material (Dawkins 1982).

Natural selection should favor behaviors that enhance survival and reproduction. Thus the occurrences of self-sacrifice (altruism), infanticide, adoption, etc., are evolutionary puzzles. Attempting to resolve them constitutes the life's work of many behavioral ecologists. This requires long-term observations of animals in their natural habitats, supplemented by molecular genetic analyses to determine kinship and comparisons among related species differing in relevant aspects of their physical (e.g., climate) and biotic environments (predators, parasites, and competitors).

Interest in behavioral ecology has grown rapidly, as chronicled, for example, in two primary journals (*Behavioral Ecology* and *Behavioral Ecology and Sociobiology*), three textbooks (Krebs and Davies 1993, 1997; Alcock 2001a), and an anthology (Sherman and Alcock 2001). At Cornell, about half a dozen faculty consider themselves behavioral ecologists. Undergraduates are exposed to relevant concepts and case studies mainly through topical seminars and two regularly scheduled courses. The first is Introduction to Behavior, which is a large (300-plus students), sophomore-level lecture course taught yearly by a team of five to seven faculty. Discussion sections are offered for all majors, each one limited to fifteen students. One or two sections are taught in the writing-intensive format. These meet twice per week, under the guidance of a senior teaching fellow. Students keep a journal of their thoughts and reactions to lectures and assigned readings and also write topical essays biweekly. In return, participants are excused from formal examinations. The other course, Animal Social Behavior, is a lecture and discussion course designed for thirty to thirty-five upperclassmen. It is taught in alternative years, and always in the writing-intensive format. This chapter focuses primarily on the latter class.

## Ontogeny of a Writing Instructor

Writing is an essential part of scientific communication. Scientists routinely must explain their research questions, results, and practical implications to close colleagues, the broader scientific community, and the public, who support their efforts through tax dollars. Unfortunately, however, writing does not come "naturally" to most people, including scientists. Writing practice in science starts in middle school and high school classes, but often ends in college. It should not. Realizing this has led to restructuring of courses in many fields of science, especially chemistry (Burke 1995) and biology (Kirkland 1997), to not only impart facts and concepts but also to encourage students to practice writing about them.

Teaching biology students to write clearly and effectively is obviously a worthy academic goal. However, I began teaching writing-intensive courses more out of frustration than inspiration. I was not very good at writing multiple choice and short-answer questions that revealed students' conceptual understanding. And I disliked having interactions with students focus on disagreements over test questions and grades (i.e., the negative aspects of evaluation) instead of understanding and generating new ideas (the positive aspects of learning). Also, I realized that I was more interested in getting students to *think* like behavioral ecologists than to memorize factual information. Finally, I regretted not being able to gauge my own teaching effectiveness and the students' progress until the academic term was half over (i.e., after the midterm exam), by which point it was nearly too late to rectify the situation.

So, about a decade ago, I began experimenting with teaching through writing. Gradually the following general format has taken shape, with input from senior colleagues, graduate teaching assistants, and, of course, my undergraduate clientele.

## Teaching Behavioral Ecology through Writing

Animal Social Behavior meets twice per week (two hours per session) for lectures and discussions of assigned readings. Students are told at the outset that their grade depends (40 percent) on oral participation but, more importantly (60 percent), on frequent (weekly or biweekly), short writing projects (one to two thousand words). Essay questions are open-ended, and they require creative thinking and synthesis of readings and lecture materials to answer. Questions are provided several weeks in advance of the due date so students have plenty of time to work on them.

In formulating their essays, students are allowed—indeed, encouraged—to consult any conceivable sources of information (e.g., books, articles, classmates, professors, or parents). The only requirement is that the actual essays be written by the author. Writing assignments are so specific to the class that appropriate essays are never available commercially (e.g., on the Internet).

When students turn in their first drafts (usually on Thursdays), my teaching assistant and I pounce on them. We both peruse each one, make extensive comments and suggestions for improvements, and return them to authors the *very next* class period (the following Tuesday). We put a grade at the end of our comments—almost as an afterthought—and encourage students to discuss their reviews with us individually.

After consultation, students may rewrite their essays and resubmit them for further consideration and regrading. The process is iterated multiple times (with or without further oral discussion), until the student terminates it. The final grade for that assignment is the one he or she received on the last rewrite they offered, regardless of when in the term it was resubmitted. So, students stop when they are satisfied with their level of understanding and their grade.

These evaluation policies and procedures strongly encourage collaboration among classmates and virtually eliminate competition. Students know that success is determined primarily by the time and effort they invest in reading, thinking, and revising their essays. It is possible for every student to earn a high grade on every essay, and thus in the course. In fact, I frequently state my desire to have every class member earn "A" or "A-" grades. And, by golly, this sometimes happens!

Of course, the "down side" is the time and effort required to read and comment on five to six hundred short essays per semester. Indeed, this class is all consuming! However the students' enthusiasm for this evaluation format helps sustain my own.

### PEER REVIEWS

A pillar of the scientific process is peer reviewing. So, once students are used to writing and revising essays, I ask them to e-mail their first draft to two classmates and to me. Commentators e-mail back brief reviews and I act as an "editor," encouraging authors to treat peers' commentaries with the same seriousness they treat mine. On a subsequent essay the tables are turned, and the original author reviews the commentator's essay, and so on. The idea is to teach students how to give and accept constructive criticisms, as occurs daily in the "real world" of science.

### GRANT PROPOSALS

University researchers are expected to obtain extramural funds to support their studies. It is useful for students to learn how to conceive a feasible project and present their ideas forcefully to funding agencies. So, as one of their assignments, I require students to "propose" a field study in behavioral ecology, using the National Geographic Society's form (seven pages) as a template. To receive "funding," students must identify a research question, develop testable alternative hypotheses to address it, specify methodologies to gather appropriate data, and suggest interpretations of the likely outcomes. Proposals also include an up-to-date bibliography and a reasonable and accurate budget.

Every year some class members "catch fire" and get so excited about their research proposal that they actually submit it. Some have received funding and conducted the research the following summer. Several have, with my assistance, even carried their project through to publication (e.g., Judd and Sherman 1996).

In the following sections I present a detailed treatment of a few topics covered in Animal Social Behavior, to give something of the flavor of the class and illustrate why writing has become indispensable to pedagogy here.

## Adaptation and Natural Selection

Darwin's (1859) theory of evolution by natural selection, which is the unifying conceptual framework of all biology, can be summarized in five steps:

(1) Variation: Individuals in every species differ in their characteristics.

(2) Heredity: Many variations can be passed from parents to offspring.

(3) Differential Reproduction: Some variations result in greater reproductive success than others.

(4) Competition: Populations tend to be stable over time, implying that there is a struggle for existence (i.e., not every individual that is born survives to reproduce).

(5) Evolution: Variations that lead to the greatest reproductive success predominate over time.

Although this seems straightforward, students often are surprised to realize that natural selection and evolution are not synonymous. Whereas natural selection is differential reproduction, evolution is gene-frequency change. Evolution can occur without natural selection (if gene frequencies change due to drift, migration, or recurrent mutations), and natural selection can occur without evolution (if variations leading to differential reproduction are not heritable). However, selection is the only evolutionary process that leads to adaptation, the "fit" between an organism and its environment.

Students also are surprised to discover that behaviors do not have to be inborn ("genetic") to be adaptive. For example, learned behaviors can certainly enhance fitness and they often are passed from parent to offspring, but they are not "heritable" genetically. In these cases, selection has favored the brain structures and capacities ("Darwinian algorithms") that enable individuals to learn well (see, e.g., Alcock 2001b).

Compared to Darwinism, some other key concepts in behavioral ecology are unfamiliar and nonintuitive. Here are two examples.

### LEVELS OF ANALYSIS

There is no consensus among biologists about how to answer questions of the general form "Why does individual A perform behavior X?" Confusion arises because behavior (and other traits) can be explained from four different, non-mutually exclusive perspectives or "levels of analysis" (Sherman 1988). Two provide "proximate" (immediate cause) explanations and the other two provide "ultimate" (long-term) explanations. Proximate explanations focus on how a behavior (1) *develops* in an individual (i.e., its ontogeny) and its underlying physiological and cognitive (2) *mechanisms*, whereas ultimate explanations focus on how the behavior affects (3) *reproduction* and its (4) *history* through evolutionary time.

To illustrate this conceptual framework, consider the (deceptively) simple question: "Why does a male bird sing?" Possible answers are that he has high hormone levels in the spring (physiological mechanism), he is amorous (cognitive mechanism), he learned to sing from his father (ontogeny), he is defending his territory (fitness value), and he is expressing a form of communication that is evolutionarily ancient, since it is shared by all passerine birds (history). All five answers are complementary, not mutually exclusive (Sherman 1988). This means that any of them may be right—or wrong—without jeopardizing any others. Competition among hypotheses that are truly alternatives only occurs within a level, not among them.

For example, the idea that male birds sing because they have high hormone levels is *not* an alternative to the idea that singing repels rival males. Both may be true simultaneously. However, the idea that males sing primarily to attract females *is* an alternative to the rival-repellant function (i.e., these hypotheses are at the same logical level).

Initially students (and many colleagues: see Mitchell 1992) are confused by this pluralistic approach, apparently because they are used to seeking the one "right" answer to every scientific question. To encourage students to accept and appreciate the levels of analysis approach, I developed a four-part sequence of lectures and essays.

First, I give students a series of hypotheses to explain a familiar behavior, the use of spices in cooking (below). The assignment is to group them into competing and complementary categories. Recent information on probable functions of spice use is provided in lectures and associated readings (e.g., Sherman and Billing 1999).

> All the following have been proposed to explain why we cook with spices. Which hypotheses are alternatives (on the same level of analysis) and which are complementary (different levels)? Spices (1) taste good, (2) provide essential micronutrients, (3) are aphrodisiacs, (4) inhibit food-spoilage microorganisms, (5) cool the body off by increasing perspiration, (6) disperse kidney stones, (7) are eaten by children because of parental pressure, (8) signal social

status because they are rare, expensive, and exotic (9) have been used for thousands of years, (10) disguise the smell and taste of spoiled foods, (11) are culturally determined.

Through writing and rewriting their essays, students discover that (1) and (5) are alternatives (mechanisms), (2), (4), (6), and (8) are alternatives (fitness effects), (7) describes an ontogeny, and (9) an evolutionary history. The last three hypotheses are (purposely) ambiguous: (3) and (10) could describe mechanisms or a fitness effects, and (11) could describe an ontogeny, fitness effect, or an evolutionary origin. Grappling with this ambiguity as they formulate their essay helps students to appreciate the importance of presenting hypotheses so the level of analysis to which they apply is clear.

Step two in this unit involves analyzing a real-life disagreement that can be traced to mixing up levels of analysis. Unfortunately, there are many protracted, acrimonious examples to choose from. The one I find most interesting and illuminating is the "clitoris debate."

Stephen Jay Gould (1987a) argued that females' clitorises are a developmental side effect of selection on males for penises, and that clitoral orgasms therefore are not adaptations. John Alcock (1987) responded that because clitorises are neither inert nor imperfectly formed, as expected under Gould's hypothesis, functional explanations should be sought. Alcock championed the idea that clitorises facilitate orgasm, which, in turn, "acts as a mechanism of discriminating mate choice and paternity control in females" (e.g., see Baker and Bellis 1993).

In his rebuttal, Gould (1987b) claimed that "Alcock misunderstood my major point, that it is logically incorrect to equate current utility with reasons for historical origin" and that "developmental explanations are more expansive and operational than the necessarily fruitless and untestable adaptationist speculations that continue to permeate our literature." In the most recent rejoinder, Alcock (1998) stated, "The adaptationist approach is science and it works. The richness of the record puts the lie to Gould's claim that adaptationists are satisfied with untestable speculations." In view of all this, I ask students to: "Analyze the clitoris debate and explain why Gould and Alcock talked past each other for more than a decade."

Most students realize that Gould's and Alcock's hypotheses are on different levels of analysis (history versus fitness effects), and therefore not alternatives. They also realize that Gould is caricaturing adaptationists and mocking them as "storytellers." Nonetheless, students often agree with Gould that if clitorises originated as developmental by-products of penises, it is unnecessary to consider hypotheses about their effects on fitness. My comments on their essays help to clarify why an answer at one level of analysis cannot logically supercede answers at another level (Sherman 1989). In this case they must explain why the clitoris persists, regardless of how it originated. Explicitly distinguishing levels of analysis limits competition between alternative hypotheses only to those framed at the same logical level (Alcock and Sherman 1994).

The third assignment in this unit encourages students to creatively use the levels of analysis framework to formulate their own hypotheses. The essay topic is: "Describe a behavior of any animal (including humans) and develop as many hypotheses as possible, both alternative and complementary, to answer the question 'what causes this behavior?'"

Often students pick behaviors of friends, family, or their own pets, and usually they come up with at least one hypothesis that correctly applies to each level of analysis, and several alternative hypotheses at one or two levels. They discover for themselves that which level of causal explanation is most interesting or satisfactory is largely a matter of personal taste and training, which also is a truism among professional biologists (see Bass 1998).

Once students learn to separate hypotheses at different levels of analysis, I move to the fourth and final step in this unit by asking: "How would you test each of the hypotheses you developed in your previous essay?"

This assignment challenges students to think more empirically, and allows me to introduce in lectures two powerful conceptual tools, strong inference and parsimony, both of which are useful in behavioral ecology—and in life.

## STRONG INFERENCE

Strong inference is the method of choice for approaching scientific questions. It consists of three steps: devising alternative hypotheses, deriving "critical predictions" from each hypothesis, and gathering the appropriate data (Platt 1964). A critical prediction is one that must be true if the hypothesis is correct. Therefore, a test of a critical prediction always will exclude one or more alternatives from further consideration. After every test the three steps are repeated, until only one hypothesis is left standing at each level of analysis.

Using strong inference is like climbing an intellectual tree: if at the first fork critical observations exclude the left branch (hypothesis), we take the right branch; if at the next fork critical observations exclude the right branch, we go left; and so on. Strong inference also is valuable in developing critical hypotheses because it forces one to ask, right at the outset, "What observation or experiment would indicate that my idea is wrong?" This focuses attention on framing hypotheses so that they are falsifiable, an approach that distinguishes science from religion. Whereas religious practitioners do not seek ways to falsify their beliefs, scientists always must be able to specify what observations would prove them incorrect.

### PARSIMONY

Parsimony is a long-standing general principle that to explain a given phenomenon the smallest set of novel theoretical entities should be postulated. In a famous example in evolutionary biology, Williams (1966) invoked methodological parsimony to explain why it is unnecessary to propose a special theoretical principle (adaptation) to explain how an airborne flying fish gets back into the sea (gravity is sufficient).

In general, a methodologically parsimonious explanation is one that takes all available data into account and minimally disrupts the preexisting, established body of knowledge. It does not require us to favor explanations that minimize the number of theoretical (unseen) forces or events. For example, if the Hubble Telescope reveals a new celestial body, it is not methodologically parsimonious to assume the object does not possess gravity just to minimize the number of attributes ascribed to it. A "no gravity" assumption obviously would be contrary to established physical theories and facts, and would require some new, mysterious gravity-suppressing mechanism. The parsimonious assumption would be that the object possesses gravity, even if there is no direct evidence for it.

Through writing and revising the fourth essay, students practice developing alternative hypotheses, and using strong inference and methodological parsimony in testing them. Throughout the rest of the course, students are expected to hone these skills.

### HUMAN BEHAVIORAL ECOLOGY

Many behavioral ecologists study humans, and they are contributing to new understandings of such diverse topics as marriage systems, mate choice, nepotism, reciprocity, parental care, warfare, and even morality (e.g., Betzig et al. 1987; Betzig 1997). Heretofore, variations in social and reproductive behaviors between populations often were regarded merely as nonadaptive cultural nuances and studying them was left mainly to social scientists. Today, behavioral ecologists also are building bridges to health sciences through the development of a new subdiscipline known as Darwinian medicine (Nesse and Williams 1994, 1998). Whereas medical researchers traditionally study *how* symptoms are brought about (their underlying mechanisms) and attempt to discover more effective ways to eliminate them, from a Darwinian perspective the questions are *why* particular symptoms occur (their reproductive consequences) and whether or not it is advisable to eliminate them. These two approaches are complementary, not alternative (because they are on different levels of analysis).

At first, students are amazed that principles of behavioral ecology relate so directly to issues they face daily. They are eager to hear about all these advances, and enthusiastic about applying the conceptual framework they have learned to human behavior and medicine. To start off, I ask students to discuss: "How would you determine if smoking is an adaptation?"

Answering this requires careful thought as students attempt to bring various concepts of adaptation (e.g., Reeve and Sherman 1993, 2001) to bear on a burning health and legal issue. Often they suggest a straightforward approach: to decide if smoking is an adaptation, look for correlations between frequencies of smoking by men and women and measures of their lifetime reproductive success. Positive correlations would imply that smoking is adaptive (due, for example, to enhancement of smokers' status) despite its potential to shorten life (e.g., due to emphysema or lung cancer), whereas negative correlations indicate nonadaptation. If smoking is nonadaptive, its persistence must be due to some nonselective cause, such as the recency of widespread availability of tobacco products and a physiological susceptibility to addiction, the mechanisms underlying which evolved in a different physiological context.

Some students adopt an interesting alternative approach to the question, taking cues from another rapidly developing field called "evolutionary psychology" (Barkow et al. 1992). These students hypothesize that our brains were designed by natural selection in ancestral environments to detect risk-takers (i.e., during the Pleistocene). Perhaps risk-taking was an honest indicator to potential mates of an individual's physical health and genetic quality. Under this hypothesis, successful risk-takers should be more attractive to members of the opposite sex than cautious individuals. Many modern-day behaviors involve taking serious risks, including drug use, bungee jumping, car racing, motorcycle riding, etc. Do individuals who engage in these behaviors attract and impress potential mates? To evaluate this possibility, one would observe when people smoke and, in particular, whether individuals (especially men) are more likely to do so when members of the opposite sex are nearby than when they are alone, or more likely to smoke when they can raise their status by impressing the "audience."

As students are formulating these essays, I raise the general question in lecture, "What is the most appropriate methodology for testing hypotheses about the adaptiveness of human behavior?" Should we (1) measure how a behavior affects reproduction today, and assume that relevant aspects of past environments were similar enough to modern environments that the behavior had the same effects on fitness back then, or (2) attempt to infer what past environments were like and see if the behaviors that are performed today indeed occur in circumstances that would have been appropriate in those past environments? Each approach has numerous advocates, the former calling themselves "Darwinian anthropologists" (Betzig et al. 1987) and the latter "evolutionary psychologists" (Crawford and Krebs 1998). Serious contention has marred interactions between these developing subdisciplines (Crawford 1993; Smith et al. 2001), but increasingly it is being realized that the two approaches complement rather than mutually exclude each other (Sherman and Reeve 1997).

At the least, evolutionary psychologists and Darwinian anthropologists agree that our psyches should bear the imprint of past selection. Therefore the criteria we use to choose mates, many of which are unconscious, should somehow relate to fitness. Interestingly, men and women are attracted by different attributes of the opposite sex (Barber 1995; Buss 1994). In general, men favor physical attributes that are associated with youth, health, and high fertility, including symmetrical facial and body features, full lips, small noses, and a waist-hip circumference ratio of 0.7 (the "hourglass figure"). In contrast, women generally favor attributes in men associated with abilities and willingness to invest in the woman and her offspring, including age, wealth, and high social status.

After introducing students to these studies and their associated methodologies, I ask them to do their own detective work for their next essay: "What attributes do men and women seek in partners, and what attributes about themselves do they advertise?"

To answer this, students work in pairs to gather data from several hundred "lonely hearts" ads in newspapers that I have accumulated biweekly for the previous six months from two big cities (San Francisco and New York), two middle-sized cities (Syracuse and Binghamton), and two small towns (Ithaca and Jamestown, N.Y.). Students are asked to summarize the information and e-mail the data to me. My teaching assistant and I collate the information (from 3,000-plus ads!), perform preliminary statistical analyses, and e-mail everything back to each student.

The assignment is to develop and test a hypothesis about human mate preferences, presenting their results in a "scientific paper" format that includes an abstract, introduction, methods, results, discussion, and conclusions. The idea is similar to Eisen's (1996) "Disease of the Week" assignments, and like his students, mine often get very interested and involved in this project, and carry it well beyond the scope of the assignment.

For example, some students investigated whether men and women seeking same-sex partners have the same preferences as individuals seeking opposite-sex partners, whether preferences vary with size of the city, and whether the disparity between an advertiser's age and the desired age of his partner increases with age in men (it does) or women (it does not). Through this project, students come to see for themselves how preferences may be interpreted as unconscious outcomes of adaptive mate choices by each sex.

The last three weeks of the course are devoted to Darwinian medicine. This involves readings, lectures, and a student-led symposium (requiring fifteen-minute PowerPoint presentations by each student). Among the topics covered are the evolution of diseases and virulence (Ewald 1994), including HIV and AIDS, uses of naturally occurring pharmaceuticals such as spices, evolution of mental disorders (McGuire and Troisi 1998), morning sickness (Sherman and Flaxman 2001), menstruation, menopause, and senescence, or aging (Austad 1997). The promise of Darwinian medicine is that it will lead to improved medical practices in the twenty-first century. Decisions about whether or not to eliminate particular symptoms chemically or surgically will be better informed if they include consideration of whether those symptoms are aiding or hindering the individual's recovery. The idea behind Darwinian medicine is that in order to fix something, it often is helpful to know what it was designed to do.

For the final essay, I ask students to discuss a contemporary social and philosophical dilemma: "Under senescence theory, aging is the inevitable result of youthful fecundity and death is unavoidable. If there never will be a medical 'fountain of youth,' how should our government allocate funds to aging research?"

Students' responses range from arguing that all funding for research into prolonging life should be terminated because of the inevitability of senescence to suggesting that funds should be reallocated to focus on improving the quality of life for the elderly, and not the average "quantity" of life. Some feel that the only long-term solution to problems of aging is minimizing the number of elderly citizens, either by reducing the birth rate (e.g., by investing in contraceptive programs) or liberalizing assisted suicide laws.

The point of this essay is twofold: to encourage students to consider the consequences of senescence theory for social policies and also use their "basic" knowledge to address "applied" problems, as they will be doing for the rest of their lives. Students relish this challenge, especially those planning careers in the health sciences. Their abilities, scholarship, and enthusiasm give me hope that these students will use the various conceptual tools of behavioral ecology, internalized through intensive writing, to change their world.

## How Writing-Intensive Courses Pay Off

Writing-intensive courses in behavioral ecology at Cornell are consistently oversubscribed, and faculty are committed to this nontraditional pedagogical format. There are several reasons. Traditional course formats enable students to demonstrate progress only twice, on the midterm and final exams, and to give the instructor evaluative feedback on teaching effectiveness only after the term is over. By contrast, frequent writing assignments enable faculty to evaluate students' development in "real time." This makes it possible to adjust the pace and level of lectures to students' comprehension, to backtrack when necessary to revisit topics that were poorly explained or otherwise misunderstood, and to initiate dialogs with students who are especially enthusiastic and those requiring extra assistance. Students appreciate multiple, unhurried opportunities to synthesize and demonstrate what they know. Whereas the traditional evaluation format emphasizes quick recall of specific facts, the writing-intensive format emphasizes thorough information gathering, careful thought, and clear and concise exposition. Students readily accept the challenge to rework their essays in light of faculty reviews, and to resubmit them to demonstrate greater understanding (and, probably, improve their grade!). After reading numerous assignments and revisions, instructors can gauge each student's motivation and progress accurately and fairly. Such knowledge is essential for assigning grades and writing letters of recommendation.

# Cultivating Dialectical Imagination

JENNIFER E. WHITING

Philosophy

᷎ I found myself so daunted by the task of saying what is characteristic of philosophical writing, as distinct from writing in other disciplines, that I turned to some of my colleagues for help. Their responses—which may say more about the philosophical circles in which I travel than about philosophical writing as such—tended to emphasize the virtues of "argument": virtues like "precision," "clarity," and "rigor." (I take it that precision and clarity are primarily matters of making things explicit—of saying exactly what one means, no more and no less. And I take it that rigor is primarily a matter of attending to, and respecting, what does and what does not follow logically from what.) And while I, too, pride myself on my commitment to these virtues, I found these responses disappointing for various reasons, including not only their myopic vision but also their arrogance and transparent falsity. Surely philosophers do not have a monopoly on the topic-neutral virtues of precision, clarity, and rigor. Think, to take just a few examples, of legal writing, or of much writing in the natural and social sciences. Some philosophical writing seems to me far inferior with respect to these virtues to much writing in these and other fields: indeed some philosophical writing seems to me not even to aspire to these virtues. And while the failure to do so is often, perhaps even usually, a defect, I do not think it always a defect. If one of the points of philosophical writing is to provoke philosophical thought—whatever exactly that is—and if philosophical thought is sometimes better provoked by cryptic or paradoxical remarks like those of Heraclitus or the later Wittgenstein, then there should be room within our conceptions of good philosophical writing for cryptic and paradoxical remarks, perhaps even for treatises composed largely or entirely of such remarks. One might, however, reasonably resist saying this—let alone teaching it—in a First-Year Writing Seminar.

Should philosophers then settle in teaching freshmen, or undergraduates in general, for precision, clarity, and rigor? Or at least for fostering these ideals? I think not. For exclusive attention to precision, clarity, and rigor can both inhibit imagination and encourage reductive habits of mind that may impede philosophical insight. It is no use objecting that emphasizing precision, clarity, and rigor need not have these effects. For the point here is not about what follows logically from what; the point is that emphasizing precision, clarity, and rigor—especially as ends and not simply as means—can and in many cases does have these effects. But truths, if I may speak of such things, may be messy or paradoxical, and there is little reason to suppose that they will always be susceptible of capture, or of communication to others, in clear and precise language. So vagueness and indirection may in some cases serve truth-respecting and/or communicative functions. Plato, for example, may have chosen to write dialogues, rather than treatises, for pedagogical reasons. He may, for example, have written aporetic dialogues in order to induce philosophically fertile confusion in his readers. Or he may have thought it important for readers to draw their own conclusions. Or, even if there were specific conclusions he wanted his readers to draw, he may have thought it more effective if they drew these conclusions for themselves. Think, for example, of F. M. Cornford's suggestion that Plato omitted any reference to Forms in the *Theaetetus* because he wanted his readers to see for themselves how impossible it was to solve certain problems without the Forms. One need not accept Cornford's view in this particular case to see that it points to a possible and philosophically respectable motivation for one sort of refusal to state one's view as clearly and precisely, or as explicitly, as possible (Cornford 1935, 28).

One might still object to preaching this in an undergraduate writing class, if only for self-interested reasons. Who wants, week after week, to try to understand, and to write helpful comments on, fifteen or so *Will to Power* or *Philosophical Investigations* wanna-bes? It is one thing to have to puzzle endlessly over Nieztsche or Wittgenstein, and quite another to have to puzzle endlessly over fifteen or more undergraduate imitations. So the question is: is there any way to cultivate philosophical imagination and insight without undue sacrifice of precision, clarity, and rigor?

I think there is, if we adopt a different conception of what is characteristic of—even if not peculiar to—philosophical writing. (By "characteristic" here, I mean what helps to make philosophical writing philosophical.) It is not, I think, an accident that so many great philosophers chose to write dialogues—either explicit ones (like those of Plato and Hume) or implicit ones (like those of Descartes and Wittgenstein). For it seems to me that what is most characteristic of philosophical writing—at least of good philosophical writing—is its dialectical nature. I am using the term "dialectical" here in a broad sense, to refer to the way in which philosophical views are typically developed in opposition or response to one another. Sometimes the oppositions are resolved, as for example in Hegelian synthesis; sometimes they are not, as, for example, in the sort of dialogical writing that Bahktin distinguishes from dialectical writing in this narrower Hegelian sense (Bahktin 1973, 22). But in any case, philosophical views are typically articulated—not simply in presenting them to others but even in the author's own mind—in response to other views, sometimes to sharply opposed views, sometimes only to subtly different ones. This means that understanding the views to which one responds plays an important role in one's own philosophical development. And this, I assume, is why understanding the history of philosophy is so often viewed—correctly I think—as central to the philosophical enterprise as such. It may also explain why Laura Ruetsche, one of the colleagues I polled about the distinctive characteristics of philosophical writing, responded by saying that philosophers spend more time telling you what their point is *not* than telling you what it *is*. I think she meant this partly in jest. But I took her to be on to something deep—namely, that it is partly by determining what their views are *not* that philosophers determine what their views *are*.

One might object here that this sort of progressive articulation of views, in response to other views, is common in many fields. And this is no doubt true. Think, for example, of the history of science, or of literary theory. Consider, for a concrete example, the way in which Bahktin articulates his view, in response to the views of his predecessors, in the first chapter of *Problems of Dostoevsky's Poetics*. Still, however, there seems to me to be one mode of such progressive articulation that is more characteristic of philosophy (even if not peculiar to it) than of other fields—namely, articulation of one's own views in response to imagined views, views that have not (so far as the author knows) been held by any actual interlocutor.

The ability to imagine plausible objections and plausible alternatives to one's own proposed views is essential (even if not peculiar) to good philosophical thought and writing. Indeed, it is partly because it is not peculiar to philosophy that it is so useful: although a lawyer, for example, needs in the end to respond only to the arguments actually raised by her opponent, her ability to do so is greatly improved by her ability to imagine and so to anticipate the various sorts of arguments, especially the improbable ones, that her opponent *might* raise. And this sort of imagination is something I think we can seek to culti-vate—without undue sacrifice of precision, clarity, and rigor—in undergradu-ates. Moreover, this sort of imagination is something we need to cultivate in undergraduates, since it tends to be relatively new to them. While they are often able to report some actual person's actual view and to say what they themselves actually think is wrong with it, they are much less often able to imagine objec-tions that someone else, with a different and perhaps only imagined point of view, might raise against their own views. They are sometimes able to appreci-ate such objections when they are pointed out, and even, in some cases, to imag-ine what sort of objection a specific sort of opponent might raise. They are, for example, reasonably accomplished at anticipating and preparing replies to the sorts of practical objections their own parents might raise against their various behaviors. But except for those who have participated in something like debate, they seem to me less able to anticipate the sorts of objections—especially more theoretical ones—that might be raised by less familiar interlocutors. Yet this ability is crucial to their ability to develop their own views and to modify them in light of their perceived inadequacies. For one hopes in modifying a view in response to one objection not to fall prey to other possible ones.

How, then, can we seek to cultivate such dialectical imagination? One way is to provide students with models to study. It is useful to walk students slowly through a text like Descartes's *Meditations*, asking them at various points whose voice a particular claim is in—Descartes's or his imaginary interlocutor's—and then asking them to identify the devices the author uses to signal in whose voice a particular claim is. Many students do not even understand this question. I have often had students reply, "What do you *mean* 'In whose voice?'" Even explicit dialogues pose a challenge here. For students often falsely assume that anything a particular character says is in that character's own voice. But characters often represent the views of others before attacking these views, or use the views of others as foils for presenting their own views. So it is instructive to ask students to distinguish among the claims of a particular character that are in the character's own voice and which are not. Learning to recognize these distinc-tions in the work of others is a step toward learning to signal them clearly and precisely in one's own work, which is crucial to good philosophical writing, es-pecially given the way in which the articulation of philosophical views so often proceeds by way of response to other views. So exercises of this sort allow one to cultivate appreciation of the dialectical situation while simultaneously de-manding precision, clarity, and rigor—rigor, too, because one can always point out when a particular interlocutor's precise conclusion does not follow from his clearly and precisely articulated premises. Note, however, that clarity, precision, and rigor function here primarily as *means* to what really matters—namely, to understanding the dialectical situation and thence communicating it (either directly or indirectly) *to* others.

A more active exercise that I find useful is to ask students to defend views they do not hold, sometimes even views with which they strongly disagree. This is useful because most of them, except for those who have been involved in something like debate, find this difficult. One way to do this is to take a student's paragraph (or short paper) with an identifiable thesis, and then to ask the student to write a second paragraph (or short paper) attacking the thesis, and later a third paragraph (or short paper) defending the thesis against the second's attack. (I mention both paragraphs and papers here because I typically begin the term by asking students to master paragraph structure before moving on to short papers, so I do this first with paragraphs then eventually with short papers.) This task presupposes that the paragraph has an identifiable thesis, so one exercise I do early on is to ask students to prepare two copies of their paragraphs—one with the thesis statement underlined and one without underlining. I then divide them into pairs and ask them to give their unmarked copies to their partners. I then ask each student to underline what he or she takes to be the thesis statement of his or her partner's paragraph. Finally, I ask them to compare notes to see if their partners have correctly identified the statements that they themselves have underlined. If not, I ask them to discuss with their partners why the partners identified different statements instead, and then to rewrite in ways designed to avoid the sorts of misunderstanding exhibited by their partners.

A similar method, which has the additional advantage of facilitating class discussion, is to ask each member of the class to identify his or her position on the issue we are discussing by sitting in a designated part of the room—for example, those taking a liberal feminist position on pornography on one side of the table and those taking a radical feminist position on the other. (I also tell them that they can move to different seats at any point if they change their minds during the course of discussion. The idea of this is to encourage open-mindedness together with a sense that it is perfectly acceptable to change one's mind.) I find that this facilitates discussion, perhaps because students feel that they are not alone but have identifiable allies, perhaps because they feel more inclined to defend a view with which they are visibly identified. When discussion lags, as it rarely does when I proceed this way, I can always call on a student who, in virtue of her location, ought to have something to say in response to a point made by the other side. But this is rarely necessary, as a team spirit tends to develop among the various groups, with members coming to one another's assistance in the discussion. I then record who is sitting where, and ask them to write a defense of a view they in fact opposed. (I tell them this after the discussion, so as to prevent deceptive seating, and they usually groan when I do this.) Later, I ask each student to write a reply to his own defense of the view he originally opposed, the idea being for students to learn what it takes to rebut alternatives to their own views in the course of defending their own views. I use this method because I believe that the most successful attacks on a target view are those borne out of appreciation of—or even better out of temptation toward—whatever it is that moves proponents of the target view. And I believe that the most successful defenses of one's own views are those that appreciate and accommodate as far as possible the driving forces behind one's opponents' views.

It is, of course, true that cultivating appreciation of views opposed to one's own can lead to ambivalence of a sort that may muddy one's own mind and hence one's own writing. But this is not necessarily a bad thing. It encourages students to recognize the complexity of issues and to resist superficial solutions to deep problems. It encourages intellectual integrity. It even encourages a kind of rigor—namely, not claiming to have shown or supported more than one has in fact supported or shown. Moreover, such ambivalence is often philosophically fertile: many important philosophical developments are the fruit of someone's seeking to do justice to each of two (or more) allegedly competing intuitions and refusing to secure one neatly at the expense of the other. Think, for example, of Kant's "Copernican revolution" and the way in which he sought to synthesize aspects of the rationalist and empiricist traditions that had previously been viewed as irreconcilable. The result was hardly crystal clear; but it was a great (and highly influential) achievement.

I do not mean to advocate encouraging undergraduates—or even graduates—to model their writing on works like Kant's *Critique of Pure Reason*, though I might consider letting a precocious student start with Descartes's *Meditations*. Stage-appropriate models are important, as I learned with one of my graduate students some years ago. This particular student was a great admirer of the relatively mature work of several eminent philosophers, and he seemed to me to be modeling his work (perhaps unconsciously) on work these philosophers had done in their forties and early fifties. As a result, he tended to make ambitious claims he was not yet prepared or entitled to make. I decided eventually to share my diagnosis with him and to prescribe that he read a number of works that these mature philosophers had written when they had been (like him) in their twenties. I handed him a reading list of such works. He soon began to do the sort of work I had been encouraging him to do, with a view to doing the sort of work he eventually wanted to do, and he later remarked how instructive this reading exercise had been for him. I often ask graduate students who are struggling with writing to do something like this: I ask them to think explicitly about whose writing they admire and why, with a view to helping them find appropriate models. With undergraduates, who are less familiar with philosophical works, I prefer to provide them with a few good models and to encourage them to think explicitly about what makes a model good (as well as about how even it might be improved). Models are important, especially with weaker students, many of whom claim that comments about their work are not enough. And once again, stage-appropriate models are important; I've found that many students benefit more from seeing a solid student paper of a sort they can reasonably hope to write than from seeing a professional piece or even too exceptional a piece of student writing, either of which can be demoralizing if it is presented as model for them.

Genre- and scale-appropriate models are also important. I once taught a freshman writing seminar in which we read a series of short stories, each of which raised issues of moral and/or legal responsibility. We discussed each story in class, both with a view to the issues involved and with a view to the question of whether positions about such issues might not be more effectively conveyed by means of narratives like those we had read than by means of more straightforward argument. The problem was that the students were writing primarily expository and argumentative pieces but were reading primarily narrative ones. When one of the students requested that I provide them with short models of expository/argumentative writing, I found a treasure in the volumes that collect Stephen Jay Gould's columns from *Natural History*. The pieces were just the right length, superbly organized (typically, for example, making one key and clearly identifiable point per paragraph), masterfully argued (always raising, and dealing clearly and concisely with, objections), and sublimely written (their rare uses of the passive voice, for example, all clearly motivated). Still, however, some students despaired of having such lofty models and I had to supplement my use of Gould with the use of anonymous student papers.

One reason for encouraging more advanced students to come up with their own models—and for providing less advanced students with multiple models— is to discourage the imagination-inhibiting idea that there is one uniquely correct way to do things. This idea tends, no doubt, to be more prevalent among freshmen, who have often been brought up on purportedly exceptionless rules, like "never use the first person" (which, incidentally, often makes it more difficult to identify whose voice a particular claim is in). So I prefer to speak in terms of guidelines rather than rules, and I try to get students to focus on the various pros and cons—for there are usually both—of doing things a particular way in a particular instance. For example, while I generally think it is easier to read a piece that contains a clear statement of its thesis at the outset—largely because it is easier to evaluate the relevance of particular claims as one proceeds—there are cases in which I think it is worth sacrificing this advantage in the interests of dramatic and/or pedagogical effect. This is one sort of choice that I often struggle with in my own work, and I find that speaking openly with students about such struggles of my own—sometimes by showing them radically different drafts of bits of my own work—is an effective device for opening their minds to alternative ways of doing things. It also cultivates an atmosphere of mutuality.

Talking about such choices as if they might be reasonably resolved in a number of ways has other benefits as well. It can help to remove one of the primary sources of writer's block—namely, the idea that there is a single best way to do things. It is also a good way to open students' minds to the potential benefits of radical revision. For I find that students are too often wedded to what they start with, and tend to think of revision simply as a matter of changing a few words—or adding a sentence or two—here and there. So I ask them early on to practice radically restructuring both paragraphs and sentences. Students find it much more difficult to do this with sentences than with paragraphs, and I am still looking for a good method to help them restructure sentences: I would welcome suggestions here.[1] With paragraphs, I ask them to write several different paragraphs, each with the same content but a different structure, and then to evaluate the various paragraphs for relative effectiveness. And I encourage them to think in terms of costs and benefits, so as to discourage the idea that the choice between one paragraph and another is always clear-cut. I have not tried anything like this with whole papers yet, but writing this piece has given me an idea I would like to try in the future. I would like to ask students to write two radically different pieces, each intended to convey the same view—one a dialogue and one a straightforward argumentative piece. It would be interesting, also, to see if it were easier for students to "translate" in one direction rather than another—i.e., from dialogue to straightforward argument or vice versa. And it would be interesting to see if starting with the dialogue and then moving to straightforward argument resulted in dialectically more interesting argumentative papers. I suspect it would. If so, asking students to move from dialogues to argumentative pieces would be another way to cultivate dialectical imagination.

Still the main way—one might say the "generic" way—to cultivate dialectical imagination is to provoke students to engage in dialectic for themselves.[2] And the first, and perhaps most important, step is in the classroom. For while novices may be able to appreciate dialectical interplay as it appears on the written page, especially if you give them pieces by authors who are responding directly to one another, written dialectic is less likely to come alive for them if they have not already participated in it first hand. The best remedy is to draw them into dialectical discussion with themselves and with each other. And one good way to do this is to guide them, in a Socratic way, in developing hypothetical examples of their own, examples that are designed either to defend or to defeat particular points. This is an excellent way to cultivate dialectical imagination while simultaneously encouraging precision and rigor. For asking them to develop their own hypothetical examples affords freer play to their imagination than does asking them to produce actual or historical examples. But the license to invent their own examples is not carte blanche: they must produce examples with the relevant features.

This sort of task is typically new to undergraduates; the closest they are likely to have come to it is in seeking to design just the right sort of scientific experiment to test a given hypothesis (which is a useful analogy to get them going). So I find that it works best in class dialogue, where I can guide the discussion. A typical exchange goes something like this. I set out a view and ask for a counterexample to it. Often there are several false starts and I probe the class about why the proposed counterexamples do not work, sometimes giving them hints. Eventually someone proposes something that is in the right ballpark but not quite on the mark. I ask other members of the class what is right and what is wrong with the proposal, and try to get them (sometimes with hints from myself) to modify it so as to get it right. I find that students can really get into this sort of exercise when it is carried out in a friendly playful way—as if, for example, they were playing a game like Twenty Questions.[3]

This sort of immediate guidance and feedback is something you must provide: textbooks cannot do this job. (It may in fact have been Socrates' appreciation of this that led him to eschew writing.) You can, of course, provide some of this in written comments on your students' work. And you can invite students to do it for one another by asking them to write comments on one another's work, which is something I frequently ask them to do in order to prepare them for the more difficult task—and eventual goal—of commenting on their own work. But there is no better introduction to philosophy than the immediate give and take of dialogue with your students. So, although I am generally wary of letting students know what I think on an issue they are supposed to be thinking through themselves, I have found that asking them to engage in debate with me—sometimes even by asking them to comment on bits of my work—is a way of drawing them into dialogue not only with me but with the broader philosophical community as well. By situating myself for them in a debate with my peers (or predecessors) I can draw them, through their debate with me, into debate with my peers (or predecessors). This serves, I think, to bring the activity of philosophy alive to them in a way in which simply reading texts—as if philosophy is something that goes on "out there"—does not.

Philosophy is an activity; it is something you do. One of the greatest obstacles to novice philosophizing is the common conception of college papers as glorified reports—reports about someone else's views. Although a few philosophically inclined students can pick up the idea of how to do philosophy simply by reading written examples of it, most students need to be goaded out of reporting philosophy and guided into doing it. This requires dialectical interaction with others—both with skilled interlocutors and with their peers. Then, having learned how to argue with live interlocutors, they should find it easier to argue with dead (or imaginary) ones: to think of their own objections to Descartes, for example, and to imagine how Descartes (or an imaginary interlocutor sympathetic to his view) might respond to such objections. Finally, having mastered this, they should be well on the way to acquiring the benefit that the Cynic Antisthenes is reported to have said he acquired from philosophy— namely, the ability to converse with himself (Laertius 1925). There is an additional—and discipline-neutral—benefit here as well. For this should move students closer to the ideal to which I think all writers should aspire—namely, the ability to comment on one's own work *as if* it were the work of another.

I once had a freshman who struggled all term, both with philosophical ideas and with their written expression. But I felt that I had made great progress when, toward the end of the term, she said, as if light had suddenly dawned upon the whole, "Why, philosophy is just like one big conversation, isn't it?" I am sure, by the way, that this student had never read—nor even heard of—Richard Rorty. I am also sure that she had little idea just how true this is of philosophy's distinctive "disciplinary culture." I have often heard people from other fields remark with curiosity on the percentage of time that philosophy colloquia typically award to commentary and discussion. I have also heard philosophers who have participated in colloquia in other fields muse that others seems to regard the sorts of questions philosophers routinely ask of one another as hostile or unacceptably impolite. Such remarks and musings seem to me to reflect the way in which philosophy, perhaps more than any other discipline, is fundamentally dialectical. It proceeds largely by way of discussion (both written and oral) with other philosophers (live, dead, and imaginary) and ultimately with ourselves. The task of teaching philosophy is thus one of initiating students into the practices of such discussion, the task of making them participants and not simply observers.

# Writing (Not Drawing) a Blank

MARILYN MIGIEL

Romance Studies

⌒ Freshmen who sign up for my First-Year Writing Seminar at Cornell—or who, more likely, find themselves signed into it—are puzzled. The course, entitled The Craft of Storytelling, bears an Italian Literature number, ITALL 101. The single assigned book (excluding a volume on style) is a Western European classic with which they are almost certain to be unfamiliar: the *Decameron*. Some students shift uncomfortably in their seats. Why does this course have an Italian literature number? I explain that the course is classified as Italian literature because I am, by training, an Italianist, and my department home is Romance studies. The answer does not entirely reassure them. If I am a real Italianist, what I am doing here? Or more to the point, I suppose, if I am a real Italianist, what are they doing there? Perhaps I opted to become an English teacher? One young woman narrows her eyes. "What *are* you?" she asks.

I have occasionally joked that I am an "Italianist in search of another identity," but this formulation misfires, as it suggests that I would happily renounce my "Italianist-ness" if I could construct another professional mode of being. What I would prefer to escape instead is a restrictive notion of what it means to immerse oneself in the study of a foreign literature and culture. Yes, I have assumed a place in an institutional hierarchy, and yes, I have assumed the professional voice of an Italianist literary scholar. But I do not take this to mean that I profess in the classroom only those issues strictly related to Italian studies. Nor do I wish to be deprived of my special affiliation with a foreign culture that shapes my view of language, writing, culture, intellectuals, institutions, and the public sphere.

I used to feel more comfortable within the intellectual territory that I had set for myself; it was, after all, territory that felt readily recognizable and appreciated within the curriculum. In my late teens, twenties, and early thirties, happily entrenched as I was in studying and teaching in Ivy League universities where the value of a humanities education was simply self-evident (so it seemed to me at the time), I had a rather different idea of what I studied and why. It was carefully delimited: by the year 1400 *ad quem* in my youth, when I not only studied but lived the Middle Ages with semimonastic vigor, and by the geographical bounds of the Italian peninsula and islands during my grad school years and first decade in the profession, when I considered it a primary objective to transmit a deepened knowledge of Italian language and culture, and to do so in the target language. These defining limits certainly made it easier for me to state what I was doing.

Many factors contributed to the erosion of such boundaries of thought during the second decade of my professional career. Two emerge with particular weight. In 1991, I participated in a John S. Knight Faculty Seminar on Writing directed by Jim Slevin. Although my mentor in graduate school, Paolo Valesio, had brought our entire graduate student cohort to consider methodological issues in our research, in our writing, and in the Italian language classroom, this was the first time that I was encouraged to reflect on the principles and the methodology of what I did in the *English*-speaking humanities classroom. (I do believe that what we learn in one cultural and linguistic context can be transferred to another context, but that transfer across languages and across different areas of activity is never completely smooth.) The following summer, in August 1992, I gave birth to my first child, a son. Soon thereafter, I experienced what could only be called a massive paradigm shift: teaching centered not on what I knew but what somebody else needed to know.

Like all of us, I hold views about writing that have been forged in diverse academic, community, and personal settings. My scholarly publications are not my lone writings; they do not sum up what I think about writing either as process or as circulated product. I have written an array of individual and collaborative pieces, including policy manuals, reports and minutes for not-for-profit boards, notes for interviews on the radio and in newspapers, and countless e-mails. I am sure you know of what I speak.

Similarly, I promote writing in my university courses, but my mission does not stop at my classroom or office door. During the spring of 1999, for example, when I was on sabbatical leave, I devoted my pedagogical skills to my son's first-grade classroom, where I volunteered about forty minutes daily in a writing workshop. There, as I helped six- and seven-year-olds "publish books," I had the opportunity to see how early narrative styles and rhythms develop. With that in mind, I did the same things I do in a college classroom, modified for another developmental stage. I offered tips on how to begin composing—different tips for different children. I introduced the idea of necessary revision, by addition, deletion, substitution, and reorganization. I reinforced principles of clarity, organization, and style. I helped young authors develop a sense of audience, and I sought to instill in them a sense of pride in their own authorship. I also had the opportunity to respond to an intelligent and highly verbal child who developed a bad case of writing trauma, and claimed he could not write in his school journal because he "had no ideas." As it turned out, this distraught child was my own son. Perhaps not coincidentally, I also developed a bad case of writing trauma caused by "no ideas," and I managed to reemerge into narrative just as my son did.

Again, you may not volunteer in first-grade classrooms or have six-year-old sons, but I am reasonably sure that many of you will share my sense of teaching as a mode of responding to others in the world.

Sooner or later, our students will deal with writing and teaching on similar multiple fronts. They may well have a profession in which they write in a variety of languages, both specialized and accessible; they may well engage in other activities, especially civic and community ones, which will require yet another range of languages; they will always have to make decisions (even if implicit) about what it means to use language responsibly; and many of these freshmen, especially if they become parents, will be involved in teaching language and communication arts to the next generation of young people.

To teach writing and the humanities in the university is to place students in environments where they can, through their repeated engagements with reading and writing, also reflect on what it means to use language effectively and responsibly in diverse contexts. At best, each of us is positioned to do this in a way that is necessarily partial. All the more imperative, then, that each of us seeks to articulate the theories that invest our teaching of writing and the humanities. The phrase that comes to mind is an Italian one with Marxist overtones: *pensare in generale, agire in particolare*, which in a literal translation would probably come out as "Think in general, act in particular." Recasting this translation, I would say, "Think globally, act locally." And in light of this maxim, let me offer some thoughts on what this process, dialectically conceived, has looked like in my most recent freshman classroom.

ॐ Philosophically, I am of a class of teachers that believes it is impossible to teach writing without teaching reading. I am convinced not only by my experience, but also by testimonies that the better writers have well-honed reading strategies and are able to use their awareness of rhetorical possibilities and alternatives as they write.[1] I also believe that people do not learn these strategies only in classrooms; as Paulo Freire reminds us, people who are learning to read and write are already experienced in "writing" the world, touching it, changing it (Freire 1987, 49). Most importantly, I believe that teaching reading and writing does not simply offer people the possibility of surviving in a world that requires alphabet literacy, but also allows people to see the possibility of transforming their world. As Ann Berthoff states, "Liberation comes . . . when people reclaim their language and, with it, the power of envisagement, the imagination of a different world to be brought into being" (Berthoff 1987, xv).

Why, then, do I teach the *Decameron*, of all texts, to freshmen?

The reasons are many, not all of them terribly altruistic or noble. The *Decameron* is the subject of my current published research and my forthcoming book, *A Rhetoric of the* Decameron *(And Why Women Should Read It)*. Its stories seem designed to entertain more than to instruct. (Probably relevant here is the calculation of an Italianist who found that 67 percent of the *Decameron's* one hundred stories are focused on sexual relationships [Bergin 1981, 289–90].) But the rock-bottom reasons are the three I shall give below:

*The* Decameron *takes as its subject language itself.*
The *Decameron* is about a lot of things, of course, so this may seem presumptuous. It has been called a "Human Comedy," in contradistinction to Dante's "Divine" *Comedy*, because it portrays the complexity of lives of people of all stations. Much of the *Decameron* seems to be about love and sexuality, since these are dominant themes, and the author claims his book is written for lovesick women. But I would insist still that the *Decameron* is about language. In the *Decameron*, seven young women and three young men, all Florentines, look to language, to their own narrative powers, to console themselves and to recreate a community that they have lost to the Black Death of 1348. They explore how language can be used to create and shape realities, how communication can promote happiness and well being, how miscommunication can bring tragedy.

*The* Decameron *is a casebook for critical reflection; it asks questions to which there are no God-given right answers.*
Peculiarly situated astraddle the Middle Ages and the Renaissance, the *Decameron* charts the tensions in a society that is caught between a set of noble and aristocratic ideals, on one hand, and the managerial thinking of a new class of banking- and businessmen on the other. Despite Francesco De Sanctis's claim that Boccaccio never engages in the studied reflection that leads to true knowledge, and despite the fact that some of my freshmen have jokingly referred to the *Decameron* as a medieval porn novel, I would propose

that the *Decameron* is a perfect text for critical reflection because it consistently poses problems that require the judgment of an informed audience. Further-more, the *Decameron* places personal responsibility and the question of virtu-ous character at the heart of moral reflection; in this way, it goes counter to the expectations that students may have about what moral reflection is.[2]

*The* Decameron *calls on us to achieve a balance between accepting languages and belief systems and striving to improve on them.*
This is a mean task. We have to be willing to be "pushed into" a community of speakers and "pulled out of" certain ideological biases. We have to accept cer-tain limitations on our language (because we are historical heirs to a debate) and we have to try to see the limitations of our belief systems. The *Decameron* does this by thinking about how our stories are rewritings of and responses to other stories that have been put into play. It tells us something that many of my students would rather not hear: that our stories are never really "original" and they are never really "free." They are deeply influenced by gender; class; race; national, civic, political, and religious affiliations; education. But the *Decameron* also shows that within these constraints that we have no choice but to accept, there is the possibility of thinking another way. And it encourages us to respond, to rewrite.[3]

&#x2E2; In order to take stock of what I had done (largely on creative intuition) in my last freshman writing course, I organized the assigned readings and writings in a table format, which included the goals and objectives that the individual as-signments served. The main goals, as I noted above, were to explore: (1) how the *Decameron* takes language as its subject; (2) how the *Decameron* serves as a case-book for moral reflection; and (3) how the *Decameron* calls on us to achieve a balance between accepting languages and belief systems and striving to improve on them. (Space limitations make it impossible to reproduce the full table here, but I would be happy to send it to interested readers.) I began to ask: How well do specific tasks and assignments achieve the goals and objectives I have? Did I give enough weight to each goal? How might I rethink my approach in the future?

This reorganized syllabus reveals to me the constraints within which I op-erate. For one thing, my assignments are partially restricted by what I have done in the past, since I suspect that some students may have access to writing assign-ments that were produced for my courses some years ago. More important, how-ever, I see the limitations of my teaching abilities, or at least my imagination, at a particular historical moment. I personally am most interested in encouraging a metacritical awareness of language and storytelling.[4] But I realize that I have difficulty bringing this subject to a level appropriate for freshmen, probably because I am highly invested in these questions and I have written on them in much more technical language. So until I come up with an improved communication style, I keep exploration of this goal within classroom discussions. There, if students express bewilderment, I can modify my approach on the spot.

The syllabus also documents two crucial shifts in my pedagogical approach: one in the sequence of assignments, the other in use of writing assignments that are personal and creative rather than traditionally "analytic." Both of these shifts have affected the way I teach my upper-level courses as well as my freshman writing seminar. Given the limitation on space, I shall expand on the first point, leaving the exploration of personal writing to another time.

Since my prime focus was on the goals I have outlined briefly here (whether or not I had articulated them explicitly to myself at the beginning of the course), my students and I did not proceed through the *Decameron* from page 1 to page 689 consecutively. Rather, our experience of reading—and rereading—began to mirror the nonlinear processes of composing, revising, and rewriting. I visualized this process as a spiral, a wheel turning back on itself.[5] Students read and write first about a single story. Then they must relate it to other individual stories, reconsider it as part of a larger unit (e.g., ten stories in a day), and relate various larger units to each other. This progression "from micro to macro" appeared repeatedly throughout the course.[6]

In order to illustrate what kind of work students might produce as they work through these overlapping units, I offer in the appendix to this chapter the final paper that a freshman named Jessi King wrote in December 1998. She is already known to us in part, for she is the same student who, upon meeting me in September 1998, asked point-blank, "What *are* you?"

Thoroughly memorable are Jessi's outspokenness, her circumspect evaluations of arguments, and her willingness to cast a critical eye on any assertion I made. She came to a reading of literary texts with lenses that she had drawn from courses in philosophy, government, and psychology, and she struggled to integrate the various languages and modes of argument she had acquired along the way. Although her prose started out thick with superfluities, I had the sense that she liked words. She thought about how words looked on the page, as she changed fonts and formatting styles often. She liked puns and colorful turns of phrase, and she worked them into her writing when she could. She had some degree of familiarity with the way pre-twentieth-century English might sound, and she was willing to try out a more refined and syntactically intricate style, even if the results were unpredictable.

Jessi's final paper is entitled "Feminism in the Decameron??? Why a Woman Just Can't Win." Arguing against readers of the *Decameron* who had proclaimed it feminist, Jessi sets out her thesis statement at the end of the first paragraph:

> Women are not dominant in the *Decameron*; on the contrary, it is impossible for a woman to outsmart a man in this book. My reasoning is twofold: first, in order to "outsmart" there must be a presupposition that the woman's opponent is smart, which will prove false; and second, when a woman encounters a man of comparable wit, she inevitably loses to him.

After considering evidence in seven paragraphs, she concludes:

> Readers of the *Decameron* who hold that many women are portrayed as stronger or more dominant are attributing these characteristics to women incorrectly. While many women do defeat men, their wins are never based on their own wit or argument, but rather on their counterpart's lack in some integral aspect. When a woman encounters a man who is not deficient she inevitably loses to him. Because of the evidence that stacks up on both sides of this issue, I conclude that a woman is never allowed to overcome her male equal in the *Decameron*. How's that for a glass ceiling?

By 8 December, the date of the final paper, Jessi has made tremendous progress in formulating statements like these. Compare her thesis statement for an essay (dated 22 September) on class issues in *Decameron* VI: "When the lines denoting social "boundaries" are examined in the *Decameron*, it is interesting not only to look at interaction between members on different sides of those lines, but also what happens when those lines are crossed." Or her conclusion for a paper (dated 5 October) that she wrote on men, women, and truth in *Decameron* II: "When a woman acts for love, the truth doesn't matter so much, while because a man's blithe playfulness is of less importance than the strength of love, he is punished for straying from the truth."

Three paragraphs from the body of the final paper are reworkings of ideas that appeared in Jessi's previous submissions. Paragraph 2 on Andreuccio da Perugia (II, 5) and paragraph 5 on Madonna Filippa (VI, 7) draw some of their insight from one-page responses that Jessi wrote in September. Paragraph 6, on Salabaetto (VIII, 10), includes observations that Jessi had formulated in a creative writing assignment from early November: writing in the persona of Fiammetta, the female narrator of *Decameron* II, 5, she had drafted a letter to Dioneo, the male narrator of VIII, 10, to tell him that he seemed to be mocking her and her story of Andreuccio.

By the final paper, Jessi has gained some measure of control over her delight in colorful phrases and puns. She shifts to a twentieth-century phrase at the very conclusion of her paper, where I would argue it works, precisely because that is where we have to come back to thinking about what "Feminism in the *Decameron*" means for us. Earlier essays had seen Jessi struggling to find a way to temper the potential outrageousness of these colloquialisms or puns. She had described Madonna Piccarda, who avoids the sexual advances of a clergyman by substituting an ugly maidservant for herself, as someone who gets "a nagging man off her back, so to speak." Of Andreuccio da Perugia, Jessi had written that the reader "very quickly gets the impression that he isn't the brightest crayon in the coloring box, so to speak." Of Lorenzo, secretly buried by his murderers, Jessi had written, "Just as he was accepting his new 'lot,' he felt his soul begin to rise and saw his brutally mangled body beneath him." In the final paper, there is one place where Jessi is punning mercilessly, but it is so subtle that, unless you know the *Decameron* well, you will miss it.[7]

Jessi's argument holds from sentence to sentence, and paragraph to paragraph, but her paper is not without some wobbly stylistic and rhetorical choices. She occasionally slips into writing about "wins" and "lacks" where choices like "victories" and "deficiencies" would serve her better. She offers that Salabaetto "is successful beyond the scope of his original downfall," which leaves even me puzzled, and I know to what she might be referring.

And there are at least two possible criticisms that strike to the heart of this paper's argument. First, since Jessi remains focused on stories in which individual qualities of characters are important, she is not thinking about stories where women are limited by things for which no single person can be held accountable: e.g., the legal and judicial systems, codes of honor and proper behavior, the use of authorized violence. Second, Jessi begins with the claim that a smart woman should be able to outsmart her male equal—only to conclude that this does not happen in the *Decameron*. I wonder whether it is ever possible to represent as one's true equal someone that one tries to overcome.

These, I would say, are questions that I would pose for Jessi's consideration, not ones for which I would hold her accountable in December of her freshman year. Very few freshmen have the critical tools to ask questions at this level. But I think Jessi shows promise for the future.

To those readers who might see Jessi's final paper as compelling evidence that I, a progressive teacher, have successfully transmitted my openly declared feminism, let me say: I would not be so confident. What I know from reading the *Decameron*, among other things, is that writing never serves ideology so neatly and tidily. There is a good chance, in my opinion, that Jessi did not intend her essay to expose an injustice to women in the *Decameron*. After all, Jessi was a student who, describing one of her own stories where women's behavior was mocked, wrote, "I don't believe that my story could in any way be perceived as pro-woman. . . . Women just don't come out on top in this story." She was also a student who, to my bewilderment, used the masculine generic to describe all authorial figures—including, at one point, a female narrator of the *Decameron*. (I conceded temporary license to Jessi, noting however that in this day and age, a copy editor might simply intervene to make her language gender-neutral.)

But I remain fundamentally optimistic that in my course, Jessi, and other students like her, heard reinforced a message about what it means to learn—most especially what it means to learn about language. Jessi chose, at the end of her freshman year at Cornell, to apply to the College Scholar Program, an honors program that permits about forty Arts and Sciences students a year to develop their own programs of study, free from all normal distribution requirements. In part of the draft statement she gave me after I agreed to write her a letter of recommendation, she had written:

> I started out, in high school, thinking that I wanted to major in something concrete, something where you can get the answers and know them. My interests have developed into something much less concrete, [where it is] impossible to ever truly put a finger on some "answer." I love people. I love the way people interact and communicate . . . through speaking, writing, and the universal languages of mathematics and logic, and the way they think about all this. I am curious to see what such fields as government, psychology, social science, psychology, English, and philosophy have to say about how people think and communicate.

Needless to say perhaps, I found it mildly ironic that the student who asked me "what I was" was applying to a program that would almost certainly require her, for the foreseeable future, to repeatedly define herself. I suppose Jessi might still argue that underclassmen are permitted to be undecided about their intended fields of study, and College Scholars are authorized to be outside rigid disciplinary boundaries, whereas college professors like me should have better defined areas of competence. But I would prefer to believe otherwise. Jessi has discovered that the acquisition of knowledge—especially knowledge about language and communication—is not limited to a single discipline. She has also discovered that the presence of multiple answers is not proof of no answer. Most important, Jessi has clearly made a crucial developmental leap in realizing that, just because there are no quick answers to the big questions, doesn't mean that you have to draw a blank, have no credibility, no identity. It means that you have to speak and write yourself through one.

## *Appendix*

Jessi King, Cornell University class of 2002
ITALL 101—The Craft of Storytelling—Final Paper
8 December 1998

"Feminism in the *Decameron*???
Why a Woman Just Can't Win"

Many readers have focused on the pro-woman tendencies of
Boccaccio's *Decameron*. They see the women characters as "feminists" who dominate and outsmart men. But I would argue that
these victories are not won without ample aid from the very men
they outsmart, for these men are not formidable or even worthy
opponents. Often, the women are not witty, intelligent or dominant
in their own right, but rather lucky that their male counterparts are
utterly inept. Each time a woman succeeds in winning over a man,
he seems to be lacking in some quality that would have been
beneficial to him. Women are not dominant in the *Decameron*; on
the contrary, it is impossible for a woman to outsmart a man in this
book. My reasoning is two-fold: first, in order to "outsmart" there
must be a presupposition that the woman's opponent is smart, which
will prove false; and second, when a woman encounters a man of
comparable wit, she inevitably loses to him.

Andreuccio da Perugia (II.5) is clearly an example of a man who,
by his dim wits, allows a woman to take advantage of him. His
naiveté is first introduced when the narrator depicts his actions upon
arrival in Naples: waving his money around for all to see, thinking
that would establish him as a serious merchant; following a strange
woman into an obviously bad part of town; and believing that an
even stranger woman was his long-lost sister, who just happened to
recognize him. These examples, the other "falls" which follow and
his inability to learn from any mistakes are testaments to his
ineptitude. It is not by taking advantage of her own wits that allows
the prostitute victory over Andreuccio, but by taking advantage of
his lack thereof.

The next in the line of stupid men is Gianni Lotteringhi (VII.1)
who actually allows his wife to convince him that her lover is a
ghost and that they have exorcised it. This woman is allowed to win
and to keep her lover, even after a mistake on her part (or possibly a
servant's) when she should have rightly been caught red-handed.

Instead, she offers a completely asinine excuse for the knocking, pacifies her husband (who, incidentally, never thinks to open the door), and gets a message to her lover all in one little exorcism. Very similar to him is the father of Brother Rinaldo's godchild (VII.3). This man was also tricked into believing that an exorcism was taking place, when in fact his wife was having an affair. Both women are indeed witty to some degree, but are placed against men whose wit does not match their own. The men just simply aren't smart enough to stop them. Should this not have been the case, the outcome would have been different and these men would have seen through this thin veil of deceit.

Two men whose witty comments are rebuked by women, Madonna Oretta's knight (VI.1) and the Bishop of Florence (VI.3), both lacked in qualities other than wit. This lacking allowed both Madonna Oretta and Monna Nonna de' Pulci to "win" in their encounters. The knight, because he lacked in ability to engage an audience, was rebuked by Oretta and discontinued his horrible tale. The Bishop of Florence, in keeping with the other clergy described in the *Decameron*, was extremely rude and ill mannered. Because of this lacking, Nonna was able to "vindicate her honor" (*Decameron* VI.3, pg. 389) with a witty remark. While both of these women were obviously witty as they were featured on the day of witty remarks, they did not succeed in outsmarting anyone since their counterparts were obviously lacking.

Besides lacking wit, courtesy, or ability, men also are described as lacking rationality. In two cases, a woman is allowed her triumph because a man is taken over by emotion. Madonna Filippa (VI.7) not only succeeds in saving her own life, but in changing the law in favor of women. This seems like a clear victory on the part of Filippa and a feminist achievement. This reading would, however, be misleading if it were to attribute the success to Filippa's wit or argument. Filippa's charm, beauty, and charisma are the factors at play in this story. Were she lacking in these features, neither the podesta nor the masses would have taken her side. The fact that her beauty overcame the podesta is the important issue, since it shows once again that the woman was allowed to win because of a lacking on the man's part. Another such man found himself in quite a bit of trouble by acting out of anger. Arriguccio Berlinghieri (VII.8), the husband who found a string tied to his wife's toe and beat another woman in her place, is a fine example of a man overcome by emotion. He could have escaped the punishment he received had he taken the time to look at the woman he was beating. Once again, his wife went free of the punishment that he ended up bearing on himself. Both men, one acting out of lust and one out of anger, allow themselves to be defeated.

In contrast to these female victories against faulty foes, there are a number of occasions where women are set up against worthy adversaries. In each of these accounts, the woman fails miserably thereby proving on the second note that women are incapable of outsmarting men in the *Decameron*. This is shown most readily in the story of Salabaetto (VIII.10), in which Dioneo rewrites the story of Andreuccio. In this rewrite, the "Andreuccio" character, Salabaetto, is indeed a witty man and while his female opponent succeeds just as the prostitute did, Salabaetto comes back to take revenge and is successful beyond the scope of his original downfall. This story is the prime example of how, when a woman is set against a dimwit, she may be allowed to win, while when set against a shrewd fellow, she is sure to lose.

Another such incidence is that where Master Alberto (I.10) shames the object of his love. Since he is a very old man, she and her friends take pleasure in teasing the doctor because of his hopeless love. While they were most courteous in their jest and many a foolish man would have allowed himself this harm, the doctor was witty and well spoken. By using a metaphor that criticized women for their eating habits, he was able to embarrass the lady as she wished to embarrass him. This metaphor was particularly effective since it rebuked the young ladies for their rudeness as well as teased them in return, explained his point, and verified his wit.

Finally, in the story of the scholar and Elena (VIII.7) we see just what happens when a lady tries to outsmart the smartest kind of man—a scholar. In the beginning, as in Salabaetto's story, Elena did manage to take some fun at the expense of this scholar and seemingly achieve her goal. However, as this suitor was a very intelligent man who did not sit idly by thinking that some mistake of fortune was the cause of his dismay. The scholar quickly learned that it was the object of his desire that caused his treacherous night and he was not swayed by love's hand to forgiveness. Ultimately, it was Elena who suffered and the scholar who took revenge.

Readers of the *Decameron* who hold that many women are

portrayed as strong, dominant, or overcoming some obstacle are attributing these characteristics incorrectly. While many women do defeat men, their wins are never based on their own wit or argument, but rather on their counterpart's lack in some integral aspect. When a woman encounters a man that is not her lesser, she has been shown to inevitably lose to him. Because of the evidence that stacks up on both sides of this issue, I conclude that a woman is never allowed to overcome her male equal in the *Decameron*. How's that for a glass ceiling?

# Writing as a Sociologist

MICHAEL MACY

Sociology

With support from the Writing in the Majors program at Cornell, I have developed a sociology course that uses writing exercises not to teach writing but to teach sociology. The course is titled Group Solidarity and it explores questions about the "glue" that holds groups together. The course addresses these questions by looking at the problem from alternative theoretical perspectives: one centered on collective interests, the other on social identities. From the interest perspective, groups are held together because the members are interdependent and thus benefit from cooperating in a common endeavor. This perspective draws heavily on economics and game theory in which social life is analyzed as a problem of exchange. The interest paradigm directs our attention to three fundamental problems: "free-riding" ("Let George do it"), efficacy ("One person cannot make a difference"), and over-cooperation ("Too many cooks in the kitchen"). It also points to possible solutions. For free-riding, the solutions are formal and informal social control and reciprocity. For efficacy, the solutions are trust, coordination, and influence. But social control and peer pressure can also lead to oppressive conformity and needless sacrifice.

Social psychologists, in contrast, argue that solidarity is based on social identities that demarcate "us" and "them." Groups are held together because the members see one another as similar in some way that becomes highly salient. The identity perspective draws heavily on psychology and portrays social life primarily as interaction rather than exchange. We focus on two core problems: personal identity (a focus on "me" rather than "us") and over-conformity. For the former, the solution is identification with the group. Group identity motivates members not by self-interest but by (1) concern for the welfare of others, (2) normative obligation, and (3) emotional expression (indignation, revenge, martyrdom, etc.). But group identity can also lead to irrational over-conformity and ethnocentric hatred, as manifested in lynch mobs, religious crusades, race wars, terrorism, and the like.

These debates and dilemmas are addressed in a series of readings that range from highly theoretical accounts (including game theory and computational models) to empirically grounded case studies. About every three weeks, I ask students to write short papers from the point-of-view of the sociologist we are reading that week, as this author might engage contending ideas encountered in previous weeks. Two sociologists now interact with one another through the medium of a reader-become-writer. The student must climb inside the author's head and find this author's voice. A few of the more playful students also try to capture the author's distinctive rhetoric and style, but I emphasize that this is not required.

These exercises are not intended merely as tools for evaluation. They are learning devices based on an underlying "constructionist" pedagogy (Harel and Papert 1991). In the more traditional "instructionist" approach, the curriculum aims at the didactic communication of a body of accumulated knowledge, through readings and lectures. Writing assignments then provide feedback needed to monitor the fidelity of transmission as information flows downstream, from experts to neophytes. The problem is that we may short-circuit the learning process if someone in a position of authority, such as "author" or "professor," draws conclusions on the wall. The students then become empty vessels into which knowledge is poured and stored for later retrieval.

The constructionist approach centers on the generation of knowledge, in which lectures and readings provide students not with a "finished product" but with raw material that students must actively process. Writing exercises are the medium. At the same time, these exercises are not invitations to free-wheel. When students are given too much latitude, they often confuse criticism with critical thinking. They tend to shoot first and ask questions later, criticizing the argument before they fully understand it. This is the mirror image of a lecture that packages the conclusion for them.

The challenge is to steer between too much and too little structure. Structure is not lecture. A carefully structured writing exercise provides students with a template that guides—yet does not stifle—critical inquiry. The requirement to get inside the author's argument disciplines the student to anticipate and pre-empt superficial criticism. On the other side, the requirement to apply the argument to novel cases or to challenge another point of view precludes the option to hide behind the ideas of others and forces the student to go beyond rote exegesis.

In essence, the exercises ask the student to read not as a reader but as a writer. To read as a writer, the student must take the material apart and reassemble it, in much the same way a child understands a toy by taking it apart. The text is also a toy, and upon reassembly, a few pieces are usually left out, requiring yet another iteration, until the puzzle is fully solved.

There is nothing especially sociological about the use of writing as a puzzle-solving exercise. The disciplinary link is not in the method but in its application to sociological case studies. These cases are not unlike murder mysteries, and the writing exercises invite students to become sociological detectives who use theory to hunt for clues that can help them solve the case.

For example, why were the most successful nineteenth-century communes those that enforced strict codes of abstinence? This would seem to make no sense from the rational-actor perspective of game theory. Yet one student revisited Kanter's book on commune survival from precisely this point of view. In a concise but highly effective argument, he showed how Kanter's social-psychological explanation failed to consider the "reward structure" confronted by the members. He then analyzed the decision problem as a mixed-motive game with two choices, "cooperate" (in this case, abstain from worldly pleasures) and "defect" (indulge). These two choices intersect at four possible outcomes, and each outcome has a designated payoff. $R$ (reward) and $P$ (punishment) are the payoffs for mutual cooperation and defection, respectively, while $S$ (sucker) and $T$ (temptation) are the payoffs for cooperation by one player and defection by the other. The student then showed that abstinence was the dominating strategy:

> In any commune—whether abstinent or indulgent—$R$ (abstain) and $P$ (indulge) would result in greater payoff than $S$ and $T$ simply by virtue of conformity. By this account, conformity in communes might have been not only externally regulated, but to a large extent also self-imposed. In the reward structure above, the difference between $S$ and $T$ is trivial, for they both signify forsaking the group, and hence the public good. Between $R$ and $P$, $R$ might be preferred in abstinent communes, whereas $R$ and $P$ might be equally preferred in indulgent communes.

In this short exercise, the student had to understand not only Kanter's original argument but also enough game theory to translate the "commitment device" identified by Kanter into an incentive problem and show how this translation identified an interest-driven mechanism that was missing in the original formulation.

In a longer assignment, I ask students to apply theories to cases in one of two ways. First, they can pick one case and compare two theories that they find applicable to this case. The goal is to see how different theories call attention to different aspects of a case. Alternatively, students can pick a theory and compare two cases that differ in a way that is relevant to the theory. The goal here is to see how well the theory can account for differences between the cases.

The important point I want to make here is that students are no longer allowed to choose only one theory and one case. The problem with a "one-on-one" assignment, I have found, is the invitation to be descriptive rather than analytical. Students tend to use the case to illustrate the theory, not to grapple with it. For example, a few years ago, a student used a drinking incident in high school to illustrate the Prisoner's Dilemma, a basic problem in game theory. The paper was very nicely organized, very clear, and provided a cogent example of the tension between individual and collective interests created by strategic interdependence. The student showed a strong grasp of game theory and a knack for bringing to life the highly abstract formalisms. However, while the student concluded that the cooperative outcome was consistent with the prediction for repeated games, he failed to consider the possibility that the anticipation of future interaction might not have been what motivated the cooperative behavior. He needed a second case, of "one-shot" (or single-play) interaction, to see if the outcome was less cooperative, as predicted by the theory.

Indeed, I generally find that even the one-case/two-theories assignment can become descriptive if students interpret their task as simply showing how the case illustrates concepts in each of the theories. For example, a student wrote a very thorough case study of his fraternity as an illustration of the theories of Hechter and Kanter. He carefully inventoried the monitoring and sanctioning capacities of the organization, as emphasized by Hechter, and then the six "commitment devices" proposed by Kanter. However, his final sentence shows how, in the end, his paper fell flat: "Ultimately, however, both Hechter's psychological approach and Kanter's sociological approach explain my fraternity's shortcomings and provide outlines for increasing future commitment."

The best papers are often from students who use two cases to test a prediction derived from a single theory. When properly executed, the assignment requires the student to distill from the theory a relationship between two variables, of the form "the more of this, the more of that." The cases must then be chosen carefully so that "this" varies from one to the other. The student then looks to see if "that" also varies as predicted by the theory. For example, one student compared a fraternity and an ice-hockey team to test predictions derived from a rational choice theory of group solidarity. (Fraternities are by far the most popular case, despite these groups' requirement of secrecy!) The student first identified the key idea from the theory, namely, that contributions to the group must be motivated by self-interest, that is, by the ability of the group to answer the question, "What's in it for me?" He then compared the ability of the two groups to answer this question, and the level of free-riding in each of the groups. The fraternity, he found, placed relatively little emphasis on monitoring and sanctioning the performance of group members compared to the team. Yet the level of commitment to the fraternity was as high or higher. He concluded that something besides self-interest must be involved, and he then speculated on the importance of friendship as a source of obligation that cannot be easily explained in cost-benefit terms.

The alternative "one-case, two theories" assignment has also elicited effective papers. For example, a student compared "rational choice" and "normativist" explanations of coaching strategies in high-school volleyball.

> In a contest of say, $N$ games, and a training period of $t$ days, which coach would have a higher success rate against the other? My hypothesis is that the relative success of the two coaches will depend on $N$ and $t$, because normativist theory is mainly applicable to long-lasting groups (such as communes), while rational choice theory is valid for all groups jointly producing a collective good. . . . The value of playing time increases to the players as $N$ decreases. This is because when $N$ is smaller, the amount of playing time is also smaller and hence, more valuable. However, the relationship of group solidarity of the Rational Actors with respect to $t$ is positive. Sanctions and monitoring are more effective with a longer training period. There is more time to monitor players and see who shirks practice and who does not. Hence, the distribution of sanctions will be more effective with a larger $t$. I believe that the Normativists would win a contest in which $N$ was large and the Rational Actors would win a contest in which $N$ was small (keeping $t$ constant). The relationship of relative success with respect to $t$ is more complex since both teams improve with higher $t$'s. More knowledge and empirical data is required before a conclusion on the effect of $t$ can be determined.

I quote from this paper at length to convey the analytical approach the student took to the assignment. Formal theory is increasingly important in sociology, and these exercises let students practice this method of argumentation in a playful and supportive environment. At the same time, the discipline's humanist wing relies heavily on the narrative case method, which students experience in the readings they are asked to grapple with. However, my interest goes beyond exposing students to alternative approaches. The hidden agenda is for students to see how sociologists, like detectives, use theory and evidence to solve mysteries. The writing exercises require that students not simply observe this process from the back of the room but actually try it themselves.

Admittedly, not all students respond equally well. Many struggle with these assignments and admit to considerable discomfort in the process. Most students require several tries before they get it right. Students can rewrite papers, but more importantly, the use of several short assignments permits everyone to iterate their work. Some students also complain that the assignments are too constricting and do not let them express their own point of view. I remind them that these are training exercises, not performances. That distinction seems to provide some solace to frustrated writers seeking creative outlets.

The distinction between training and performance is also a nice point on which to end this essay. I often hear colleagues complain that too many of their students "do not know how to write." I have not found that to be the problem. Actually, matters are rather more serious. Among undergraduates, I find that very few students come to Cornell knowing how to *read*. Accordingly, in mounting a Writing in the Majors course I am not trying to teach students to write, or for that matter, to write like a sociologist. I save that for graduate seminars. Here, I am using writing exercises to teach students to *read* like a sociologist. Mostly it works, and when it does, students find that they no longer learn by remembering what they read. Real learning begins when students are able to reconstruct what they read, and to that end, writing can be an effective tool.

# Afterword

## *Writing Writing*

JONATHAN MONROE

Normal usage is the art of channeling weapons so the majority
of sentences willingly enforce the current meaning of money
with a minimum of state body revealed in the headlines.

BOB PERELMAN, *Virtual Reality*

Topic sentence. However; but; as a result. Blah, blah, blah. It
follows from this. Concluding sentence.

CHARLES BERNSTEIN, *Content's Dream*

1. There is no Topic Sentence. . . .
2. Possible Topic Sentences or Opening Remarks at the Party

ANN LAUTERBACH, "The Night Sky"

Whose words they were
we couldn't say.

They spoke to us from
another time,
not ours,
*noch nicht*
anyway,

though we were told
someday
they'd be our own.

Then they'd be ours.
We'd pass them on to

we                ourselves

### *What Do We Talk about When We Talk about Writing?*

ℐ To begin, a question, a response—not yet an answer, a thesis—more questions.[1] *Doing*, as everyone knows, isn't *knowing* (exactly). Coming to a certain level of self-awareness about a particular practice, including the practice of writing, invariably changes it, both the awareness and the activity, not to mention the self, more or less permanently. There is something about the activity (not state) of awareness that changes everything. Knowing leads to unknowing, doing to undoing, writing to revision, revision to more writing, forwards and backwards and sideways, *dans tous les sens*, as the French have it, "in all directions (senses, meanings). . . ."

Florentino Ariza, the flowery yet awkward, eloquent yet errant protagonist of Gabriel García Márquez's *Love in the Time of Cholera (Amor en los tiempos del cólera)*, wants nothing more, growing up in his unnamed South American country, than to be a poet. What he becomes, instead, in order to survive, is a businessman. Having steeped himself as a youth in Golden Age sonnets, Florentino grows up to understand that, in real life, nothing could be more desirable and helpful than to be able to write a good business letter, an ability as it turns out much further beyond Florentino's reach than winning the local sonnet-writing contest decided by oral performance in the town square. Had Florentino grown up to be a student at a university such as Cornell, or a faculty member there in, say, comparative literature, my home department since joining the Cornell faculty in 1984, perhaps he would have written the following:

AS IT IS

The first discipline
of a discipline is, or
should be, not to forget
that it has not always been
a discipline.
         It is this
forgetting that makes up
the discipline, makes it
what it is, a thing
unmade and not

made up in the eyes
of those who
really make it,
hear it as it is,
necessarily fictional,
but a thing they need
to forget in order to
get on with remembering
what it is they don't need
to forget to go on with.

It is a thing
not itself not a thing that claims
things are the way they are,
have been and will be
always as they never were,
never can be again
once the forgetting starts
getting remembered, once
the dismembering
of its members achieves
a critical
mass, a celebration
perhaps of the need
to congregate, to gather
together under future stars
whose covert revelations
have yet to be revealed,
which is to say, re-
membered as if
forgotten.

As a comparatist by training, I've enjoyed the rare privilege of directing for the past ten years at Cornell, with course relief from my usual comparative literature teaching responsibilities, a time-honored and time-tested Cornell institution. I say enjoyed "as a comparatist" because the Knight Institute's interdisciplinary character has always felt to me of a piece with concerns I take to be at the heart of the comparatist's métier. It's this interdisciplinary orientation above all that led me to accept the invitation to direct the Knight Writing Program in 1992, and that continues to make the Knight Institute to this day such an intellectually rewarding local culture to inhabit and explore. As anyone familiar with what I have called the local knowledges and local practices of comparative literature knows, a comparatist is virtually, by definition, one who moves between and among, an exile of sorts who takes pleasure in in-betweenness, in not belonging to any one place, in a kind of ceaseless oscillation between contexts and cultures that requires never-ending translation. In this sense, being a comparatist is analogous to, and coincident with, being an eternal student. Like the field of writing instruction, comparative literature is a discipline that tends sometimes to be located within, sometimes outside English departments, sometimes to its comparative institutional advantage and sometimes not. Speaking from within a discipline, then, that almost as a matter of principle wants not to have an inside, a discipline that has always defined itself by a certain refusal to be at home anywhere—and in as many languages, cultures, and disciplines as possible—we could say that writing as a comparatist means writing as a perpetual outsider, no matter the geographical or institutional location. In this sense, of course, the comparatist is far from being alone. I take writing as a comparatist to be allegorically coincident with writing generally, and in particular with the multiple roles and writing cultures both undergraduates and graduate students must negotiate within the university, and thereafter in the world at large. It seems fair to say that it may be more the rule than the exception for students at all levels to feel outside of the disciplines they seek to inhabit. If writing is about anything, it is about connection, understanding, exploration, but also unavoidably, fortunately, about missed connections, misunderstandings, getting lost, learning to negotiate and learn from difference, conflict, lack of resolution. To help students more fully engage these open-ended negotiations, to find ways to encourage them to take the risks involved in that process, is perhaps the central task involved in the teaching of writing. It is a task that belongs most integrally to faculty members writing and teaching within their particular—always conflicted, always to some degree unsettled—disciplinary cultures.

As Florentino has his scenes of writing as a poet and as a businessman, often painfully and comically confusing the one with the other, what diverse scenes of writing do our students encounter from faculty representing their particular disciplines? Where does that writing take place, and for whom? When is one writing within a discipline and when not? When is a discipline not a discipline?

Open to a wide range of energies and discourses from different fields whose interaction it seeks to encourage, the Knight Institute supports thinking about writing as a continual process of self-revision and self-transformation. While it relies to some degree on the contributions of a small core group of writing professionals, its peculiar, hybridized identity and the greater part of its strength, stability, and resiliency have evolved from a farsighted interdisciplinary model created in the late sixties that has since expanded to include participation from some thirty departments each semester. Writing has thus come to be institutionalized at Cornell as, of all things, a kind of anti-discipline, a discipline that is and is not a discipline, in much the sense that Schlegel intended when he advised that it is necessary both to have a system and not have one. It is, perhaps, the single most convincing example I have encountered within the university of Friedrich Schlegel's desire to put poetry and philosophy into close relation with each other (and biology, and government, and history, and linguistics . . .) and to do this on a regular basis.

DEFINING TERMS

So many paths
in every word,

yet only two
seemed open, prose

and verse, at
least that's what

Jourdain would say
were he alive:

*"C'est tout! Enfin,
Il faut choisir!"*

The character of any field or culture of inquiry is perhaps best understood by what that culture or field makes manifest, including, perhaps above all, the processes of explicitation through which it brings to light not only new information about its objects of inquiry, but its own assumptions, conventions, and procedures. Under the directorship of my two immediate predecessors, Fredric Bogel and Harry Shaw, the Knight Writing Program had come to articulate and represent, at least as I understood it, three primary emphases: (1) thesis development, closely aligned with a corollary emphasis on critical thinking; (2) assignment sequencing, an emphasis indebted to James Slevin, former Chair of the Georgetown English Department, who first came to Cornell in 1986 at Harry Shaw's invitation to help redesign Teaching Writing, and (3) responding to— not merely grading—student essays. Through my combined experiences with the Knight Writing Program as a teacher of one First-Year Writing Seminar each year as part of my regular teaching load in comparative literature; as a course leader in comparative literature between 1987 and 1992 for the dozen or so graduate students from the department teaching in the program each semester; and, finally, a veteran of the program's annual Faculty Seminar in Writing Instruction, I had come to admire and agree with these three emphases wholeheartedly. Yet if thesis development and sequencing had become two of the Program's manifest values, I found myself drawn as director especially to what Cornell Russian professor Pat Carden called, in her contribution to *Teaching Prose,* "finding cruxes" (37–39). The importance of this emphasis resides especially in encouraging students, perhaps in a more aleatory and intuitive way than the idea of the sequence might suggest, to generate their own questions. Its purpose is not to minimize the importance of the thesis, but rather to stress the importance of arriving at a thesis and then questioning it further, to discourage the kind of premature settling on an answer—a thesis being nothing else than the answer to a question—that tends to inflect undergraduate writing, and first-year writing in particular, toward what we might call forms of "expository correctness."

Beyond this questioning of the thesis statement as in and of itself a reliable index of the quality of a piece of writing, one of my first priorities in my first year as director was to address the issue, as I felt it strongly at the time, of Cornell's centrally isolated location, not only geographically but in relation to the national topography, as it were, of the rapidly developing, heterogeneous field(s) of composition and rhetoric, fields with which the Knight Program had previously had comparatively little contact. By my first year as director, the diverse fields or cultures of composition and rhetoric, WAC (writing across the curriculum), and WID (writing in the disciplines) had developed to the point where it seemed important to engage them more fully, beyond the helpful connection Harry Shaw had established in bringing in James Slevin to help redesign our summer training programs. Persuaded in my first year as director in 1992 of the distinctiveness, if not the uniqueness, of what had come to be called the Cornell model, I began considering the possibility of hosting a national conference on (as I already then preferred to call it) writing in the disciplines, only to discover that Clemson, the College of Charleston, and the Citadel were then preparing to host what would become, in January 1993, the first biennial Writing across the Curriculum Conference in Charleston, South Carolina. Initially conceived as more a regional than a national affair, the first Charleston conference is significant in the history of WAC in marking in effect the national institutionalization of WAC as a movement after some two decades of development by that name. So successful was the first conference, drawing around two hundred participants from all over the country, that by the second national conference in 1995, where I chaired a Knight Writing Program panel on what I called our "decentralized center," attendance had grown to over four hundred. Following the third conference in Charleston in 1997, which drew some seven hundred participants, Cornell was selected by the three cofounding schools as the first university to host the event in another venue.

The field or culture of writing across the curriculum, or writing in the disciplines, is itself no more a meta-field than any other, but one field among many. It continually runs the risk, as does every field, of devolving into something more parochial than it aspires to be. In bringing the fourth national WAC conference to Cornell in June 1999, I hoped the Knight Writing Program's experience might help inflect the WAC movement, while honoring its history and traditions, more strongly in the direction of a discipline-based approach to the teaching of writing. To that end, I organized and hosted a special three-day series for the 1999 meeting on the topic of Disciplinary Cultures. Like *Local Knowledges, Local Practices* and its companion volume, *Writing and Revising the Disciplines*, the Disciplinary Cultures series was based on the premise that the strength of WAC and WID continues to reside in its (or is it their) closeness to the rich, ever-changing variety and depth of writing practices that go on within, among, and across particular fields, each parochial to its others, if not to itself, each in danger of becoming captive to the enchantment of its own self-representations. As the unreconciled, unresolved proliferation of professional terms within the discipline suggests—composition, rhetoric, WAC, WID, etc.—what we talk about when we talk about writing and the teaching of writing remains, happily, resistant to the idea of a unified field, the more so (often less happily) owing to institutional factors—perhaps most notably what has been called the adjunctification of writing instruction—that remain in flux within higher education generally. From this more global, as well as the more local, Cornell, perspective, the great strength of writing and the teaching of writing at Cornell clearly lies in its embeddedness within the particular disciplinary cultures the Knight Institute seeks to support. The three keys to the Institute's success in this regard have been three fundamentals: (1) a field-based approach, (2) faculty participation, and (3) funding, all of which are inextricably bound up with one another. Above all else, it is the faculty's shared commitment to the teaching of writing, understood always as writing located within and across the disciplines, that has allowed the Knight Institute to flourish.

At the core of the Institute's longevity and success in this regard is the principle of dialogue: whether the internal dialogue that constitutes writing as a self-reflexive activity, and which I've meant to imply by the idea of "Writing Writing"; the ongoing dialogues—typically more fractured and unsettled than they may appear from the outside—that go on within the disciplines; or the dialogues that take place, manifestly and often in more subterranean ways, between and among disciplines and across various discourse communities. With this expanded understanding of dialogue as a given, the primary goal of a decentralized center of writing instruction, as it has been conceived at Cornell, is, in a fundamental sense, to give back to the faculty (or better, help bring to the surface, make manifest) what has been theirs all along, expertise in their own disciplinary languages, their own discourse communities—plural, internally fractured, diverse, hierarchical, changing, etc. In this way, a decentralized writing center can be of service to, not colonize, faculty and graduate students, helping them to develop greater self-awareness of the writing practices of their respective fields in ways that will facilitate student access to them. It has been our experience in the Knight Institute that some of the most effective ways to generate and sustain interest among the faculty are: (1) to appeal to disciplinary self-interest; (2) to help make explicit ways in which thinking about writing can enhance discipline-based learning; (3) to encourage ongoing dialogue among the faculty, and so ensure that our knowledge base in the teaching of writing is broad, deep, and openly shared; and (4) to cultivate an understanding of the teaching of writing as a nexus of interaction, a forum for the exchange of a diverse range of perspectives and approaches that encourages intra- and cross-disciplinary cooperation, self-reflection, and innovation.

## From *Writing in the Majors* to *Writing in the Disciplines*

Prior to the founding of the Knight Institute's upper-division Writing in the Majors program in 1988 by Harry Shaw and current director Keith Hjortshoj, a program that effectively remained in an extended pilot phase prior to its expansion in 1997, the writing program remained for the duration of its first two decades a first-year program only. The addition of Writing in the Majors represented a crucial step in the Knight Program's evolution beyond this original limitation. Thanks to the Knight Foundation's December 1999 grant for endowment, coupled with a dramatic increase in the university's own commitment to upper-division writing courses, Cornell is at last poised, after three decades of experimentation, refinement, and development, to offer a fully-articulated undergraduate writing program, one broadly committed to the teaching of writing at all levels of the curriculum. While the idea of "writing in the majors" remains important to the Institute's commitment to teaching and mentoring undergraduates in their chosen fields, my own preferred emphasis on the term "writing in the disciplines" stems in part from the recognition that if the teaching of writing is to retain the commitment and respect of faculty across the disciplines, it can do so only by appealing to faculty working at the highest levels of disciplinary sophistication within their chosen fields. Anything less, ultimately, will likely contribute to the increasing adjunctification of the teaching of writing—a fact the field of composition must confront increasingly—and the consignment of the teaching of writing to a remedial activity. One of a writing program's critical functions in this regard is to help students develop a more acute awareness of discursive constraints and options, engage their own critical/institutional formations in ways that are integrally self-revising and open-ended—aleatory despite being programmatic, programmatic despite being aleatory—and so turn the discourses and writing practices of the various disciplines they encounter to use in ways that might contribute even to the self-revisioning of the disciplines themselves, as well as the social uses of disciplinary practices beyond the academy.

As our students intuitively understand—and sometimes more than just intuitively, on the basis of past experience—there may be many reasons to fear writing, yet those who most fear it, who most procrastinate about writing as a project, may do so because they understand very well that mastery is an impossible, open-ended, potentially self-complicating, if not self-harming project, and that although everyone needs language to survive, the task of writing writing is far more complex than merely getting it right, a process involving often difficult self-questioning and intricate negotiations within and across fields of inquiry. Given the risks involved, we might ask, not, "Why do some students (and not only students) find writing so difficult?" but "Why commit to the task of writing at all?" In the university, as in life, the answer to the second question depends on the answer to a prior one: "What do you care about?" The history of writing at Cornell is deeply informed by this question. In the university-wide decision, arrived at through intensive faculty dialogue nearly three decades ago, to move away from the then standard composition, theme- and form-based model of teaching writing to a content- and thus discipline-based model, Cornell committed itself to the fundamental and complementary principle that students are likely to write most effectively when they care about what they are writing. At Cornell, this principle led not to a centering of the teaching of writing, but rather to a deliberate decentering that would locate it in a thoroughgoing way within and among the disciplines. The program's financial and administrative structures were initially conceived and have since been elaborated with three fundamental principles in mind: (1) that writing is the property of all disciplines, (2) that writing takes place in the university within the particular contexts defined by the disciplines, and (3) that effective writing within the university involves cultivating the ability to engage in increasingly complex disciplinary negotiations.

What may be more interesting and instructive from an institutional perspective than the history of tensions over the past several decades involving the terms "theory," "creative writing," and "composition"—tensions that reached their peak in the 1980s and that have since largely played themselves out—is the fact that all three areas of specialization grew up together as sibling rivals, as it were, on parallel tracks in the development of what Peggy Kamuf has called the "Division of Literature" (Kamuf 1995, 53). From the perspective of this division—at once internal and external—what I have called elsewhere antigeneric or multigenre writings, such as those associated perhaps most readily with the diverse energies of Language Writing and multicultural, multilingual poetries, have been especially significant in carving out spaces for writing outside the university that have slowly opened up opportunities for alternative writing within the academy as well. As a consequence, the academy has itself become increasingly receptive in recent years to attempts to write past institutionalized divisions of writing that have tended to compartmentalize and delimit the writing process.

When I began as director of the Knight Program in 1992, one of the first items of business for me to pursue to understand what the position might involve was a questioning of what struck me at the time as one of the iconographic phrases of the field of composition and of higher education generally, one of those phrases that could almost immediately establish currency and a sense of belonging. The term "critical thinking," compelling as I found it (and I used it as much as anyone) began to feel to me in the ways it was used as if it were the Unthought itself, a kind of mantra that teachers and administrators of writing and others could use with almost invariable success to affirm the value of our activities within the university. What happens when critical thinking itself (as value) becomes the Unthought? Why critical thinking as the apparent *raison d'être* of all reading and writing? Why not understanding? Why not compassion? Why not cooperation?

Given the university's position as the cultural embodiment of what Jacques Derrida has called, in an essay based specifically on Cornell's topography, "the principle of reason"—at once *Grund* and *Abgrund*, ground and abyss of community—how does the university's image of itself get reflected, in Derrida's words, "in the eyes of its pupils" (Derrida 1983, 11). What is the "other" of "critical thinking"? Is it dumb thinking, ritualized thinking, normative thinking, routinized thinking, rote thinking, thinking otherhow? What if, not only in the university but earlier in grades K–12, the educational system were to use all its resources, including the teaching of poetry and philosophy, to question the dichotomies that currently structure university curricula between reading and writing, between the creative and the critical, between instrumental and playful uses of language? What if the goal of teaching/learning were not so much mastery—understood in a limited sense as the routinized acquisition of particular language games, of genres and modes of thinking/feeling/writing—but something like awareness, as exemplified through particular modalities of attention (including mixed modes), not for the sake of innovation as an end itself, but toward something like a more genuine freedom, not as the other of what counts as discipline or rigor, but as its companion?

> In Providence, you can encounter extinct species, an equestrian
> statue, say, left hoof raised in progress toward the memory of
> tourists. Caught in its career of immobility, but with surface intact,
> waiting to prove that it can resist the attack of eyes even though
> dampened by real weather, even though historical atmosphere is
> mixed with exhaust like etymology with the use of a word or bone
> with sentence structure. No wonder we find it difficult to know our
> way about and tend to stay indoors. (Waldrop 1993, 17, 27)

While it is of course true that, as Stanley Fish has argued, human beings are "always in a particular place" and so cannot hope to achieve anything like a "universal perspective" (Fish 1995, 81), one of the goals of teaching innovative, anti- and multigeneric writing might be to help enable students to resist the passivity of remaining within one discursive location and instead cultivate a capacity to move with more fluency and fluidity among various discourses. Although Fish asserts that we "do not wake up in the morning and announce as our programme for the day 'I will now see beyond my horizons'" (81), isn't this in fact what we ask our students to do? Isn't this in fact perhaps the most vital task to which intellectual life and critical thinking invite us, i.e., to *keep moving*? The "hope and the dream of critical self-consciousness" is not conceived in this sense, in the way Fish asserts, "as a mental action independent of the setting in which it occurs . . . that would deny its own limits by positioning itself in two places at the same time" (104). Critical thinking does imply, however, that we cannot help but occupy positions that involve overlapping contexts, agendas, choices. It's not a question of occupying what Fish calls a "disembodied place" (104). On the contrary, critical thinking involves, if anything, a more concrete sense of where we are, of the multiple locations from which we speak, the multiple identities that occupy us much more than we may be said to inhabit them. Nor is it a question of "relaxing the grip of forms of thought and categorization specific to particular disciplines" (104), except where these forms threaten to inhibit exploration, as forms sometimes will when they cease being enabling and instead become enforced. It's not a matter of moving out of settling into a particular location, in other words, but of moving among settings in a more or less unsettled and unsettling way, of refusing the allure of becoming a stable, or at least static, identity that can be easily consumed as such. Underlying Fish's defense of professional correctness is a disciplinary anxiety in the most fundamental sense, the fear of the loss of discipline itself as leading to the loss of a recuperable identity, fear of chaos, fear of the loss of identity as previously constituted, fear that the very thing we ask most of our undergraduates as well as graduate students and of ourselves as teachers—call it intellectual growth— may bring genuine discomfort precisely because it challenges the identities we bring into the classroom, where the classroom may be understood not only as an individual but as a community project.

Each poem, each theory, has its own marketing niche. If what the late eighties and early nineties came to within the academy was not so much an ongoing revolution of discourses as the manufacture of new discursive commodities and field economies, this fact is of consequence not only in the loftier reaches of graduate seminars but also in the trenches of what might be called, with a parodic nod to the currently fashionable jargon of "outcomes assessment" and "quality management," Academic Discourse Acquisition (ADA). In such a climate, the essays in the present volume remind us that it is important to encourage a sense of the multiplicity and heterogeneity of writing practices across the disciplines at all levels of the curriculum (not merely in advanced undergraduate and graduate seminars) in ways that will challenge the stupefying regimentation of the standard expository essay, cultivate the capacity to respond to various non-normative text(ure)s, and so begin to close the gap between innovative reading and innovative writing practices.

> Though the way I see you depends on I don't know how many
> codes I have absorbed unawares, like germs or radiation, I am
> certain the conflicting possibilities of logic and chemistry have
> contaminated the space between us. (Waldrop 1993, 19)

To the extent that ADA encourages a culture of discursive standardization as the desirable alternative to our reigning culture of distraction, it becomes itself a reaction formation.[2] The best antidote to a culture of distraction is not discursive standardization, but an enhanced awareness of discursive choices, the ability to move in and out of the varying discourses or speech genres that make up our daily life—worlds both inside and outside the academy. With the age of the personal computer barely entering its adolescence, it may seem almost quaint to invoke the memory of Robert Frost in a discussion of innovative writing and disciplinarity. While Frost—he of the two roads—could stand before the country as "the figure of the unified poet speaking to and for the unified nation," representing poetry as an "insistence on individuality" and "an enclave of privacy," whose political corollary was "an antipathy to explicit collectivity" (Perelman 1996a, 114), the pervasive digitalization of culture over the past de-

cade has created an irreversible context for writing that Frost could scarcely
have imagined. The option of transforming, in Marjorie Perloff's words, "what
is usually thought of as prose into what is usually thought of as poetry, simply
by hitting the 'indent' key and lineating the text," has contributed to a situation
in which "Not only the boundary between 'verse' and 'prose' . . . but also the
boundary between 'creator' and 'critic'" appears increasingly unstable (Perloff
1991, 17). As Charles Bernstein has written in his poem "Of Time and the
Line":

> . . . Every poem's got
> a prosodic lining, some of which will
> unzip for summer wear. The lines of an
> imaginary are inscribed on the
> social flesh by the knifepoint of history.
> Nowadays, you can often spot a work
> of poetry by whether it's in lines
> or not; if it's in prose, there's a good chance
> it's a poem.

> (Bernstein 1991, 42–43)

   At a time when poetry no longer figures in K–12 curricula, much less in the
academy, as it did, say, in 1960, a poem such as Frost's "The Road Not Taken"
might be read less as a pious celebration of issues of responsible choice than as
an emblem of the limited choices the educational system offers students in an
attempt to prepare them to take their places in an economy or polity that offers
them less and less security. Given the distracted syntax of contemporary culture,
poetry's marginalized position may have less to do with radical departures
within poetry (e.g., in Language Writing) from narrativized norms—norms
that still dominate more mainstream poems—than with the fact that the larger
culture has become habituated to modalities of perception and language use that
have rendered such norms outdated or irrelevant:

> My linguistic environment might include, within the space of an
> hour . . . street fights in several languages, a Beethoven quartet with
> commentary, calls to the phone company followed by intimate
> discussions of personal affairs followed by a computer-voiced
> marketing survey—with a Weill song interpreted by John Zorn in
> the background, segueing into close readings of Spinoza followed
> by a recitation of the Brothers Grimm.
>    When a poem includes some of these varieties of language use,
> it's not as if this is a totally synthesized experiment: you're listening

to what you're hearing, charting the verbal environment of the
moment. Of course, there are many choices you make . . . .
(Bernstein 1992, 176–77)

Strange as it may seem to poetry lovers brought up to think of Frost as a central
figure for understanding what might be considered normal and normative in
poetry, students today at all levels, from K–12 to graduate school, may find the
disjunctive syntax of what Ron Silliman has called "new sentence" poems at
once more familiar and more intriguing than the relatively seamless styles of
more traditionally narrativized, Frost-like poems. It is illuminating in this regard to note that although Bob Perelman's brief poem, "China" (only mildly
disjunctive by Ron Silliman's "new sentence" standards), became for a time in
the aftermath of Fredric Jameson's infamous reading of it a kind of poster-
poem for Language Writing's supposed symptomatic fragmentation (Jameson
1991, 26), the poem has been defended by its author, not at all as a schizophrenic
exercise designed to test the hermeneutical skills of advanced graduate students
in literary theory, but rather as a poem that "touches on the matter-of-fact uto-
pian feelings that early education can evoke":

> The opening line—"We live on the third world from the sun.
> Number three. Nobody tells us what to do."—combines rudimen-
> tary astronomy with an assertion of complete independence, as if
> learning about the solar system in second grade marks a liberation
> from older narratives of fate. But despite the ingenuous tone of the
> poem, irony does appear in the assertions of collectivity. Nobody
> (from other planets or from heaven) tells us what to do: but that
> doesn't mean that "we" don't tell each other what to do. (Perelman
> 1996a, 78)

In light of such an explanation, and without discounting too polemically
and categorically the potential appeals of a more normatively poetic style
rooted, like Frost's, in a particular location during a particular period of the
country's history, we may usefully ask what the effect might be of asking not
only graduate students but third-graders to read a poem like "China" alongside
a classic Frost poem? What roads would students take and not take in reading
the two together? What would be the likely consequences of a sustained pedagogy in this way for the formation of adult language practices and the
positionality of poetry in relation to other discourses? Which would offer both
younger and older students a potentially more useful encounter with the contemporary world(s) they live in and are bound to encounter every day? What
questions does each poem stage for critical apprehension? What sense of the

possibilities and limits of discursive contexts and life-choices would each one give? What image does each poem provide of the relation between reader and writer and what does each imply about questions of democracy, writing, and authority?

## Digital Persons

### I

| | |
|---|---|
| How many codes | converged in the |
| urbane words my | teachers said to |
| me? What choice | did I have? |
| Their senses passed | by clear enough |

| | |
|---|---|
| I took what | advice they had |
| to give did | what they said |
| would cause less | grief make it |
| possible to think | a little less |

| | |
|---|---|
| produce much more | and better still |
| to good effect | especially with the |
| groups I would | want to belong |
| to move past | where I thought |

| | |
|---|---|
| I'd want to | be a better |
| job the right | kinds of attention |

### II

| | | |
|---|---|---|
| How many codes | converged in | the |
| urbane words my | teachers said | to |
| me? What choice | did I | have? |
| Their senses passed | by clear | enough |
| I took what | advice they | had |
| to give did | what they | said |
| would cause less | grief make | it |
| possible to think | a little | less |

| | | |
|---|---|---|
| produce much more | and better | still |
| to good effect | especially with | the |
| groups I would | want to | belong |
| to move past | where I | thought |

I'd want to     be a     better
job the right     kinds of     attention

III

How many codes    converged    in the
urbane words    my     teachers
said to me?     What    choice did
I have     Their    senses passed

by clear     enough I     took
what ad-     vice they     had

to give did     what     they said would
cause less grief     make it     possible to think

a little less     pro-     duce much
more and better    still to    good effect especially with    the groups    I'd
want to be-     long to     move past where

I thought I'd    want to    be a better job     the right    kinds of attention

By the time students reach the university, much less graduate school, the interpretive communities they belong to will already have been shaped in ways even the most effective professor may barely be able to alter. Such a recognition underlies much of the force of Ann Lauterbach's "Misquotations from Reality: Poetic Value, Choice, and the Beautiful Tree," a satisfyingly uncategorizable piece that issues a call to contemporary poetry to awaken different modalities of attention and in the process serve critical thinking in powerful ways that are as political as they are aesthetic. As Lauterbach reminds us, these categories are inseparably bound up with the discursive choices writers (not just authors) make as to the kinds of relationships they want to establish with potential readers. In a culture of distraction, if critical thinking is not to be opposed to the personal, to understanding or compassion—poets and not only poets need to continue to see it as their task, in Lauterbach's words (paraphrasing Yeats), "to be fascinated with what is difficult" (Lauterbach 1996, 148). In lieu of a "narcotics of release," poetry has the potential to offer "an experience of intimacy . . . linked to or folded onto social discourse" (146). At a time when reading is often perceived, in Lauterbach's words, not as an act "that expands and extends knowledge to order of unfamiliar experience" but as a means by which to "substantiate and authorize claims and positions which often mirror the identity bearings of the reader" (153) a time as well when Americans make political choices "as if they were surfing channels, changing for the sake of change without investment," teachers of writing (as of "literature," "theory," etc.) need to draw on all available resources to demand "our engaged attention, in order for judgment, for choice, to occur" (156).

What Bakhtin has said of meaning generally applies as well to what we talk about when we talk about writing: "A meaning only reveals its depths once it has encountered and come into contact with another, foreign meaning: they engage in a kind of dialogue, which surmounts the closedness and one-sidedness of these particular meanings, these cultures" (Bakhtin 1986, 7). Against the either/ or, avowedly tautological constraints of Fish's anti-interdisciplinarity (Fish 1995, 50)—a model all the more confined by its exclusive focus on the reception of literary works from the past and its neglect of contemporary relations between reception and production—Bernstein's counter-model of "Optimism and Critical Excess" implies a rejection of the idealized monolith of the Public Sphere in favor of tactical engagements with diverse public spheres, including, potentially, those represented by various academic disciplines:[3] What is most likely to be helpful to students in the present context is an emphasis not so much on a single-minded mastery of normative writing practices within any given discipline as on mental agility and a self-conscious coming to terms with the stylistic constraints of various disciplines. In pedagogical terms, this would mean making use of multitextured, antigeneric writing, not instead of but alongside familiar hegemonic prose and verse forms such as the plot-governed novel or the autobiographical lyric, to counter the image many students have of the educational process as a matter of appropriating a one-size-fits-all academic style they can translate with minimal effort and equal success from one discursive, disciplinary context to another. Such an approach might be used in literature/theory/composition classes and elsewhere as instances of a self-conscious engagement with the multiplicity of discursive choices that have become not only available but unavoidable in contemporary life and that the anti-compositional (disjointed, atomized, fragmented) culture of distraction demands we engage and negotiate or else. This is one way of imagining, in any case, what Perelman calls with reference to the idea of the new sentence a "different cultural function for poetry" (Perelman 1996a, 63), one that would allow it to reconfigure its role within the academy—where it is often regarded by all but those relative few who choose to engage it as the softest and least intellectual relevant of disciplines—in a way that would do greater honor to its potentialities.

DIFFICULT PLEASURES

Stooping to Words
When I Was Done Sweeping

So many roads
impinged on words,
reopened, closed, some

kind of form.
And now you're
here, exactly, stooping

to words when
you're done at
the gates of

the Genre Hotel,
some slow shift
where lies as

much as lives
to tell in
lieu of love

enforcing labor, lines
the balance, sets
the ceiling high:

*"Cuidando La Fruta
Ganamos Todos" (Cortadero—
Correro—Calificacion—Viajes),*

Somebody's cows. Some
thing they said
they'd left undone

so you wouldn't
feel so lyrically
divisive, divided, alone.

If in academic writing, as Fish says, "discipline is the real author" (1995, 136), a certain disciplinary excess of pleasurable difficulty is the shadow- or co-author. Fish is clearly right that "the crucial issue in interdisciplinary studies" is "the issue of difference." As he goes on to say: "It is in the name of difference—of the recognition of perspectives, materials, and interests excluded from the disciplinary focus—that one calls for interdisciplinary work . . ." (136). Students learn, we all learn, by what we initially don't understand, or have difficulty understanding, by what we have difficulty identifying in ourselves. "Interdisciplinarity" names the desire for a continual engagement with the others in ourselves, including those parts of ourselves from which we have split ourselves off. Anti- and multigeneric, interdisciplinary writing encourages students to understand that what is to be valued is not prefabricated or forced synthesis, not homogenization or harmonization of syntax, texts, textures, and contexts, but a calculated dissonance and irresolution that takes difference, in Fish's words, "seriously rather than as a regrettable and temporary situation" (138).

It would be politically naive to feel it is necessarily a problem that, in Fish's words, "the energies generated in the effort to undo disciplines, and by undoing them to transform academic work into work that is truly political (that is, truly interdisciplinary), are continually being absorbed . . . by their supposed object" (Fish 1995, 139). The choice between legitimation and effective critique is a false one. It's not a question of refusing institutions, but of transforming them. From this perspective, the desire "to be something other than what [one] is" (139) might be seen not as a disciplinary problem, but as a desirable project of ongoing self and community transformation. The interest of such a practice would not be to "learn how to live with ourselves" at the expense of "a self we dream of becoming" (139), but to maintain these in close relation. In this way we might give up the "pleasures and consolations" of tautologically sustaining self-identities (139) in favor of an acceptance and understanding of what we've been and are in light of what we might hope to become.

To take interdisciplinarity and interdiscursivity seriously, and playfully, is anything but to give up "rigor," except to the extent that term might imply a certain normatively discursive rigor mortis. In lieu of rigorously normative readings and writings, why not, as Rachel Blau DuPlessis proposes, "a theory of education access, or of elaborate playfulness in small groups or coteries, or a theory of interactive and conflictual communities, or a theory about agency through mastery of narrative and song, or a theory of resistance to colonization through deformation of linguistic markers, or a theory of writing the silent and the silences, or a theory of adding to work by transmitting it—I am gesturing to a variety of social explanations of poetic production" (DuPlessis 1996, 42)? Why not, as both the "how" and the "what" of recent innovative writing suggest, a kind of writing that involves continual movement between the particular and the general, between the local and the translocal (not "universal"), between instantiation and abstraction?

## Possible Persons, Community Projects

The possibility of a democratic formation of reading and writing habits begins not in the university, but at home, in earliest childhood, in the early years of acculturation in the school system. If greater freedom of language use is the goal, students are likely over time to have as much to unlearn from previously acquired, routinized relationships to the act of writing (poetry included), as they do to learn:

> Learning to read and write is
> not a mechanical operation
> but a social,
> & in Bataille's sense
> erotic,
> experience. ("What was your first textual experience?")
> Many poets I know
> had, like myself, "learning"
> difficulties
> in this area: I would call them
> resistances—a dread,
> or refusal, of submission
> to a rule-governed wor(l)d,
>
> the inscription of "regulated social order"
> into language.

(Bernstein 1992, 73)

While innovative writing may still have a fighting chance of suggesting alternative practices beyond normative prose syntax, the obstacles are likely to be severe. The task then is to help students become aware, as Bernstein says, that there are "different/modes of relationship/to language/that are/constantly potentially copresent & constantly/potentially blocked off" (Bernstein 1992, 74). In helping to desublimate and thus make visible habitual, institutionalized reading and writing practices—even as students are learning these practices in other courses—the teaching of innovative writing has the potential to offer students a greater sense of discursive freedom. The chances of such a denormativizing pedagogy are much better the earlier they begin. By the time students have reached the university, it will already be too late for many, and not only for those who set out to "get the picture" in philosophy or whatever discipline, that is to say in whatever gets called by these names within a given institution or classroom. Innovative writing continues to retain the potential, nevertheless, to offer resistance to what Bernstein has called the "sclerosis" (74) of genres in any and all disciplines, the potential to contribute, in other words, not toward the development of a New Literacy, but rather toward the development of *new literacies*. Such a project involves developing a kind of "hyperattentiveness" (83) to the traps of language, the discursive pictures that otherwise may hold us and our students captive. From this perspective, "Unmastering language is not a position of inadequacy; on the contrary, mastery requires repression and is the mark of an almost unrecoverable lack" (146).

The point of a pedagogy based on this understanding would not be to "re-trace the steps" but to "respond to the process of discovery" (Bernstein 1992, 175), to allow students not merely to reproduce a particular discursive still-life, as it were, but to create their own moving pictures, "not to display imagination but to mobilize imaginations." Against the steady diet of "deadening cyclic narrativity" to be found in "those most diverting of contemporary/absorptive genres, the TV series . . ." focusing on the "how" of the work is critical, as Bernstein points out, if the goal of writing is to help students free themselves from the entrapments of the culture of distraction and its "simplistic reduction/ of everyday life, the distractions of reading/'entertainments'—the fastread magazines &/fiction & verse" that offer "the banalities of everyday life" with-out "reflecting its elusive actualities" (84). In a culture where distraction and normativity figure not as opposing terms but as complementary repressive forces, it is useful to recall that, as Gordon Bearn has remarked: "At the begin-ning of the *Investigations*, when Wittgenstein is describing how we acquire mas-tery of our language, he insists that 'the learning of language is not explanation, but training [*ein Abrichten*]'. Training in the sense that we train animals to do tricks, or the sense in which we break a horse. An *Abrichter* can be a horse-breaker" (Bearn 1995, 21). In just this sense, as Bearn points out, the nostalgia for a disciplinary mastery of philosophy that never ceases to inform even Wittgen-stein's most adventurous writing involves attempts to arrive at "perfect ostensive definitions [which] are made possible by the violence of our being broken in," or what Derrida has called "the pure originary violence of our training"(21).

With respect to the teaching of my own area of disciplinary specialization, such violence might suggest one way of understanding why, where poetry is still taught at all in the early grades, a poet like Frost would tend to be preferred over, say, Gerard Manley Hopkins. More easily amenable to the instrumental end of acculturating children into the norms of standard prose usage, Frost's more nar-rative style might still be (mis)taken as the road to a better job, a more secure place in the economy. Yet the increasingly distracted, disjunctive syntax and unsettling displacements of an ever-accelerating global economy suggest the need to anticipate and respond to other rhythms, other modes. Remarking the

Derridean notion of being "scarred by the violence of our linguistic training," Bearn writes: "The devious will have smelled an inconsistency between the form of my presentation—an argument which attempts to be clear and precise—and the conclusion of my presentation—that we must always mean something other than what we mean, always say something other than what we say, always understand something other than what we understand. . . ." By contrast: "Those of Derrida's texts which are the most slippery are also the most authentic presentations of his critique of the dream of authenticity. Were it possible, they might be authentically inauthentic; they are, perhaps, beyond authenticity and inauthenticity" (Bearn 1995, 22). With a similar understanding, Bernstein writes:

> Poetry is necessarily theoretical and it can evade this no more than
> it can evade its historicality. . . . I am interested in increasing
> differentiation of writing forms. But that means we can't take our
> conventions for granted, else they become markers for distinctions
> no longer having any necessity. The writing style of most theoreti-
> cal prose, like most nontheoretical poetry, is inert. I am looking for
> ways to keep the genres active, alive, aware of themselves.
> (Bernstein 1996, 183)

For the institution of poetry, writing "otherhow" may be said to constitute a similar practice, one that acknowledges what Kamuf has called "the possibility of a certain exteriority, or difference, within institutional space" and the "unsettled relation literature maintains to its own institution," understanding as well the importance of the "question about the relation between literary pedagogy and political practice" (Kamuf 1995, 69). In this spirit, what Bernstein has called the "modular style" and "disjunctive collage or serial ordering that characterizes much recent poetry" has much to recommend it, and not only for work in poetry:

> Essays can also be combinatorial, marking a sharp break from
> essays that are developmentally narrative. We are trained by
> expository writing models not to think of essays as combinatorial;
> that is, that you could, and might well, reorder all the sentences.
> You have an outline and there's supposed to be some sort of quasi-
> logical development.
>   This is specifically not what I am interested in doing. (Bernstein
> 1992, 152)

Writing of the efforts of deconstructive thought to think "the limits of institutions," Kamuf has emphasized that such a project does not imply a stance "against institutions as such," including disciplinary institutions, but rather against "an unworkable concept of institution as self-defined and self-limiting space of inclusion/exclusion" and on behalf of "the transforming destabilization of such a structure" that would take into account "the relation of institutionality to the trace of its difference from itself" (Kamuf 1995, 67). Similarly, against the inertia of normativity that institutional and disciplinary compartmentalization tend to enforce, innovative writing has the potential to operate in what Perelman has called "institutionally defined spaces," while making use of the "mediating academy, destroyer of magic though it may be . . . as a means to a wider common audience" (Perelman 1996a, 87, 93). In this regard, Aldon Nielsen justly draws attention to what the black critic, theorist, and poet Russell Atkins calls "the value-context" of learning and the ways in which "dominant modes of education have the effect of leading students away from analysis of how something has been created-into-knowledge and of convincing many of them that all that can be created has been created already, perhaps even 'always already'"(Nielsen 1996, 89). The object of the minority student, in this sense, may be better served by resisting the lure of such dominant modes—even as they speak "a language of diversity and identity politics"—in favor of "an oppositional poetics, new forms of heterodox creating-into-knowledge." Even with the emergence of a new cadre of "public intellectuals," it is likely that the most sustainable and vital location of what Nielsen calls "cultural work" will continue to be "within the academies," including the work that goes on in "college and university writing courses." Whether it is a question of "poetry" or "theory," as Nielsen says: ". . . true creating-into-knowledge moves from tradition into the newly creative; it never just applies tradition to the new circumstance" (91). Atkins's understanding of what he called "deconstruction" as "an act of composition," has implications in this respect for all levels of writing instruction, and not only at the university level.

> When the rain breaks through, the bright sun
> shatters in prisms of light
> the hundred roads among the trees,
>
> a thousand flowers blooming in layers of dust

"Words reveal," as Rosmarie Waldrop has observed in "Form and Discontent," "their own vectors and affinities" (Waldrop 1996, 61). Despite and even because of its marginalization in the culture of distraction, poetry may be seen as in many respects an important and even necessary location for such struggle, a kind of writing "as a multiple dialog with a whole net of previous and concurrent texts, tradition, schooling, the culture and language we breathe and move in, which conditions us even while we help to construct them" (Bernstein 1992, 160). The larger questions involved are the questions of a truly open democracy: What counts as reading? What is writing? Whose literacy? Or better: What literacies are available? Whose community? Schooled in such questions, which open onto many more than just two roads, may a thousand rhetorics (poetries, philosophies, humanities, disciplines, sciences, investigations, explorations, pleasures, freedoms) bloom.

Next

It's not easy not to drown in
the same question twice.

Step lightly
against it, boulder to

shoulder, slide out,
slip down.

What bears
repeating is the way

the handlebars' streamers
went wild in the wind,

rounding the corner
where the hydrant

sprayed its slick
across the sky.

*Sans teeth, sans eyes*—
What was the question,

and who was it for?
The generic white vase

with its purple lip
pressed against the bookcase?

What contains is contained
in a matter of moments

only to be dispersed
like milkweed vessels

in a manner of vestibules.
Nanoseconds foretell

another black hole
where the newly disappeared

reassemble their luxuries
by the airport van.

Such stock in
securities as we

exchange, begin to
displace us (baryons, mesons,

hyperons, quarks), I meant
to say *use*, unmentionable

values, dementias,
forms, multi-

mensions to come
beyond particles, waves.

# NOTES

*TAs and the Teaching of Writing at Cornell: A Historical Perspective*

1. Parts of this chapter appeared, in somewhat different form, in Gottschalk 1997. For further discussion of graduate student teacher training at Cornell, including Sarah Day O'Connell's assignment sequence for Music 111: Famous Performances, see Gottschalk 2001.

2. In 1915–16 Professor Strunk began teaching an advanced course called English Usage and Style that continued for many years. Presumably he found his little handbook useful for that course.

3. The seven colleges/schools are the College of Agriculture and Life Sciences; the College of Art, Architecture, and Planning; the College of Engineering; the School of Hotel Administration; the College of Human Ecology; the School of Industrial and Labor Relations; and the College of Arts and Sciences.

4. The phrase "decentralized center" was coined by the current Knight Institute director, Jonathan Monroe.

5. The Freshman Seminar Program became the John S. Knight Writing Program in 1986 when the first director, Fredric V. Bogel, helped the program receive a major endowment from the John S. Knight Foundation. It is now the John S. Knight Institute for Writing in the Disciplines, following further endowments received under the directorship of Jonathan Monroe.

6. We also published and began to enforce—by means, for instance of normalized evaluations, review of syllabi, and the preparatory seminar—a set of program-wide guidelines for all writing seminars, and we produced and published a guidebook, *Teaching Prose: A Guide for Writing Instructors,* for the use of all instructors, especially those taking the preparatory seminar.

7. Shaw's task was made easier in that his predecessor, Rick Bogel, had succeeded in getting the Knight endowment for the program, which gave Shaw access to substantial funds.

8. It's a comment instructors need to hear frequently; see Gottschalk 1995, 6.

### *"You* Can *Make a Difference":*
### *Human Rights as the Subject Matter for a First-Year Writing Seminar*

1. Montejo's book differs in that he wrote it himself and supervised the translation. He was serving as a rural schoolteacher in the village of Tzalalá when it was attacked by the military on 9 September 1982. His book was written in the United States, to which he and his family fled as exiles. Like many Mayan exiles of his class, Montejo attained a level of formal education unheard of in his own country. He completed a Ph.D. and became an anthropologist and is teaching in the United States. Montejo describes the events in Tzalalá in a straightforward narrative style with little figurative language or political rhetoric.

2. Menchú's story was first published in 1983 in French and then in Spanish under the title: *Me Llamo Rigoberta Menchú y Asi Me Nació la Concienca* (My name is Rigoberta Menchú and this is how my [political] conscious was born) in 1983 by Elisabeth Burgos Debray, who also edited the English version. Menchú, winner of the Nobel Peace Prize in 1992, told her story without the benefit of extensive formal education and with the intervention of several people in the production of the book. Rigoberta, as she is universally called, had fled Guatemala to Mexico where she spoke publicly about the fate of Mayan people. She was so effective that leftist political Guatemalan exiles in Mexico arranged for her to join a tour of Europe. When she recounted her story to Burgos Debray in 1983 in Paris, she was twenty-three years old.

### *Writing from (Field) Experience*

1. The terms "capstone" and "cornerstone," which are used in this chapter, are borrowed from the title of the closing panel of the 1999 John S. Knight Summer Consortium for Writing in the Disciplines, "From Cornerstone to Capstone."

### *Writing in Cognitive Science: Exploring the Life of the Mind*

We would like to thank past teaching assistants Leon Rozenblit, Lisa Libby, Whitney Postman, and Wil Readinger for contributions to the development of the writing section of this course. We are grateful to Elizabeth Tricomi for making the course look good by winning the John S. Knight Writing Award, to the Cognitive Studies in Context grant for providing support for the course as a whole, to Steve Knowlton for help with the chess fonts, and finally to Keith Hjortshoj, without whom this writing section would not have existed.

1. Elizabeth Tricomi's essay was included in the third volume of *Discoveries*, the Knight Institute's annual publication of prize-winning student writing by Cornell undergraduates in Institute-sponsored courses.

2. We should note that relieving the mind of sole responsibility for the body's actions *does not* imply that criminals should go unpunished for their destructive actions. On the contrary, it implies that the question of whether or not the criminal is "responsible" for his/her actions is irrelevant, if not ill formed. If we acknowledge that the (at least indirect) causes of human behavior are external, then we can

recognize that culturally caused preferences for peaceful and sharing behavior are to be encouraged over culturally caused preferences for aggressive and selfish behavior. Part of that encouragement quite naturally involves deterrents such as institutionalized punishment. See Honderich (1988) for a version of strict determinism in which moral responsibility is not eschewed.

3. Nonetheless, it will soon be necessary to begin a scientific and philosophical dialogue on the ethical considerations surrounding the development of "conscious" robots.

4. In fact, one might even chide the Turing test for its basic assumption that humanlike intelligence—or more precisely, humanlike conversation style—should be the sole benchmark for measuring whether an entity is "capable of thought" (Spivey, 2000).

## Freshman Rhetoric and Media Literacy

1. Historically, cultural studies began with the work of Raymond Williams, E. P. Thompson, and other British critics and historians in what is now known as the "culturalist" approach to cultural studies, who took as their object culture as a total, though infinitely various and particularizable, system through which one could lay bare the "lived experience" of humans in different historical periods, including the present. Their followers and successors at the Birmingham School combined the culturalist approach in varying degrees with the insights of left-wing social and political philosophers in France—primarily Louis Althusser, Roland Barthes, and Michel Foucault—who became associated with the "structuralist" approach to cultural studies. Unlike the culturalists, who tended to view cultural expression as emerging unproblematically from "lived experience," structuralists view cultural forms as impersonal embodiments of ideology. Whereas in one approach, people produce culture, in the other, almost the reverse occurs: cultural forms produce, or constitute, individuals as subjects, typically without their conscious participation. To put it differently, subjects are "interpellated" (called, summoned, placed—the word is from the French of Althusser) by their culture, which is a system of representations working to uphold systems of power.

## Writing Political Science: Asking a Question Then (Actually) Answering It

1. The course has been structured in different ways over the years, depending in part on the size of the class. With twenty-four students, a teaching assistant read and graded all the short papers and I worked with each student on their long research paper. I have also experimented with assigning long papers in a class of thirty-six students in which I worked with two teaching assistants. We planned the course together over the summer; each of us taught three four-week modules, through which small sections of twelve students rotated, and the class came together for a week in the beginning and a week at the end. The modules were closely integrated around the theme of liberalism. One module focused on equality, one on privacy, and one on difference. Each student, that is, took each module and worked with each of us

although they had only one of us as a research paper supervisor. What I have tried to do in these different formats is to create a close-to-tutorial-like structure embedded in a larger class setting.

### Teaching Behavioral Ecology through Writing

1. I thank Jonathan B. Monroe for inviting my participation in several Knight Institute Summer Consortia, and for his comments on an early draft of this chapter. I thank the John S. Knight Institute for Writing in the Disciplines for supporting my teaching assistants, and my students and colleagues for their enthusiastic participation in developing nontraditional approaches to teaching and learning behavioral ecology.

### Cultivating Dialectical Imagination

1. What students need to learn is to take a different point of view not simply on their own thoughts but on their attempts to express them. Students can sometimes achieve this with respect to the expression of their thoughts by reading their own papers out loud, slowly and with feeling, while listening carefully and marking anything awkward or problematic that they notice in doing so. So I typically ask them to do this once or twice a term, and then to turn in the manuscript thus marked together with their attempts to correct the marked passages.

2. Note that I do not say here "dialectical argument." I mean to allow, for example, that one story (or parable) can constitute an imaginative dialectical response to another. We need to maintain a broad conception of what counts as genuinely dialectical. There are literary as well as scientific forms of dialectic and the beauty of philosophy is that it can accommodate both.

3. If a class is too recalcitrant, I will even divide them into teams—always of course with a view to making the teams even—and let them compete against one another. That has never failed to get them going in this or other exercises (like getting them to identify ambiguities or other problems with sentences, where I sometimes play a Jeopardy-style game with them). But making the teams even results in one problem that I have not figured out how to solve: the strongest students in each group tend to carry the group. Still, however, the weaker ones want to contribute and I think they work harder to do so in the team context. Moreover, the team situation brings out the best in the capable but lazy students, whose egos lead them to contribute more here than in individual discussion. In any case, I have never found any problems with this approach so long as I set the tone for friendly competition: it works more to get the students within a team to cooperate than to pit members of the class against one another.

### Writing (Not Drawing) a Blank

1. According to Linda Flower and John R. Hayes, "[Writers] set up goals based primarily on their knowledge of the conventions of writing and the features of texts. They may be one way in which extensive reading affects a person's ability to write: a

well-read person simply has a much larger and richer set of images of what a text can look like." See Flower and Hayes 1980, 21–32; Selfe 1986, 46–63.

2. Christina Hoff Sommers argues convincingly that students have been encouraged to see moral reflection as reflection about public policy issues, not about virtuous behavior per se (Sommers 1984, 381–89).

3. Take, for example, this excerpt from Freire and Macedo (1987, 48–49):

A pedagogy becomes critical when an educator like Henry Giroux or Stanley Aronowitz has a dialogue with students and methodically challenges them to discover that a critical posture necessarily implies the recognition of the relationship between objectivity and subjectivity. I would call this critical because in many cases individuals have not yet perceived themselves as conditioned; on the contrary, they passionately speak of their freedom.

When challenged by a critical educator, students begin to understand that the more profound dimension of their freedom lies exactly in the recognition of constraints that can be overcome. Then they discover for themselves in the process of becoming more and more critical that it is impossible to deny the constitutive power of their consciousness in the social practice in which they participate. On the other hand, they perceive that through their consciousness, even when they are not makers of their social reality, they transcend the constituting reality and question it. This behavioral difference leads one to become more and more critical; that is, students assume a critical posture to the extent that they comprehend how and what constitutes the consciousness of the world.

4. This is clear from my research and publications. See Migiel 1998a, 161–77; Migiel 1998b, 1–13; Migiel 1999, 302–7; Migiel 2001; Migiel 2002.

5. Erika Lindemann uses similar imagery: " . . . recall your own writing experiences. They should tell you that the process isn't linear. It is recursive, like the forward motion of a wheel, its leading edge breaking new ground but then doubling back on itself" (Lindemann 1995, 24). This metaphor proves particularly powerful for me because it is Dantesque. In thinking about this more, I adopted a model of the structured hypermedia system ("ASK system") as it has been developed by Roger Schank at the Institute for the Learning Sciences at Northwestern University <www.ils.nwu.edu>.

6. As it turned out, nonlinear organization proved beneficial on a practical front as well. About three-quarters into the semester, when the students began to think about their final reading and writing assignments, they realized that, unbeknownst to themselves, they had read almost the entire *Decameron*. "How did you trick us into this?" one student asked, obviously surprised that reading such a long book hadn't proved as burdensome as he had feared.

7. The passage is at the beginning of the paragraph 3: "The next in the line of stupid men is Gianni Lotteringhi (VII.1), who actually allows his wife to convince

him that her lover is a ghost and that they have exorcised it. This woman is allowed to win and to keep her lover, even after a mistake on her part (or possibly a servant's) when she should have rightly been caught red-handed. Instead, she offers a completely asinine excuse for the knocking, pacifies her husband (who, incidentally never thinks to open the door), and gets a message to her lover all in one little exorcism." When Jessi writes that the wife offers "an asinine excuse," she assumes that the reader will know, as she does, about the system that the wife has set up in order to ensure communication with her lover; the wife uses the skull of an ass, which points toward Florence or toward Fiesole, depending on whether the wife's husband is at home or not.

## Writing Writing

1. "Writing Writing" is drawn from Monroe 1996. All poetry in this chapter, unless otherwise attributed, is written by Jonathan Monroe.

2. Though Bartholomae's "Inventing the University" may be reductively misread as advocating something like an indoctrination into the discursive practices of the various disciplines, or what I am calling ADA, I take his argument to be rather that these discursive practices function as a kind of reality principle that those writing in an academic environment have little choice but to negotiate, whether to conform to them or challenge them, in order to write effectively. For additional information and perspectives bearing on such issues as inflected through work in the Knight Institute, in addition to the pieces in the present collection, see Gottschalk 1995 and Hjortshoj 1995 and 1996.

3. Having recalled especially Milton, Spenser, Sidney, or Raleigh as examples of authors "whose literary achievements . . . would have provided them with a ticket of entry to the 'wider' realms of social and political life," Fish writes of the obviously very different situation today: "If someone should today aim for a position in government or commerce or aspire to become an ambassador to a foreign court, he or she (it would have earlier been only 'he') would not think to further that ambition by writing a poem or a sequence of sonnets, but that is exactly what Sidney, Ben Jonson, and Donne did." The conception of poetry's relation to the public sphere in this narrative of the decline of poetry's significance, as also in Fish's exclusively Anglo-American characterization of Romanticism, is clearly very limiting: ". . . when the answer arrives [as to 'what poets are supposed to do and for whom they are to do it'] in the form of the Romantic emphasis on inspiration and the attendant de-emphasis of social and political factors, the result is a splendid isolation that finds a place for poetry, but one that is literally out of this world. The artist now communicates not with princes and with lords but with other artists in a realm even more elite than the Elizabethan court. The circuit of communication now goes not from poet to patron (and back again) but from poet to peer and to a small group of readers whose sensibility is answerable to that visionary company" (Fish 1995, 30–31). Fish readers will recognize in this description a version of the way "interpretive communities" work within the present day academy. From the side at least of literary production, it

is important to remember in this context that perhaps the single most influential volume of poetry in English in the past two centuries, Wordsworth's *Lyrical Ballads*, began its career with only "a small group of readers," as did work by Blake, Baudelaire, Rimbaud, Whitman, Mallarmé, not to mention Dickinson, etc. . . . A more nuanced understanding is clearly called for to account for the ways public spheres of influence function, both aesthetically and politically. It is worth mentioning in this regard that, as Perelman points out: "*The Lyrical Ballads* is one of the first avant-garde works in English and, to compress its highly complex class rhetoric into a generalization, it is committed to democratic language. The poem also supports Wordsworth's affirmation, in the 'Preface,' of the ultimate identity of prose and poetry" (Bernstein 1996).

# REFERENCES

*Active Voices.* Cultural Survival. June 1998. <http://www.cs.org>.

Alcock, J. 1987. Ardent Adaptationism. *Natural History* 96:4.

——. Unpunctuated Equilibrium in the *Natural History* Essays of Stephen Jay Gould. 1998. *Evolution and Human Behavior* 19:321–36.

——. 2001a. *Animal Behavior*, 7th edition. Sunderland, Mass.: Sinauer Associates.

——. 2001b. *The Triumph of Sociobiology*. Oxford: Oxford University Press.

Alcock, J., and P. W. Sherman. 1994. The Utility of the Proximate-Ultimate Dichotomy in Ethology. *Ethology* 96:58–62.

Archdiocese of Guatemala. 1999. *Guatemala Never Again! Recovery of the Historical Memory Project*. The Official Report of the Human Rights Office. New York: Orbis Books.

Arnold, Matthew. 1865. Preface to *Essays in Criticism*. Boston: Ticknor and Fields.

Asturias, Miguel Angel. 1967. *El Señor presidente*. Translated from the Spanish by Francis Partridge. New York: Atheneum.

Austad, S. N. 1997. *Why We Age*. 1997. New York: John Wiley and Sons.

Bakhtin, Mikhail. 1973. *Problems of Dostoevsky's Poetics*. Translated by R. W. Rotsel. Ann Arbor, Mich.: Ardis Press.

——. 1986. The Problem of Speech Genres. In *Speech Genres and Other Late Essays*, edited by Caryl Emerson and Michael Holquist, translated by Vern W. McGee. Austin: University of Texas Press.

Baker, R. R., and M. A. Bellis. 1993. Human Sperm Competition: Ejaculation Manipulation by Females and a Function for the Female Orgasm. *Animal Behaviour* 46:887–909.

Barber, N. 1995. The Evolutionary Psychology of Physical Attractiveness: Sexual Selection and Human Morphology. *Ethology and Sociobiology* 16:395–424.

Barkow, J. L., L. Cosmides, and J. Tooby, eds. 1992. *The Adapted Mind: Evolutionary Psychology and the Generation of Culture*. Oxford: Oxford University Press.

Bartholomae, David. 1985. Inventing the University. In *When a Writer Can't Write: Studies in Writer's Block and Other Composing-Process*. Edited by Mike Rose. New York: The Guilford Press.

Bass, A. H. 1998. Behavioral and Evolutionary Neurobiology: A Pluralistic Approach. *American Zoologist* 38:97–107.

Bazerman, Charles. 1991. The Second Stage in Writing Across the Curriculum. *College English* 53:209–12.

Bearn, Gordon C. F. 1995. Derrida Dry: Iterating Iterability Analytically. *Diacritics* 25.3 (Fall): 3–25.

Bergin, Thomas G. 1981. *Boccaccio.* New York: Viking Press.

Bernstein, Charles. 1986. *Content's Dream: Essays 1975–1984.* Los Angeles: Sun & Moon Press.

———. 1991. *Rough Trades.* Los Angeles: Sun & Moon Press.

———. 1992. *A Poetics.* Cambridge, Mass.: Harvard University Press.

———. 1996. Community and the Individuality Talent. *Diacritics* (Fall/Winter): 179–95.

Berthoff, Ann. 1987. Foreword. In Paulo Freire and Donaldo Macedo, *Literacy: Reading the Word and the World.* South Hadley, Mass.: Bergin and Garvey.

Betzig, L., ed. 1997. *Human Nature.* Oxford: Oxford University Press.

Betzig, L., P. Turke, and M. Borgerhoff Mulder, eds. 1987. *Human Reproductive Behavior.* Cambridge: Cambridge University Press.

Boccaccio, Giovanni. 1993. *The Decameron.* Translated by Guido Waldman. Oxford: Oxford University Press.

Bogel, Fredric V., and Katherine K. Gottschalk, eds. 1988. *Teaching Prose: A Guide for Writing Instructors.* New York: Norton.

Boyer, Ernest L. 1990. *Scholarship Reconsidered: Priorities of the Professoriate.* Princeton: The Carnegie Foundation for the Advancement of Teaching.

———. 1994. *The Student as Scholar: Reflections on the Future of Liberal Learning.* Cambridge, Mass.: Academy of Arts and Sciences.

Brereton, John C., ed. 1995. *The Origins of Composition Studies in the American College, 1875–1925.* Pittsburgh and London: University of Pittsburgh Press.

Burgos Debray, Elisabeth. 1984. *I, Rigoberta Menchú: An Indian Woman in Guatemala.* New York: Verso Press.

Burke, B. A. 1995. Writing in Beginning Chemistry Courses. *Journal of College Science Teaching* 24:341–45.

Buss, D. 1994. *The Evolution of Desire: Strategies of Human Mating.* New York: Basic Books.

Cadby, Peter. 1999. The Truth About Rigoberta Menchú. *New York Review of Books,* 8 April.

Caramazza, A. 1997. How Many Levels of Processing Are There in Lexical Access? *Cognitive Neuropsychology* 14:177–208.

Chomsky, Noam, and George S. Herman. 1988. *Manufacturing Consent: The Political Economy of the Mass Media.* New York: Pantheon.

Ciardi, John. 1959. *How Does a Poem Mean?* Boston: Houghton Mifflin.

Clarke, John, et al. 1981. Sub Cultures, Cultures and Class. In *Culture, Ideology and Social Process,* edited by Tony Bennett, Graham Martin, Colin Mercer and Janet Woollacott. Buckingham, U.K.: The Open University Press.

Clifford, James. 1988. *The Predicament of Culture: Twentieth-Century Ethnography*. Cambridge, Mass.: Harvard University Press.

Clifford, James, and George E. Marcus, eds. 1986. *Writing Culture: The Poetics and Politics of Ethnography*. Berkeley: University of California Press.

Cooper, L., and R. Shepard. 1984. Turning Something Over in the Mind. *Scientific American* 251(6): 106–14.

Cornford, F. M. 1935. *Plato's Theory of Knowledge*. London: Routledge and Kegan Paul.

Crawford, C. B. 1993. The Future of Sociobiology: Counting Babies or Proximate Mechanisms? *Trends in Ecology and Evolution* 8:183–86.

Crawford, C. B., and D. L. Krebs. 1998. *Handbook of Evolutionary Psychology*. Mahwah, N.J.: Lawrence Erlbaum Associates.

Damasio, A. R., and H. Damasio. 1992. Brain and Language. *Scientific American* 267(3): 88–95.

Darwin, C. R. 1859. *On the Origin of Species*. London: John Murray.

Dawkins, R. 1982. *The Extended Phenotype*. San Francisco: W. H. Freeman.

Descartes, Rene. 1993. *Meditations on First Philosophy: In Which the Existence of God and the Distinction of the Soul from the Body Are Demonstrated*. Translated from the Latin by Donald A. Cress. Indianapolis: Hackett Pub. Co.

Derrida, Jacques. 1983. The Principle of Reason: The University in the Eyes of Its Pupils. *Diacritics*. (Fall): 3–20.

DuPlessis, Rachel Blau. 1996. Manifest. *Diacritics* (Fall).

Dwyer, Kevin. 1982. *Moroccan Dialogues: Anthropology in Question*. Baltimore: Johns Hopkins University Press.

Eisen, A. 1986. "Disease of the Week" Reports: Catalysts for Writing and Participation in Large Classes. *Journal of College Science Teaching* 24: 331–34.

Elbow, Peter. 1986. Teaching Two Kinds of Thinking by Teaching Writing. In *Embracing Contraries*. Oxford: Oxford University Press.

Elias, Helen. 1976. *Teaching Practical Writing at Cornell University*. Office of Special Programs: Cornell University, March.

Ewald, P. W. 1994. *Evolution of Infectious Disease*. Oxford: Oxford University Press.

Executive Board, American Anthropological Association. 1947. Statement on Human Rights. *American Anthropologist*, n.s., 49, no. 4:539–43.

Fish, Stanley. 1995. *Professional Correctness: Literary Studies and Political Change*. New York: Oxford University Press.

Flower, Linda, and John R. Hayes. 1980. The Cognition of Discovery: Defining a Rhetorical Problem. *CCC* 31:21–32.

Frank, Robert. 1988. *Passions Within Reason: The Strategic Role of the Emotions*. New York: W. W. Norton.

Freire, Paulo, and Donald Macedo. 1987. Rethinking Literacy: A Dialogue. In *Literacy: Reading the Word and the World*. South Hadley, Mass.: Bergin and Garvey.

García Márquez, Gabriel. 1997 [1988]. *Love in the Time of Cholera* [Amor en los tiempos del cólera]. Translated from the Spanish by Edith Grossman. New York: Alfred A. Knopf.

Giroux, N. 1991. *Postmodernism, Feminism, and Cultural Politics: Redrawing Educational Boundaries.* Albany: SUNY Press.

Gottschalk, Katherine. 1995. The Writing Program in the University. *ADE Bulletin* 112 (Winter): 1–6.

———. 1997. Putting—and Keeping—the Cornell Writing Program in Its Place: Writing in the Disciplines. *Language and Learning Across the Disciplines.* 2(1): 22–45.

———. 2001. Preparing Teachers of Writing Across the Curriculum to Teach Writing. In *Preparing College Teachers of Writing: Histories, Theories, Programs, and Practices,* edited by Sarah Liggett and Betty P. Pytlik. Oxford: Oxford University Press.

Gould, S. J. 1987a. Freudian Slip. *Natural History* 96:14–21.

———. 1987b. Stephen Jay Gould Replies. *Natural History* 96:4–6.

Gross, M. R. 1994. The Evolution of Behavioral Ecology. *Trends in Ecology and Evolution* 9: 358–60.

Hayden, Tom, et al. 1962. *The Port Huron Statement.* Reprinted in Jim Miller, *Democracy Is in the Streets.* New York: Simon and Schuster, 1987.

Herr, Michael. 1977. *Dispatches.* New York: Knopf.

Hjortshoj, Keith. 1995. The Marginality of the Left-Hand Caste. *CCC* 46.4 (December): 491–505.

———. 1996. Theory, Confusion, Inclusion. In *Critical Theory and the Teaching of Literature,* edited by James F. Slevin and Art Young. Urbana, Ill.: National Council of Teachers of English.

Honderich, T. 1988. *A Theory of Determinism.* Oxford: Oxford University Press.

Hume, D. [1739] 1978. *A Treatise of Human Nature,* edited by L. A. Selby-Bigge. Oxford: Clarendon Press.

Imai, M., and D. Gentner. 1997. A Cross-Linguistic Study of Early Word Meaning: Universal Ontology and Linguistic Influence. *Cognition* 62:169–200.

Jacobson, David. 1991. *Reading Ethnography.* Albany: State University of New York Press.

Jameson, Fredric. 1991. *Postmodernism, or, The Cultural Logic of Late Capitalism.* Durham, N.C.: Duke University Press.

*John S. Knight Institute for Writing in the Disciplines.* Cornell University. December 2002. <http://www.arts.cornell.edu/knight_institute/>.

Johnson, Sabrina. 1977. "Report on All Courses That Fulfilled the Freshman Seminar Requirement." Research study, Cornell University.

Jorden, Eleanor H., with Mari Noda. 1987. *Japanese: The Spoken Language.* New Haven: Yale University Press.

Judd, T. M., and P. W. Sherman. 1996. Naked Mole-Rats Direct Colony Mates to Food Sources. *Animal Behaviour* 51:957–69.

Kamuf, Peggy. 1996. The Division of Literature. *Diacritics* 25.3 (Fall): 53–72.

Kant, Immanuel. 1998. *The Critique of Pure Reason*. Edited and translated by Paul Guyer and Allen W. Wood. New York: Cambridge University Press.

Kirkland, W. L. 1997. Teaching Biology through Creative Writing. *Journal of College Science Teaching* 25:277–79.

Kozol, Jonathan. 1987. *Amazing Grace*. Boston: Beacon.

Krebs, J. R., and N. B. Davies. 1993. *An Introduction to Behavioral Ecology*. Oxford: Blackwell Science.

———, eds. 1997. *Behavioral Ecology: An Evolutionary Approach*. 4th Edition. Oxford: Blackwell Science.

Labov, William. 1972. The Logic of Nonstandard English. In *Language in the Inner City: Studies in the Black English Vernacular*. Philadelphia: University of Pennsylvania Press.

Laertius, Diogenes. 1925. *Lives of Eminent Philosophers*, with an English translation by R. D. Hicks. VI.6. Loeb Classical Library. London: W. Heinemann.

Lauterbach, Ann. 1996. Misquotations from Reality: Poetic Value, Choice, and the Beautiful Tree. *Diacritics* (Fall/Winter).

*Lawrence of Arabia*. 1998. Burbank, Calif.: Columbia Tri-Star Home Video.

Lindemann, Erika. 1995. *A Rhetoric for Writing Teachers*. 3rd ed. New York: Oxford University Press.

Maalouf, Amin. 1989. *Leo Africanus*. Translated by Peter Sluglett. New York: Norton.

Marcus, George E., and Michael M. J. Fischer. 1986. *Anthropology as Cultural Critique*. Chicago: University of Chicago Press.

Massey, Douglas S., and Nancy A. Denton. 1993. *American Apartheid: Segregation and the Making of the Underclass*. Cambridge, Mass.: Harvard.

McGrath, Ellie, ed. 2001. The Best College for You 2001. *Time/ The Princeton Review*, 63–74.

McGuire, M., and A. Troisi. 1998. *Darwinian Psychiatry*. Oxford: Oxford University Press.

Migiel, Marilyn. 1998a. Beyond Seduction: A Reading of the Tale of Alibech and Rustico [*Decameron* III 10]. *Italica* 75:161–77.

———. 1998b. Encrypted Messages: Men, Women, and Figurative Language in *Decameron* 5.4. *Philological Quarterly* 77:1–13.

———. 1999. How (Thanks to a Woman) Andreuccio da Perugia Became Such a Loser, and How (Also Thanks to a Woman) Reading Could Have Become a More Complicated Affair. *Romance Languages Annual* 10:302–7.

———. 2001. Domestic Violence in the *Decameron*. In *"Dangerous Love": Domestic Violence in the Middle Ages*, edited by Eve Salisbury, Georgiana Donavin, and Merrall Pryce. Gainesville: University Press of Florida.

———. 2002. The Untidy Business of Gender Studies: Or, Why It's Almost Useless to Ask if the *Decameron* Is Feminist. In *Boccaccio and Feminist Criticism*, edited by F. Regina Psaki and Thomas C. Stillinger. Annali d'Italianistica Book Series.

Mitchell, S. D. 1992. On Pluralism and Competition in Evolutionary Explanations. *American Zoologist* 32:135–44.

Montejo, Victor. 1987. *Testimony: Death of a Guatemalan Village*. Willimantic, Conn.: Curbstone Press.

Monroe, Jonathan. 1983. Blue Horses. *The American Poetry Review* 12.1 (January/ February): 46.

———. 1987. *A Poverty of Objects: The Prose Poem and the Politics of Genre*. Ithaca: Cornell University Press.

———. 1996. Poetry, the University, and the Culture of Distraction. In Poetry, Community, Movement. *Diacritics* (Fall/Winter): 3–30.

———, ed. 2001. *Writing and Revising the Disciplines*. Ithaca: Cornell University Press.

Nesse, R. M., and G. C. Williams. 1994. *Why We Get Sick*. New York: Harper Collins.

———. 1998. Evolution and the Origins of Disease. *Scientific American* 279:86–93.

Nielsen, Aldon Lynn. 1996. Black Deconstruction: Russell Atkins and the Recon-struction of African-American Criticism. *Diacritics* (Fall).

Nietzsche, Friedrich. 1968. *The Will to Power*. Translated by Walter Kaufmann and R. J. Hollingdale. Edited, with commentary, by Walter Kaufmann. New York: Vintage Books.

Orwell, Sonia, and Ian Angus, eds. 1969. *The Collected Essays, Journalism and Letters of George Orwell*. Vol. 1, *An Age Like This 1920–1940*. New York: Harcourt Brace Jovanovich.

Pannikar, R. 1982. Is the Notion of Human Rights a Western Concept? *Diogenes* 27 (1): 28–43.

Perelman, Bob. 1993. *Virtual Reality*. New York: Roof Books.

———. 1996a. *The Marginalization of Poetry: Language Writing and Literary History*. Princeton, N.J.: Princeton University Press.

———. 1996b. Poetry in Theory. *Diacritics* (Fall).

Perloff, Marjorie. 1991. *Radical Artifice: Writing Poetry in the Age of Media*. Chicago: University of Chicago Press.

Preis, Ann-Belinda S. 1996. Human Rights as Cultural Practice: An Anthropological Critique. *Human Rights Quarterly* 18:286–315.

Platt, J. R. 1964. Strong Inference. *Science* 146:347–53.

Reeve, H. K., and P. W. Sherman. 1993. Adaptation and the Goals of Evolutionary Research. *Quarterly Review of Biology* 68:1–32.

———. 2001. Optimality and Phylogeny: A Critique of Current Thought. In *Adaptationism and Optimality*, edited by S. Orszak and E. Sober. Oxford: Oxford University Press.

"Report of the College Writing Committee (The Sturgeon Report)." 1982. Commit-tee chair, Nicholas Sturgeon, Department of Philosophy. Cornell University, College of Arts and Sciences. May.

"Report of the Faculty Committee on the Quality of Undergraduate Instruction (The Kahn/Bowers Report)." 1965. Submitted to the Faculty of Cornell University, 11 October.

"Report of the Provost's Commission on Writing (The Holmes Report)." 1981. Committee chair, Clive Holmes, Department of History. Cornell University, October.

*Resources for Scientists Teaching Science*, Ann Stork, ed. National Science Foundation. December 2002. <http://instruct1.cit.cornell.edu/courses/taresources/>.

Riefenstahl, Leni. [1934] c. 1977. *Triumph of the Will*. [S.l.]: RHD Films Dist., Inc.

Rosenberg, Edgar. 1966. Address to the Trustees of Cornell University. Cornell University, 15 April.

———. 1967. Report to the College of Arts and Science on Freshman Humanities. Cornell University, May.

Rushdie, Salman. 1988. *The Satanic Verses*. New York: Viking.

Schön, Donald A. 1983. *The Reflective Practitioner: How Professionals Think in Action*. New York: Basic Books.

———. 1987. *Educating the Reflective Practitioner*. San Francisco: Jossey-Bass.

———, ed. c. 1991. *The Reflective Turn: Case Studies in and on Educational Practice*. New York: Teachers College Press.

Schwalm, David E. E-mail post to Writing Program Administrators listserve. 2 September 1996.

Selfe, Cynthia L. 1986. Reading as a Writing Strategy: Two Case Studies. In *Convergences: Transactions in Reading and Writing*, ed. Bruce T. Petersen. Urbana, Ill.: NCTE.

Sherman, P. W. 1988. The Levels of Analysis. *Animal Behaviour* 36:616–18.

———. 1989. The Clitoris Debate and the Levels of Analysis. *Animal Behaviour* 37:697–98.

Sherman, P. W., and J. Alcock, eds. 2001. *Exploring Animal Behavior*. 3d ed. Sunderland, Mass.: Sinauer Associates.

Sherman, P. W., and J. Billing. 1999. Darwinian Gastronomy: Why We Use Spices. *BioScience* 49:453–63.

Sherman, P. W., and S. M. Flaxman. 2001. Protecting Ourselves from Food. *American Scientist* 89:142–51.

Sherman, P. W., and H. K. Reeve. 1997. Forward and Backward: Alternative Approaches to Studying Human Social Evolution. In *Human Nature*, edited by L. Betzig. Oxford: Oxford University Press.

Silliman, Ron. 1987. The New Sentence. In *The New Sentence*. New York: Roof.

Skinner, B. F. 1971. *Beyond Freedom and Dignity*. New York: Knopf.

Slevin, James. 1994. Reading and Writing in the Classroom and the Profession. In *Writing Theory and Critical Theory*, edited by John Schilb and John Clifford. New York: Modern Language Association, 53–72.

Smith, E. A., M. B. Mulder, and K. Hill. 2001. Controversies in the Evolutionary
Social Sciences: A Guide for the Perplexed. *Trends in Ecology and Evolution*
16:128–35.

Sommers, Christina Hoff. 1984. Ethics Without Virtue: Moral Education in America.
*American Scholar* 53:381–89.

Spinoza, B. [1677] 1960. *Ethics*, edited by. J. Guttman. New York: Hafner.

Spivey, M. J. 2000. Turning the Tables on the Turing Test: The Spivey Test. *Connection Science* 12:91–94.

Stoll, David. 1997. The Construction of I, Rigoberta Menchú: Excerpts from a Work
in Progress. *Brick* 57:38.

———. 1999. *Rigoberta Menchú and the Story of All Poor Guatemalans*. Boulder, Co.:
Westview Press.

Strunk, William, and E. B. White. 2000. *The Elements of Style*. 4th ed. Boston: Allyn
and Bacon.

Venuti, Lawrence. 1998. *The Scandals of Translation: Towards an Ethics of Difference*.
London: Routledge.

Waldrop, Rosmarie. 1993. *Lawn of Excluded Middle*. Providence: Tender Buttons.

———. 1996. Form and Discontent. *Diacritics* (Fall/Winter): 54–62.

Walvoord, Barbara. 1996. The Future of WAC. *College English* 58:58–79.

Whorf, B. L. 1963. *Language, Thought, and Reality*. Cambridge, Mass.: MIT Press.

Williams, G. C. 1966. *Adaptation and Natural Selection*. Princeton, N.J.: Princeton
University Press.

Williams, Joseph M. 1997. *Style: Ten Lessons in Clarity and Grace*. New York:
Longman.

Wittgenstein, Ludwig. 1997. *Philosophical Investigations*. Translated by G. E. M.
Anscombe. Malden, Mass: Blackwell.

# CONTRIBUTORS

ROSS BRANN is Milton R. Konvitz Professor of Judeo-Islamic Studies and chair of the Department of Near Eastern Studies at Cornell University. His publications include *The Compunctious Poet: Cultural Ambiguity and Hebrew Poetry in Muslim Spain* (1991), which received the 1992 National Jewish Book Award in the category of Sephardic Studies. In 1996, he received the Stephen and Margery Russell Award for Distinguished Teaching.

MATTHEW EVANGELISTA is a professor of government at Cornell, where he teaches courses in international and comparative politics. He is the author of two books, *Innovation and the Arms Race* (1988) and *Unarmed Forces: The Transnational Movement to End the Cold War* (1999). He serves on the editorial board of Cornell University Press and of the journal *International Organization*.

JANE FAJANS is an associate professor of anthropology at Cornell University. She has done fieldwork in Papua New Guinea with the Baining People, and in Ithaca, New York. She is the author of *They Make Themselves: Work and Play among the Baining of Papua New Guinea* (1997) and editor of *Exchanging Products: Producing Exchange* (1993).

WILLIAM W. GOLDSMITH, professor of city and regional planning, is an authority on urbanization and regional development. He founded Cornell's program on international studies in planning and now directs Cornell's undergraduate program on urban and regional studies. His book *Separate Societies: Poverty and Inequality in U.S. Cities* (1992) won the 1993–94 Paul Davidoff Prize.

KATHERINE K. GOTTSCHALK is the Walter C. Teagle Director of First-Year Writing Seminars at Cornell University. She has previously published on TA preparation, program administration, and the teaching of writing, and is co-editor with Fredric Bogel of *Teaching Prose: A Guide for Writing Instructors* (1988).

KEITH HJORTSHOJ is the John S. Knight Director of Writing in the Majors and has taught a variety of writing and teacher training courses at Cornell since 1976. For three years he was codirector of Cornell's Lilly Endowment Teaching Fellows Program. He has published work on urban India and Islam as well as rhetoric and composition, including *The Transition to College Writing* (2001).

BILLIE JEAN ISBELL is a professor of anthropology and former director of the Latin American Studies Program at Cornell. Recent publications include "Metaphor Spun: A Conversation with Cecilia Vicuna" (with Regina Harrison, 1997); "De Inmaduro a Duro: Los Simbolico Feminino y Los Esquimas Andinos de Genero" (1997); "Time, Text and Terror" (1997); and "Violence in Peru: Performances and Dialogues" (1998).

MARY FAINSOD KATZENSTEIN is a professor of government and women's studies at Cornell University. Her books include *Faithful and Fearless: Moving Feminist Protest inside the Church and Military* (1998) and *Beyond Zero Tolerance: Discrimination and Culture in the U.S. Military,* edited with Judith Reppy (1999).

MICHAEL MACY is a professor of sociology at Cornell University. His article on "Social Learning and the Structure of Collective Action" received the ASA Theory Section Best-Paper Award and his paper on management fads (with David Strang) won the 1999 Academy of Management Best Paper Award in Organizational Theory. He is an associate editor of *Advances in Group Processes* and on the editorial board of *Social Psychology Quarterly*.

KATHRYN S. MARCH is an associate professor of anthropology, women's studies, and Asian studies at Cornell University. Since 1973 she has worked with indigenous minority peoples in the Himalayas, primarily on questions of gender and social change. Her work includes *Women's Informal Associations in Developing Countries: Catalysts for Change?* (with Rachelle Taqqu, 1986) and *If Each Comes Halfway: Meeting Tamang Women in Nepal* (2002).

ROSE MCDERMOTT is an assistant professor of government at Cornell and the author of *Risk Taking in International Politics: Prospect Theory in American Foreign Policy* (1998). Her work concentrates on political psychology in international relations. In 2002 she was the recipient of a John M. Olin Institute of Strategic Studies postdoctoral fellowship at Harvard University.

MARILYN MIGIEL is an associate professor in the Department of Romance Studies at Cornell University. Her research and publications are focused mainly on medieval and Renaissance Italian literature. In 1995, she was awarded the Stephen and Margery Russell Award for Distinguished Teaching.

JONATHAN MONROE is a professor of comparative literature, associate dean of the College of Arts and Sciences, and director of the John S. Knight Institute for Writing in the Disciplines at Cornell University. A member of the Cornell faculty since 1984, he has served as the director of graduate studies for the Department of Comparative Literature and as head of Cornell's Humanities Fellowship Board. He is the author of *A Poverty of Objects: The Prose Poem and the Politics of Genre* (1987) and the editor of *Writing and Revising the Disciplines* (2002).

ELIZABETH OLTENACU has been teaching in animal science at Cornell since 1978. She has been involved in teaching introductory animal genetics and applied animal behavior to undergraduates on campus and to off-campus audiences through Cornell's Extension Outreach programs. She served as associate director of academic programs in the College of Agriculture and Life Sciences from 1987–95.

PAUL SAWYER has been a professor of English at Cornell since 1975. He is author of *Ruskin's Poetic Argument: The Design of the Major Works* (1985).

DANIEL R. SCHWARZ is a professor of English and Stephen H. Weiss Presidential Fellow at Cornell University and a recipient of Cornell's College of Arts and Sciences Russell Award for Distinguished Teaching. His numerous books include *Imagining the Holocaust* (1999) and *Reconfiguring Modernism: Explorations in the Relationship Between Modern Art and Modern Literature* (1997).

HARRY E. SHAW is a professor of English at Cornell University and the recipient of the John M. and Emily B. Clark Distinguished Teaching Award. His publications include *Narrating Reality: Austen, Scott, Eliot* (1999) and *The Forms of Historical Fiction* (1983). Director of the John S. Knight Writing Program from 1986 to 1992, and chair of the Department of English from 1992 to 2002, he is currently a senior associate dean of the the the College of Arts and Sciences.

PAUL W. SHERMAN is a professor in the Department of Neurobiology and Behavior at Cornell, where he has been on the faculty since 1981. He studies the behavioral ecology of various mammals and birds, and he teaches animal social behavior and Darwinian medicine. He has published more than 125 papers and books on these topics.

MICHAEL J. SPIVEY is an assistant professor in the Department of Psychology at Cornell University. His research, funded by a Neuroscience Fellowship from the Sloan Foundation, is in the areas of cognitive neuroscience and psycholinguistics, with special emphasis on measuring on-line cognitive processes via recording eye movements during natural tasks.

JENNIFER E. WHITING teaches philosophy at Cornell University. She is co-editor (with Stephen Engstrom) of *Aristotle, Kant, and the Stoics: Rethinking Happiness and Duty* (1996), and has served as codirector (with Louis Sass) of an NEH Summer Institute on Mind, Self, and Psychopathology. Her current research is on ancient and modern conceptions of self.

JOHN WHITMAN is an associate professor in the Department of Linguistics at Cornell University. He teaches historical linguistics, Japanese and Korean linguistics, and syntax. His publications include *Nichieigo hikaku sensyo*, vol. 9: *Kaku to gojun to tôgo kôʐô* (with Koichi Takezawa, 1998).

# INDEX